YOUNG WOMAN'S GUIDE for Personal Success

Edited by Linda Ellis Eastman

Goblin Fern Press
Madison, Wisconsin

Published by:
Goblin Fern Press, Inc.
6401 Odana Road, Suite B
Madison, WI 53719
Toll-free: 888-670-BOOK (2665)
www.goblinfernpress.com
Specializing in personalized publishing.

Please contact the publisher for quantity discounts.

ISBN-10: 1-59598-047-7
ISBN-13: 978-1-59598-047-2

Library of Congress Cataloging-In-Publication Data
(Prepared by The Donohue Group, Inc.)

Young Woman's Guide for Personal Success / edited by Linda Ellis
Eastman.

   p. ; cm. -- (Professional woman network series ; 4)

   Includes bibliographical references.
   ISBN-13: 978-1-59598-047-2
   ISBN-10: 1-59598-047-4

1. Young women--Life skills guides. 2. Young women--Conduct of life.
3. Young women--Psychology. 4. Life skills. 5. Success. I. Eastman,
Linda Ellis.

HQ1229 .Y68 2006
646.7/0084/22

Typography by:
The Geo Group www.thegeogroup.com

Printed in the United States of America.

This book is dedicated to
Amanda Ellis,
because of the special person she is.

TABLE OF CONTENTS

TABLE OF CONTENTS
-CONTINUED-

TABLE OF CONTENTS
-CONTINUED-

TABLE OF CONTENTS
-CONTINUED-

ABOUT THE EDITOR

LINDA ELLIS EASTMAN

Linda Ellis Eastman is President and CEO of The Professional Woman Network (PWN), an International Training and Consulting Organization on Women's Issues. She has designed seminars which have been presented in China, the former Soviet Union, South Africa, the Phillipines, and attended by individuals in the United States from such firms as McDonalds, USA Today, Siemens-Westinghouse, the Pentagon, the Department of Defense, and the United States Department of Education.

An expert on women's issues, Ms. Eastman has certified and trained over one thousand women to start consulting/seminar businesses originating from such countries as Pakistan, the Ukraine, Antigua, Canada, Mexico, Zimbabwe, Nigeria, Bermuda, Jamaica, Costa Rica, England, South Africa, Malaysia, and Kenya. Founded in 1982 by Linda Ellis Eastman, The Professional Woman Network is committed to educating women on a global basis regarding self-esteem, confidence building, stress management, and emotional, mental, spiritual and physical wellness.

Ms. Eastman has been featured in *USA Today* and listed in *Who's Who of American Women,* as well as *Who's Who of International Leaders.* In addition to women's issues, Ms. Eastman speaks internationally regarding the importance of human respect as it relates to race, color, culture, age, and gender. She will be facilitating an international conference where speakers and participants from many nations will be able to discuss issues that are unique to women on a global basis.

Linda Ellis Eastman is also founder of The Professional Woman Speakers Bureau and The Professional Woman Coaching Institute. Ms. Eastman has dedicated her businesses to increasing the self-esteem and personal dignity of women and youth around the world.

Contact:
The Professional Woman Network
P.O. Box 333
Prospect, KY 40059
(502) 566-9900
lindaeastman@prodigy.net
www.prowoman.net
www.protrain.net

INTRODUCTION

By Linda Ellis Eastman

This book has been designed specifically for the teenage girl. Today's world presents many challenges and concerns for young women and it is the intent of this book to provide guidelines regarding self-esteem, manners, positive attitude development, handling peer pressure, wardrobe and grooming, confidence building, and dealing with personal anger.

Life has its ups and downs when you are a young woman living at home, attending school, and trying to have an exciting social life. Between the ages of thirteen and nineteen, hormonal mood swings and occasional self-consciousness are to be expected. There are the challenges of meeting new friends, possibly attending a new school, being a good student, and living with others within a home. Especially challenging relationships can be sibling versus sibling and the mother/daughter power struggle.

If you, the reader, are a teenage girl, know that what you may be feeling on a day-to-day, or even hour-to-hour, basis is probably very normal. There are chapters within this book that will guide you with your personal anger and frustration, as well as provide suggestions on how to deal with sadness and grief.

There are lots of fun topics within this book, too! Take a look at the chapter on your body and also the super tips for wardrobe and travel. If you are wondering which fork or spoon you should use the next time you dine at a lovely restaurant, then definitely read the chapter on etiquette and manners!

This is a great read for young women and also for the people who love them. If you are a counselor, parent, grandparent, or any other person who cares deeply for teenagers, you will be given insights into the lives of young women and how to provide them with healthy, loving support for them.

Teenage girls of today, this book is for you. May it guide you on your journey through your teen years and provide guidelines and suggestions for positive self-esteem and confidence. Remember, you are a treasure.

Linda Ellis Eastman

YOUNG WOMAN'S GUIDE
for Personal
Success

ABOUT THE AUTHOR

ROWENA BRUCE

Rowena Bruce is President and CEO of Best Achievers Inc., an organization providing personal and professional development training, career consulting, and personal coaching services. She is an entrepreneur, trainer, consultant, and personal/professional coach. She is a dynamic speaker and motivator who inspires youth and adults to pursue their passions. Ms. Bruce uses her educational background in Psychology, Human Behavior, Social Work, and Adolescent Life Cycles from Eastfield College and Dallas Baptist University in Dallas, Texas. Ms. Bruce received her Coaching Certification from The Professional Woman Coaching Institute.

Ms. Bruce founded Best Achievers, Inc. in 2003. She specializes in the areas of professional development, training, career and personal coaching, human resource management consulting, recruiting and conducting interviews. Ms. Bruce provides services to churches, universities, government agencies, and community-based youth organizations.

Currently Ms. Bruce provides consulting services for the City of Dallas, coordinating the Exxon Mobil Youth Employment programs. She is also involved in program development and training, recruiting, interviewing, and hiring youth and adults for the Youth Education and Employment programs. Ms. Bruce has over 10 years of experience with the State Department of Texas where she held the posistions of Regional Human Resource Specialist and Regional Recruiter/Trainer.

Rowena Bruce is a Certified Professional Career and Personal Coach and a Certified Entrepreneur Trainer. She is a member of the following professional organizations: The Professional Woman Network, The National Association of Female Executives, Dallas Human Resource Management Association, and the Society of Human Resource Management. Ms. Bruce will serve on the 2007 International Board of Advisors for the Professional Woman Network.

Using her dynamic personality, extensive knowledge, and her vast network of resources for teens, adults, schools, corporations, churches, and non-profit organizations, Ms. Bruce has been able to motivate and impact lives and challenge teens and adults to become Best Achievers. Ms. Bruce resides in Cedar Hill, Texas with her husband, Darwin.

Contact:
Best Achievers, Inc.
P.O. Box 412
Cedar Hill, Texas 75106
(469) 556-8053
www.bestachieversinc.com
www.protrain.net

ONE

LOVING YOURSELF AND OTHERS

By Rowena Bruce

"Faith, Hope, Love, these three, but the greatest of these is Love."
–1 Cor. 13:13 (KJV)

Love is defined in *Webster's Dictionary* as "a strong, positive emotion of regard, warm affection, enthusiasm or devotion." Love is God's greatest gift to us. When I was a child growing up with my mother and grandfather, they taught me to always treat people the way I would want to be treated. Now I raise my children with that same principle. Treat people the way you want to be treated–with love, respect, and kindness. Of course, the way you treat others is based upon the love you have for yourself.

Unconditional love means to love and accept unconditionally. It means placing no conditions as to how to behave or what to do in order to receive acceptance and love. But you can't love others until you love yourself first. You must love yourself unconditionally before you truly love others unconditionally. Love can be defined in many different ways. First, you must define what love means to you. Think about it. What's your definition of love? Be honest.

My definition of LOVE:_____

Loving Yourself

When you are filled with love, you can share the gift of love with others. Self-love means accepting yourself unconditionally, no matter what circumstances exist. It is accepting yourself (your height, weight, appearance, race, personality, etc) just the way God created you. You accept your strengths as well as your weaknesses. Self-love exists when you learn to accept yourself for who you are without attempting to be someone else.

As you grow, accept and love all things about yourself physically, mentally, and spiritually. Think of loving yourself in the same way that you would show love to someone else you deeply care about. How do you love yourself? First of all, understand that loving yourself does not mean you are conceited! A conceited person thinks that she is the best, that she stands above others, and that others are not equals. A person who loves herself has love to share with others and feels that she is equal to others.

To provide you with a solid foundation on how to love yourself, let's start by reviewing the way you define words that are significant in understanding how to begin to love yourself. Remember, love is in your heart, right there inside of you.

EXERCISE
The first step in getting to love yourself is defining the following words. Please look up their definitions and write down their meanings on the lines below:

Respect

_____

_____

_____

_____

Compassion

_____
_____
_____
_____

Happiness

_____
_____
_____
_____

Kindness

_____
_____
_____
_____

Forgiveness

_____
_____
_____
_____

Now really study the meaning of these words. All of these words have significance in defining your level of self-love. Self-love means showing yourself respect, compassion, and kindness. You must be willing to forgive yourself for mistakes both present and past. You must also be able to feel happiness inside without needing external sources to maintain your happiness. Being true to yourself is remembering that God loves you and you should likewise love yourself and not deprive yourself of the very things that you wish to show to others.

Filling yourself with love is the first step in loving yourself. The primary means for showing love to yourself is by nurturing your mind, body, and soul by developing emotional, mental, spiritual, and physical well-being. Surround yourself with kind people who believe in you. Learn and practice ways to relax and unwind. Tap into your spiritual self with special reading or classes.

The next step is for you to discover the ways in which you are already showing love to yourself. To help you evaluate this, take the time to answer the following questions. Be honest with yourself and think about each of the following questions:

EXERCISE
How do you respect yourself?

_____
_____
_____
_____

How do show compassion for yourself?

_____
_____
_____

List three things you do to make yourself happy:

_____
_____
_____

What are three things you do to be kind to yourself?

_____
_____
_____

Do you forgive yourself for your past mistakes? Why or why not?

_____
_____
_____

"Love is the highest and most powerful emotion."
–Unknown

Eight Keys to Loving Yourself

1. Accept yourself for who you are and learn to love yourself as a person.

2. Learn to understand yourself emotionally, physically, and spiritually.

3. Have respect and compassion for yourself. Don't put yourself down!

4. Encourage yourself with positive thinking daily. Post affirmations on your mirror!

5. Fall in love with yourself.

6. Pamper yourself daily.

7. Do the things you love to do.

8. Never give up on yourself or your dreams.

Below are some additional tips on loving yourself. Remember, these tips are designed to help you when you have made a conscious decision to focus on what is best for you, to lift your spirit, and to take action.

Additional Tips on Loving Yourself

1. Pray daily.

2. Give yourself permission to love yourself.

3. Treat yourself with respect, kindness, and love.

4. Realize the greatness inside of you.

5. Know and love yourself.

6. Be yourself at all times.

7. Surround yourself with people who love and believe in you.

8. Make a list of things you love about yourself and refer to it often.

9. Praise and compliment yourself daily.

10. Celebrate the small and big things about yourself daily.

Copy these lists and carry them with you to remind you of your love for yourself, or use them to create affirmations you can review when you wake up or as you're going to bed. Remind yourself what a wonderful, unique person you are.

EXERCISE
What do you love about yourself?

_____
_____
_____
_____
_____
_____
_____
_____
_____
_____
_____
_____
_____

Now close your eyes. Take a moment to consider all the things you have discovered about how to love yourself on a daily basis. What is one step that you will take today? Open your eyes. You are ready to continue.

"If God is for us, who can be against us?"
– Romans 8:31

Loving Others
To love others, you need to remember to love them the way you would like to be loved. Show others respect, love, kindness, and compassion. The love you have for others is simply a reflection of the expression of

the love you have for yourself. We will now explore and identify how you love others.

EXERCISE
How do you show love to the following people in your life? Share your feelings and emotions about these people:

Parents

_____
_____
_____
_____

Friends

_____
_____
_____
_____

People at work or school

_____
_____
_____
_____

The next step is for you to discover the ways in which you are showing love to others. To help you evaluate your love for others, please take the time to answer the following questions:

EXERCISE
How do you show kindness towards others?

_____
_____
_____
_____

How do you show compassion for others?

_____
_____
_____
_____

How do you show respect for others?

_____
_____
_____
_____

Do you forgive others for their mistakes? List mistakes that you have forgiven in others:

_____
_____
_____
_____

Are you ready to take the next step? Now consider ways that you can change or add behaviors and ways of showing others that you love them. How can you show your love to others as well as to yourself?

What are some ways you will take action to love yourself and others?

_____
_____
_____
_____
_____
_____
_____
_____
_____

I would like to leave you with the following Love Pledge. This is a pledge to love yourself and others. Use your love pledge for daily inspiration for one month. After those thirty days, review your actions and thoughts. Were you true to your pledge? How did it make you feel toward yourself and others? Make notes to yourself on ways that you can continue to improve your loving relationship with yourself and others.

My Love Pledge

I, _____(your name), pledge to love myself with all of my heart and soul.

I pledge to honor and love myself first.
I pledge to love myself with compassion.
I pledge to love everything about myself.
I pledge to love and respect myself.
I pledge to love my mind and body.
I pledge to love others with compassion.
I pledge to love and respect others.
I pledge to honor others.

This is my love pledge and I will keep my love pledge for the next thirty days. After that time, I will reflect on this pledge and sign another pledge for thirty days. I will continue this until this new behavior has become a wonderful habit.

_____

Signature   Date

Hopefully, this chapter has helped you look closely at yourself and discover how important it is to feel really good about yourself, to accept yourself just the way you are, and to love and treasure yourself. It may be difficult and a challenge at times to feel that you are worthy of love. Sure, there are difficult days, and yes, you (like everyone else!) will make mistakes. But pick yourself back up, talk to yourself in a positive way, and take a new path. You can do it! Just believe in yourself and treat yourself like your own best friend. Love yourself—starting today!

Notes:

_____

_____

_____

_____

_____

_____

_____

_____

_____

_____

_____

_____

_____

_____

_____

_____

_____

_____

_____

_____

_____

_____

_____

_____

ABOUT THE AUTHOR

JACQUELINE KINLOCH

Jacqueline Kinloch is a Certified Image Consultant who resides in Houston, Texas with her husband Leon. She is a graduate of the University of Houston, with a bachelor's degree in health and minors in biology and psychology.

Ms. Kinloch, a former educator and flight attendant with Continental Airlines, is a certified image consultant for women. She teaches others about the importance of grooming, etiquette, and overall appearance. Ms.Kinloch also stresses the importance of positive attitude, professionalism, and handling oneself with poise. Ms. Kinloch conducts seminars on Wellness and Business Etiquette for local schools, corporations, and women's organizations. She also donates her time to local charities throughout the Houston area.

Ms. Kinloch, who believes in giving back to the community, is Executive Director of Ready Women Inc., a non-profit organization that gives comprehensive makeovers to women who are transitioning from Welfare to Work. Woman who belong to Ready Women Inc. are also taught job retention skills and can take advantage of monthly seminars to assist them in becoming well-rounded individuals.

Contact:
Ready Women
3 Royal Hampton Ct.
Sugar Land, TX 77479
(281) 265-8798
readywomeninc@alltel.net
www.protrain.net

TWO

SOCIAL ETIQUETTE AND MANNERS

By Jacqueline Kinloch

Have you ever attended a party or a social event, and that certain someone seems to move about with the gracefulness of a beautiful butterfly and display the manners of royalty? You can't help but notice this person. You wonder if she was born with such a gift. Well, ladies, surprise, surprise! Etiquette is not genetic. It's not something that you are born with. It's not inherited, it's learned!

Etiquette and good manners can be had by all if practiced. Remember the golden rule taught to you by your mother or first-grade teacher? Treat others like you want to be treated. If common courtesy is at the forefront of your behavior, good manners will always prevail, no matter what the circumstances.

Graceful Dining

Many social gatherings like proms, family dinners, and later in your life, business functions, involve dining. Your behavior at such occasions can tell people a lot about your character. Having bad manners at the table can cost you the next invitation or put the brakes on your fast track career when you enter the work arena. No matter your age or your

25

aspirations, the following tips will help to put you at ease while at the dining table:

- Sit straight and upright. Don't slouch.

- Elbows do not belong on the table.

- Your napkin should be placed in your lap as soon as you sit down.

- If the dinner is formal, follow the lead of your host or hostess.

- Do not start eating before the host or hostess. If you're at a dinner party or an event with many tables, wait until everyone is served.

- Don't talk with food in your mouth or chew with your mouth open.

- Don't reach across the table. Ask politely for the item to be passed by the person sitting closest to the item.

- Do not hold your fork as if you were shoveling something.

- The two styles for holding utensils are American and European. The most common style in this country is American. The fork is usually held in your right hand (unless you are left-handed, then simply reverse the process). When cutting, the fork is placed in your left hand with tines faced down and the knife in your right hand.

- Don't cut all your food at once. Cut a few pieces, then return the fork to your right hand and place the knife on the side of the plate.

- Never place used utensils back on the table. Rest them on the plate once they are used.

- Never use your fingers to push food onto the fork or spoons. Using a small piece of bread is acceptable.

- Never smoke at the dining table.

When you're served a cup of tea, the tea bag goes in the cup. However, when served a pot of tea, the tea bag goes in the pot. When desired strength is reached, take the tea bag out of the cup with your spoon, and twist the string around the bag to squeeze out the liquid. Liquid should not be squeezed out with your hands. Never leave the tea bag in the cup; this is bad tea etiquette! Always place the tea bag behind your cup on the saucer.

While dining, if you discover an uninvited guest in your food, please don't make a scene, and don't make a big announcement. Discreetly get the attention of the table server and whisper the problem to him or her.

If you have food caught between your teeth, run your tongue over your teeth with your mouth closed or drink some water. If these actions do not release the object, excuse yourself and proceed to the restroom to remove the object. It is not acceptable to use a toothpick while at the dining table.

Lipstick may be freshened discreetly at the table. If this can't be done without the use of a mirror, excuse yourself from the table. (Use your discretion with this one; it is still part of a great debate. Some experts say it is a part of grooming, and should not be done while dining.)

Never comb your hair or apply make-up at the table. (This is definitely considered grooming.)

If you receive a call on your cell phone (that is already placed on vibrate), please excuse yourself and answer the call. It is very rude to engage in a phone conversation while dining with others.

When leaving the table, place your napkin on the seat and push the chair in. If leaving the event, place your napkin on the table and push the chair in.

Do not blow your nose at the table. You may dab a runny nose, but if more is needed, excuse yourself and make a B-line to the restroom.

Always cough into your napkin, and turn your head away from the table.

Conversation that is graphic or gory does not belong at the table. Save it for later or better yet, try to avoid it all together. Conversations as such are done in poor taste.

You're probably saying to yourself, "I'm well equipped with the dos and don'ts of gracious dining, but I still don't know what side my bread plate is on. Is my water glass to my right or to my left? Which fork do I use first?" Relax and take a deep breath. It's not that difficult. Remember the initials B.M.W. In this instance, I'm not speaking of the German automobile. These initials stand for bread plate, main plate, and water glass. Your bread plate should be at the top left side of your place setting, your main plate is in the center, and your water glass is located to the top right side of your main plate. Your utensils will be located on both sides of the main plate.

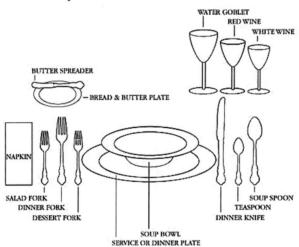

Always start the main course by using the fork and knife that are farthest from the plate, and work your way inward. If soup is being served, the proper spoon will be placed to the right of the knives. The dessert spoon and fork will be situated directly above the place setting, in a horizontal position. The spoon is usually the upper-most utensil, with the handle to the right, and the fork should be situated just below it, with the handle to the left. If this is a formal dinner, wine glasses curve from white wine, to red wine, to dessert wine. Champagne glasses are usually not set, but are presented before dessert. If you are not having any beverage that is being served, simply place your hand over the glass and say "No, thanks." For a casual meal, the coffee cup and saucer will be set at the beginning. For a formal meal, the cup and saucer are put out when dessert is served.

A Place Setting for Dinner

Social Gathering and Networking

Not all social and business events revolve around mealtime. Some functions may be more geared towards mingling, such as a networking party or some other type of gathering. Manners and etiquette are needed for introducing and greeting, and for engaging in good conversation. Introductions bring people together and stimulate networking. My father used to say that some people have the gift of gab and that they are never at a loss for words. Just like dining skills, being a good conversationalist is learned.

With a little guidance and practice, you too can mingle with ease. Let's consider introductions and greetings. An introduction is the first impression you make on someone and this impression is the lasting one. When attending a social gathering, always be prepared to give a self-introduction. You should also tell something about yourself. This shared little something usually sparks a conversation.

Don't forget to extend your hand when introducing yourself to an adult. A nice firm handshake will suffice. Remember not to squeeze the life out of the other person's hand and never give a limp shake either. When introducing others, the rule of thumb is that men are introduced to women, younger people are introduced to older ones, and people of a lower ranking are introduced to people of a higher ranking in a work setting. When introducing, always give the other person's full name, and mention something that the two people have in common or something you feel is interesting, like a hobby. For example, "Lisa, I would like you to meet John Johnson. John, this is Lisa Ginn; she just returned from South Africa."

Always mention something that will move the conversation forward and never make negative comments about someone's employment or school. After being introduced, some may request that you call them something other than the name given. By all means, address people in their preferred fashion. It is rude not to comply.

Another introduction might sound like this: "Madame Mayor, I would like to introduce to you Mr. James Bryant." Introductions are very important in most cultures and if not done, you could be considered rude. If you forget the proper way to introduce, it's better to still proceed with some type of introduction than to not introduce at all.

Now that all the introductions are out of the way, the fun begins: conversations with strangers and casual acquaintances! However fearful you are of this venture, being skilled in the art of conversation can take you a long way in life, and will help you to leave a lasting impression on people. Conversations involve listening and interchange. When conversing with others, don't hog the ball; bounce it back and forth. In other words, don't dominate the conversation, for this may give the impression that you are self-centered. You must listen to what others are saying. Without listening, you are just simply "talking" and not having a conversation. Some people have the habit of thinking about what they are going to say next instead of listening to what the other person is saying. Some like to call this bad habit "reloading."

Learning to be a good conversationalist is somewhat easy if you have the proper tools in your toolbox. Good conversationalists always have good eye contact and think before they speak. Be in tune with the people that you are conversing with, so that you will know if they are interested in what you are talking about. No one likes to be part of a boring conversation.

When having a conversation, don't put others down or correct something someone says. The only time this is acceptable is when your name is mispronounced during the introduction. This can be corrected when you respond to the introduction. You can simply say "It's a pleasure to meet you, I'm …..(And give your full name)." Someone mispronoucing the English language does not give you the license to make corrections.

Gossiping is taboo. It tells others that you have nothing else to talk about but other people. Do your best to talk about things you think are of interest, and not about other people's business.

The best advice that I could probably give you is to be well-informed. This can be accomplished by simply reading the newspaper or by watching or listening to the news. Keep abreast of current books, movies, and television shows of interest, for such topics are always great conversation starters.

Another tool is to ask others about themselves. You can ask them what part of the country they are from, if they have siblings, what school they attend or attended, their favorite food, and so on. When this technique is used, you can usually just sit back and listen.

Please don't ask rude questions. On occasion, people ask questions that are very inappropriate. Can you believe that some people ask such questions as, "How much did you pay for your dress?" or "How much was that car?" That's plain rude! Well, how do you respond if you're asked a rude question? Deflect and respond that you don't wish to share that information. You may want to respond to unwanted questions by simply saying, "I don't care to discuss that." Keep in mind that most people don't know that they've asked something rude, so try to be gentle with them.

Profanity is also something to avoid while at social or work functions. Someone once said to me that people who use profanity have lazy minds, and that they use profanity because they lack creativity.

Remember, to become a good conversationalist takes time and some effort. Always be polite and include everyone if you are in a group situation. Be yourself when conversing with others and never pretend to be someone you're not; people can see right through the façade. When interacting with new acquaintances, don't try to be their psychiatrist and give advice on how they should handle matters. Most of the time, people just want a listening ear.

There are a few topics that a good conversationalist should avoid if at all possible:

• Don't talk about someone's salary.

• Don't talk about health issues that one may be having.

• Don't talk about religion unless your conversation partner(s) bring it up.

• Don't talk about politics or someone's political party choice or lack of party choice.

• Don't ask your partner if he's wearing a toupee or if she's wearing a wig or hair weave.

Conversation brings people together. It's wonderful to learn about the differences in cultures, lifestyles, and experiences of others. When conversing with others, be absorbed in what they are saying, make them feel special and most of all, be respectful. Being a good conversationalist will take you a long way in life and open many doors.

EXERCISE
Plan a social gathering at your home. Invite family members and close friends. Have some of your family members or friends pretend to be someone that you are not acquainted with. By doing this, you can practice introducing them to the people you do know. Also practice starting conversations with them. You will also want to include a meal at this gathering, so that you can practice your dining etiquette. This should prove to be a fun experience for all involved and should help you on your way to becoming social savvy. (You could make name tags with the "assumed" name for each guest.)

Tips on Tipping

As you make your way through life and put your stamp on the social scene, don't forget to tip when appropriate. Many social occasions will involve tipping Use the following "tips on tipping" to guide you:

• Wait person: 15-20 percent of the total bill

• Bartender: $1 per drink

• Buffet service: 10 percent of the bill. (This is done only if something is brought to you).

• Coat check: $1 per item

• Delivery people: $1 to $3

• Taxi driver: 10-15 percent

• Bellhop: $1 to $2 per bag

• Maid: $1 to $2 per person a night

• Room service: 15-20 percent, unless already included

• Valet: $2 to $3 when a car is picked up, or $ 1 to $2 when the car is dropped off

• Doorman: $1 to $2 to flag a taxi

• Concierge: $5 to $10 for special service such as acquiring theater tickets to sold-out shows

• Tour guide: $1 to $2 per person per day

• Limousine driver: 15-20 percent, unless the tip is already included (be sure to check)

• Hairstylist: 15 percent of cost for the service

• Shampoo person: $1 to $5, depending on amount of services

• Pedicurist: 15-20 percent

• Manicurist: 10-20 percent

The amount you tip is based on the quality of service and the country in which you live. Tipping is more common in the United States, so if you travel abroad, please research the tipping guides for the country you plan to visit.

The art of social graces and good manners is acquired and learned. You will find that by having a solid understanding of etiquette, doors will open much more easily for you in social and business arenas. Remember, etiquette is simply using common courtesies to have others feel at ease. Knowing the right thing to do and say in any given situation will give you lots of confidence and create an image for yourself that is polished!

Good luck!

ABOUT THE AUTHOR

Ruby M. Ashley, MBA

Ruby Ashley is Chief Executive Officer of Ruby Ashley & Associates. She is a leader in personal and professional development, specializing in the delivery of workshops, seminars, training programs, and assessments. Her workshops and training programs are highly interactive and stimulating with focus on improving employee performance. She firmly believes that as long as individuals are willing to learn, change, and grow, they will always reach high levels of achievement.

Ms. Ashley is an accomplished motivational keynote speaker, facilitator, trainer, and consultant with more than 26 years of experience in the corporate environment. As a Certified Customer Service Trainer, she delivers an outstanding Customer Service Excellence program. Other training program topics include: personal and professional development, women's issues, diversity and multiculturalism, self-esteem, leadership development, strategic planning, road map to retirement, and team building. Teen topics are Save Our Youth, Teen Image, and Leadership.

Ms. Ashley earned Bachelor's and Master's degrees in Business from Brenau University in Gainesville, GA. She is a member of The Professional Woman Network (PWN), is a certified trainer, and member of The PWN International Advisory Board. Ms. Ashley holds memberships in other professional organizations, including the American Business Woman Association, Toastmasters International, Les Brown Speaker's Bureau, and is an affiliate of Leadership Development Group, Inc. She is a youth mentor and an active volunteer in her community.

Ruby Ashley is also a co-author of *Becoming the Professional Woman* and *Self-Esteem & Empowerment for Women* in the PWN Library.

Contact:
Ruby Ashley & Associates
1735 Chatham Ridge Circle #206
Charlotte, NC 28273
(404) 316-5931
rbyash@aol.com
www.protrain.net

THREE

"I'M MAD!" HANDLING ANGER AND FRUSTRATION

by Ruby M. Ashley

Everyone gets angry and frustrated. Anger is just a part of being human, especially when you're a teenager. Usually when you experience anger and frustration, it is because something is wrong in your life or something is not going your way. There are many methods for expressing your anger and frustration. Unfortunately, most are disrespectful to others and do not help you grow and learn from the situation. Understanding your negative emotions will help you make the proper choices when you are upset and need to express how you feel.

The teenage years are a frustrating time for both teens and their parents. As a teen, you may find this time frustrating because you are too young to be out on your own, yet you think you are too old to accept all of your parent's decisions and rules without question. Also consider that your parents' expectations of you are constantly changing. Try to understand that because you are growing up, your parents are experiencing a wide range of emotions, too, including anger, excitement, pride, and happiness (along with many other positive and negative feelings). Your parents may feel frustrated that they're no longer able to protect you and keep you safe like they did when you were little. Your growing maturity means they have to revise their ideas about what you need and what their responsibilities are regarding you.

As you go through your times of unexplained anger and frustration, be aware that most other young people your age feel the same way you do. Some of what's bothering you may just be "the teenage blues," the normal frustrations of trying to figure out your new values, attitudes, and abilities as you are growing up. However, if your anger/frustration is leading you in a destructive direction or if it is getting in the way of your relationships with friends, family, dating partners, or people at school, you may want to take a closer look at these negative feelings.

Which of the following describe your feelings when you are angry or frustrated? Circle the words that apply:

disturbed	annoyed	bothered
irritated	upset	depressed
"just don't care attitude"	low self-esteem	hopeless

Since anger can cloud your judgment and cause you to make bad decisions, it is important to learn how to manage your anger. Doing so will help you mature and better understand yourself.

One way to deal with your feelings, negative or positive, is to write about them. You may find it helpful to write something in a journal or diary every day. Turn to your diary when you find yourself feeling angry. Your anger log is a place where you can express your true feelings and thoughts. Every time you find yourself getting angry, jot down why you feel that way. The following is a sample entry of a time when I was really mad at my mom during my teenage years:

EXERCISE

Time and Date:	5 o'clock, Saturday, March 16th
What Happened?	My girlfriend spent the weekend with me, and my mom said we could not go to a dance with our dates. (I was so sure we could go to the dance that I didn't ask in advance.)
How angry was I?	9 (on a scale from 1 to 10)
How did I express it?	Talked loud so my mom could hear me.
How long did it last?	All night and part of the next day.
Problems with my anger:	I couldn't sleep and felt frustrated the next day.
Was my anger justified?	No.
Additional notes:	I know I should have asked in advance, but I was so sure that Mom would say yes because I had a guest for the weekend. I even asked her a second time, and she still said no. My friend and I were sad and mad, not only at my mom, but also at our dates. After they arrived and found out we couldn't go, they left us.

Your Turn

Time and Date: _____

What Happened? _____

_____

_____

How angry was I? _____

(on a scale from 1 to 10) _____

_____

How did I express it?   _____
_____
_____

How long did it last?   _____
_____

Problems with my anger: _____
_____

Was my anger justified?   _____
_____

Additional Notes: _____
_____
_____

After you've kept your anger log for two weeks, read it over and see whether you can find any patterns. Ask yourself the following questions:

• What kinds of things make me angry most often?

• How do I usually handle them?

• Does a particular person (or other people) keep popping up?

• Is there any type of treatment I am upset about?

• Reading over my log, what's my first reaction?

• My second reaction?

• Do I like what I see?

Use a separate section in your anger log to write about how you feel. After two weeks, determine if writing about your anger is helpful to you. If so, continue keeping your log.

Does your log give you any ideas for changes you want to make in your life? Can you think of new ways for handling your anger? Do you have issues you want to discuss with a particular person?

If you can't handle your anger or frustration on your own, it's okay to seek HELP! Talk to a counselor, friend, or therapist. These people can help you get in touch with what's really bothering you and can advise you about things you can do to cope with your anger.

Anger with Parents
The relationship between parents and teens is often a difficult one. It seems like you are always at odds with each other. While you want to assert your independence and spend a lot of time with friends, your parents want to make sure you are safe by keeping you at home. Here is a typical example of the kind of conflict a teenage girl might experience when she asks her father if she can go to a party:

When Joy receives an invitation to her friend Clarissa's party, Joy's father says she can't go. Joy gets so mad, she wants to scream, "I'm going because you are being unfair," but the last time she made a similar statement, her father yelled back, "I don't have to be fair! It's my house!" So Joy decides to try another approach.

Even though Joy is angry, she takes a deep breath and counts to ten. She has learned that talking to her father in an angry tone does not work! Joy really wants to go to the party, so she focuses on trying to get her father to change his mind by talking to him in a calm manner. She lets him know she has heard him and asks again in a different way, "I understand that you don't want me to go, but I'd really appreciate it if you'd tell me why."

Her father says to her, "I don't know who those people are; I don't trust you; and you're always staying out late." Joy is frustrated and wants to start screaming, but she focuses her anger on achieving her intention. She presents the situation to her father as a problem and asks him if they can solve it together. She promises him she will be back on time and asks him if he would feel better if Clarissa's mother called him. "You will like her; she's really nice. Would that help?"

Joy's father is still unsure and says, "I don't know." Again, she wants to scream; instead, she uses her anger to focus on what she really wants. She lets her father know she hears his concerns and is responding to him. "So if Clarissa's mom calls you, and I promise to be back by twelve, would that make you feel better?"

Joy leaves the room so her father will have time to think about his response. She is feeling proud because she kept her temper and helped her father move from being angry to listening to her. When Joy's father finally gives her permission to go to the party, she makes sure he knows she has returned home before twelve. The next day she thanks him for trusting her and letting her go to the party.

As a teenager, I used to get mad at my mom, because even when I would plead my case like Joy did, my mother would usually still say "NO!" Unlike Joy's father, my mother would not change her mind. Have you ever experienced a similar situation? Below are some ways of expressing anger to parents:

• "What you just said really hurt my feelings."

• "Right now, I'm feeling like nobody is listening to me or taking me seriously. It's a lonely feeling."

• "I get that you're upset with me right now, and I'm upset, too! What would make you feel better?"

Anger with Brothers and Sisters

Relationships with siblings can be difficult even if you are close. Anger can emerge in these relationships for many reasons. One of the biggest is due to competition for your parents' attention or limited resources like computer or TV time.

It is possible to express anger with a brother or sister while avoiding any type of power struggle. Remember, you have the right to set limits. You'll be more effective if you express your own feelings and don't focus on what other people have done wrong. Knowing that you have a right to set limits means that sometimes you can walk away from a fight. Here are some ways of expressing anger to brothers and sisters:

- "You know that kind of teasing makes me feel angry."

- "I know you like playing that music, but I really don't like it. This room belongs to both of us. What do you think we should do?"

- "I see you've worn my favorite sweater without asking my permission, and I'm really upset. I would appreciate you asking me before wearing any of my clothes."

- "I don't talk to people who talk to me that way. When you're ready to be polite, then we'll talk."

By saying how you feel and standing up for yourself with your siblings, you will feel better about your abilities to deal with any potential difficult situation and conflict in your life.

Anger with Friends

It may be hard to express anger with your friends because sometimes you feel closer to them than to your own family. Even though you feel you need them too much to risk telling them you're mad at them, they will become targets of your anger from time to time. When expressing anger to a friend, keep the following points in mind:

- Express your anger even if you believe it is unjustified.

- If you can, try to separate how you're feeling from what you want your friend to do.

- Remember that your friend is on your side; he or she is not an enemy.

- Talk about your own feelings, rather than saying what the other person has done wrong.

- If you talk about the other person, describe his or her behavior, not character.

- If you talk about the other person's behavior, be specific, not general.

- When possible, say what you do want, instead of what you don't want.

You should realize that even the best of friends will have disagreements. The important thing to remember is that you don't want to say or do something in anger that will cause permanent damage to your relationship. Try to understand the other person's point of view even if you don't agree with it, and to accept the fact that the other person has reasons for his/her behavior that may have absolutely nothing to do with you or your friendship.

Anger with Strangers

Being angry with strangers is somewhat different than getting upset with people you know. Because you don't have an ongoing relationship with strangers, you will probably handle getting mad at them differently than you do with your friends and family. It is important to know what your expectations are. How do you think people should be treated? Do you believe it's important to treat others with courtesy and respect? If so, you can make sure that you treat strangers properly, even if you're angry with them about some problem that you need to solve. Make sure whatever standards you set for others are the same standards you have for yourself and that you can live up to them.

When you get angry with others, make sure you express your feelings and wishes by using "I-messages." Say, "I'm feeling very frustrated" rather than, "You're really screwing this up." Be specific. Say, "I've been waiting for my sandwich for half an hour," rather than, "Is it going to take you all day to complete my order?" By carefully wording what you say to others, you are more likely to reduce the amount of conflict in the situation and get the results you want.

Anger at School

Do you have a difficult time expressing anger with your teachers and principals? Do you think these authority figures have all the power, making you feel small and helpless? If you are having a problem at school, seek help from an objective third party like your counselor, another teacher, or another principal. Just remember that there are people at school who really care about you and want to help you, so don't be afraid to ask them. Don't let your anger over what you perceive to be unfair situations get the best of you. Try to come up with a reasonable solution that will minimize conflicts or arguments with a person in authority over you.

For example, if your teacher gave you a zero on a paper you believe you turned in, it won't help to argue about it. Find out if the teacher will allow you to do the paper again or if you can do some extra credit work to make up for the bad grade. If not, then ask what options the teacher has for you to improve your grade. Maybe the teacher wants you to go to tutorials or has another suggestion. Be ready and willing to do what the teacher asks of you even if it means extra work. Once the teacher sees that you are trying and doing your best, he or she will probably be more understanding in the future if the same situation arises. Stay focused on the positive things you want, just like Joy did in the earlier example with her father. It is important not to lose your temper and to keep trying to resolve the situation so that both you and the teacher are satisfied with the result.

Proper Communication is Important

Anger can propel you to take a stand that you have not had the time to think through carefully. You must be able to recognize any negative advice from people around you, especially if you are in a heated argument with someone. When someone is angry, he or she has the tendency to judge, blame, criticize, or act strangely. Anger can have severe consequences.

Some teens have an easier time expressing their anger than others. What happens when you vent your anger depends on how well you handle your emotions, what the circumstances are, and who you are with at the time. Some common expressions of anger include staring at the victim, calling someone names, starting untrue rumors, making fun of others, and bumping or pushing people while walking by them. Many girls never overcome the hurtful experiences inflicted on them by their classmates, causing some women to have emotional scars that last a lifetime.

Other scars are physical ones caused when teenagers cut themselves to try to deal with stressful situations. According to T. Suzanne Eller in *Cutting Edge*, "1.5 percent of all Americans deliberately harm themselves, and 60 to 70 percent of self-injurers are female. Also, 90 percent of self-injurers begin cutting as teens, and their struggle often extends into their mid-20s to early 30s (between five to ten years–longer if untreated)." (http://www.christianitytoday.com/tcw/2006/001/11.38.html)

The most common reasons for cutting include trying to calm yourself, trying to gain a sense of control in your life, or just trying to feel something other than numbness. In an insightful article at http://www.coolnurse.com/self-injury.htm, the author suggests that "self-injury usually indicates that somewhere during development, a person didn't learn good ways of coping with overwhelming feelings or stress." Obviously, cutting is not a healthy coping strategy, so if you or someone you know is engaging in this dangerous behavior, please seek professional help.

How do you deal with the anger and frustration that causes stress in your life? Can you think of a healthier way to handle it? Perhaps you could take a nap, go for a walk, listen to some music, talk to a friend, meditate or read a book, etc. Find something you enjoy that is soothing and doesn't cause harm to your body or spirit. Try the following exercise to determine what you are currently using for coping mechanisms and what alternatives you might consider instead.

EXERCISE

Problem (example)	Current Coping Strategy	Healthy Alternative
Stress	Eat junk food	Go for a walk

REMEMBER, anger can be a powerful vehicle for continued personal growth and change, especially when it helps you recognize that you are not clear about something. During your teen years and throughout life, you are going to experience anger and frustration. What will make the most difference in your life is how you handle yourself during these trying situations.

REMEMBER, when you are angry or frustrated, you should watch what you say and what actions you take. You don't want your words and actions to burn a bridge you may need to cross at a later time.

My hope for you is to have a life filled with your dreams and aspirations coming true. Your attitude about whatever you decide to do in life will always make the difference. So stay sharp, work hard, and keep a cool temper.

You Can Do It!

Sometimes analyzing the causes of your anger and frustration can really help you. The Institute for Mental Health Initiatives has developed the RETHINK acronym to help people deal with their anger. Think of the last time you were mad with someone and complete the following exercise:

Meaning of acronym	Your Exercise
Recognize your anger.	Describe your angry feelings.
Empathize with the other person. thinking/feeling?	What could the other person be
Think of the situation in a new way.	How are you contributing to the problem? Can you find any humor in the situation or do something differently?
Hear what the other person is saying.	Try to paraphrase the other person's point of view.
Indicate respect and love with your words.	Think of some "I" statements you could use to communicate how you feel.
Notice what works to control your anger	What activities could you choose to calm you down?

Keep your attention
on the present.

What can you do today to make
the situation better?

Recommended Reading

Anger and Relapse: Breaking the Cycle by Jo Clancy, LMSW-ACP, LCDC.

Hot Line Anger by Laurie Beckelman.

The Struggle to Be Strong, edited by Al Sesetta, M.A. of Youth Communication, and Sybil Wolin, Ph.D. of Project Resilience.

ABOUT THE AUTHOR

JANIS SIMMS DAVIS

Janis S. Davis, Owner/CEO of Working It Right Consults, began her career as a physical therapist 22 years ago. Throughout her career he developed a desire to use her skills to address issues of woman's health. She attended Barry University in Miami and received her Master of Science degree in Physical Therapy, and a Bachelor of Science degree in Biology.

Janis has attended many seminars to strengthen her skills in providing consulting services for women. Her background as a therapist, and her God-given gift of wanting to help others, provides her with not only the desire, but also the skills, to assist women in addressing the management of stress and wellness. She has had the oppurtunity to speak before many groups and has provided workshops for the Women Ministry of several south Florida churches. Prior to her relocating from Florida to Georgia, she served as the lead servant of the HealthCare ministry of her church.

Janis is a certified trainer from The Professional Woman Network (PWN), and served on the 2006 Woman Network International Advisory Board. She is a co-author of *Customer Service & Professionalism for Women.*

Contact:
Working It Right Consults
5574 Grammercy Dr. SW
Atlanta, GA 30349
(404) 346-7750
JSimmsmspt@bellsouth.net
www.protrain.net

FOUR

IT'S YOUR BODY! NUTRITION & FITNESS

By Janis Simms Davis

You are about to start a journey that will affect you for the rest of your life. This chapter will encourage you, educate you, and give you a different outlook on the real you! You will learn about the needs of your body and how it works, which will lead you toward a different view of just who you are. You will learn that we are all different. We differ in color, weight, height, and looks, but we all require the same needs to survive. So let's start this journey of healthy living. For what you do today will affect the rest of your life.

This journey will start on the Street of Existence. Let's first answer a few questions to make you think and begin to learn about you. How well do you know your body? What makes your "engine" run? Do you know the importance of having fat, protein, or carbohydrates (carbs) in your body? Just what does it mean to be healthy? Please answer the questions the following page.

EXERCISE

1. What two words come to mind when you think about nutrition? (There are no wrong answers.)

_____   _____.

2. _____ is the fuel that helps you keep going, by giving you the energy needed to work. (Food)

3. What does healthy living mean to you?

_____

_____

_____

Don't think too hard.

DID YOU KNOW that an adult body holds an average of ten pints of blood and a newborn baby has only about one cup of blood running through its body? Without blood, our organs could not get the required oxygen and nutrients needed for us to survive.

Have you heard the saying, "You are what you eat"? Can this possibly be true? Well, in a way it is. The foods you choose to eat affect the way you look, how you feel, and give you energy to perform tasks. If you eat foods high in fats, you're at a high risk for being fat. If you eat balanced meals, chances are you will be healthier with less likelihood of being ill with diseases such as diabetes and heart disease. It's your body, your one and only God-given body, so let's start taking care of it now.

Nutrition, also known as "food" or "your diet," plays an important role in making sure your organs work. As you grow, your mind and body are changing physically and emotionally. You should know that eating a balanced diet will help make the most of your physical and mental potential. Food to the body is like gas to a car. Just like a car needs gas to run, the human body needs fuel (food) to work both physically and mentally.

Smart Eating

Know that no one food is enough to provide the required nutrients that the body needs. To eat smart, you need balance, variety, and self-control. Remember that all foods from the food groups should be a part of a healthy diet! We are going to take a look at a few of the many nutrients a growing body needs every day. Before we start, please answer a few more questions. Remember, this is a journey we are taking together so that we—you and I—can make changes for a better you.

1. What is a balanced meal?

_____

_____

_____

_____

2. Do you feel that you are living a healthy lifestyle? _____ (yes or no)

Whatever your answer was to the last questions, only you are able to change and improve. Learning about eating is the first step. To make sure that you are eating the right foods, you need to learn about the different kinds of foods. So here goes:

Carbohydrates ("Carbs")

Carbs are the body's main source of energy. There are two types of carbs: complex and simple. Simple carbs have few needed nutrients and should be eaten in limited amounts. Some simple carbs are candies and soda. Complex carbs provide fiber and needed nutrients in one's diet. Teens need to eat complex carbs, such as fruits and vegetables, every day. Make a list of the carbs you have in your diet. Circle the ones you will continue to eat and cross out the ones that you will limit. Remember: there is no one food that should be eliminated from your diet. Self-control is the key.

Simple carbs   Complex carbs

_____   _____

_____   _____

_____   _____

_____   _____

Other important food groups are fats and proteins. It's also important to pay attention to vitamins and minerals, such as calcium and iron.

Fats

Many feel that fats should totally be eliminated from a diet and are the main reason for weight gain. But did you know that fats also provide energy for the body? Your body needs fat to sustain itself. Fats build the brain, protect organs, and keep your skin and hair healthy. The key is eating just enough and not overdoing your intake of fats. Your body stores any fat that is not burned as energy. Later in this chapter we will review just how much of each food group is needed to maintain your body and keep it fit.

Proteins

Along with carbs and fats, proteins provide energy for your body. The primary role of proteins is building and repairing body tissues, like muscles and organs. Some good sources of protein are meats, eggs, and beans.

Minerals and Vitamins

Calcium is needed for strong bones and healthy teeth. As we get older, especially as teens, we stop drinking milk for fear of getting fat or just not liking it. Calcium is a vital ingredient in maintaining healthy bodies, and teens need to have two to three servings of calcium every day. Along with milk, some other sources of calcium are yogurt and cheese. If you are counting calories, fat-free, low-fat or skim milk products are the best.

> *DID YOU KNOW that the human skeleton has 206 bones and that bones are made up of calcium along with other minerals? Calcium is needed to make bones hard so that they can support your weight. The amount of certain vitamins and minerals that you consume, especially calcium and vitamin D, affect how much calcium is stored in your bones.*

Iron is another important mineral needed by your body. For your body to have the required amount of energy, and ability to think clearly, it needs to be fueled with iron-rich foods such as lean beef, cereals, beans, and enriched breads.

O.K. Let's see. To be healthy, we need to have a variety of foods. If we stop eating any one particular food, there is a great chance that we will be unhealthy and at risk for disease. So the bottom line is we need to be concerned about what we eat and how much we eat to maintain a healthy lifestyle.

Eating Right

Start every day with breakfast. This could be a cereal bar, a peanut butter and jelly sandwich, a glass of milk, and juice. During lunch, eat grilled foods rather than fried, eat small servings, have a salad, along with fruit and milk or yogurt. If you get hungry and need to eat between meals, try snacking on fruit, veggies, or cheese. Avoid empty calorie foods such as sugary drinks, cookies, cakes, and chips. If you take in more calories than you burn, then you will see a weight gain, feel tired, and lack the ability to think well. This is not all about eating to look thin, it's about eating to be healthy. By changing your eating habits, know that weight loss is a bonus, not necessarily the goal.

Suggestions

Instead of:	Choose:
Whole milk	Low-fat/skim milk
White bread/croissants/biscuits	Whole wheat bread
Regular ice cream	Sorbet/sherbet/non-fat or low fat ice cream
Doughnuts/pastries	English muffins/small whole wheat bagels
Sugary cereals	Oatmeal/whole grain cereal
Potato/corn chips	Unsalted pretzels/unbuttered popcorn
Fried tortillas	Corn or whole wheat soft tortillas/pita bread
Cookies	Fig bars/gingersnaps
Regular ground beef	Lean ground beef/ground turkey
Pepperoni/salami/bologna	Lean turkey/chicken/ham
Fried chicken	Baked, broiled chicken

So what did you learn? The dietary guidelines provided by the U.S. Department of Health Services describe a healthy diet as one that emphasizes fruits, vegetables, whole grains, and fat-free or low-fat milk.

Here are some key points to remember:

• To maintain a healthy body weight, you should balance calories from foods and drinks with calories burned.

• To prevent gradual weight gain over time, make small decreases in food and drinks and get moving. (Not to look good, but to be healthy.)

• Eat less fat (especially butter, coconut, and palm oil).

• Choose baked snacks over fried.

• Eat fewer fast foods as they are high in fat. Instead, eat more fruits and vegetables.

• Drink low-calorie drinks.

The Fitness Connection

Hey! Let's get physical. Now that you know that eating is good for you but in moderation, you need to learn how to balance food with physical activity. Know that getting physical can be as simple as using the stairs instead of the elevator, walking to the store, bus stop, or school, especially if you are already eating right and are involved in sports or other activities other than sitting.

The different types of exercise needed for a healthy lifestyle are aerobic and strengthening. Aerobic exercise makes your heart stronger, thus helping it to pump blood and bring more oxygen to all the parts of your body. Exercise can also prevent high blood pressure and diabetes. Combined with a healthy diet, exercise can speed up weight loss.

DID YOU KNOW that regular exercise also helps you burn calories faster, even when you are sitting still?

Aerobic exercise raises your heart rate, which burns calories. Some examples of aerobic exercise are: walking, jogging, running, swimming, and bicycling. Strength training includes weight lifting, squats, and lunges.

DID YOU KNOW that in the United States, 58 million people are seriously overweight and in poor physical condition?

If you think being overweight was just a matter of appearance, you are wrong. Obesity, or being twenty percent above your healthy body weight, is a dangerous condition. Those extra pounds increase your risk for developing heart disease, diabetes, and even some forms of cancer. With this knowledge, let's consider how not changing might affect your life.

Health Status Now	Health Risk Later
Excess weight	Heart disease/diabetes/ high blood pressure
Inactive lifestyle	Osteoporosis/diabetes/stroke

The Benefits of Exercise

Exercise:

• Improves your self-esteem

• Gives you energy

• Strengthens your heart and muscles

• Relieves stress

• Prevents bone loss

Calories Used in Various Activities:

• Running (11 minutes/mile)	Up to 10.5 calories
• Swimming (crawl/slow)	Up to 12.0 calories
• Walking 30 minutes	Up to 6.2 calories
• Basketball	Up to 10.6 calories
• Weight lifting	Up to 7.1 calories
• Cleaning 60 minutes	Up to 4.5 calories
• Cooking 60 minutes	Up to 3.5 calories
• Cycling	Up to 4.9 calories
• Dancing	Up to 4.9 calories
• Gardening	Up to 8.6 calories

(Source: Shape Up, America, a not-for-profit organization committed to raising awareness of obesity as a health issue)

The best way to guarantee you will stay on the road to healthy living is to eat foods you like and do physical activities you enjoy. By doing this, chances are you will not return to old habits and will begin to enjoy your new way of living.

Now our journey is coming to an end. I hope you have learned enough to start living a healthy lifestyle, and are also motivated to do further reading on improving the new you. Remember, you are doing this for you. It's not all about looking good, but feeling good as well. You should be able to look in the mirror and say, "I know I've got it together." By incorporating simple changes into your life, like drinking more water and moving more, you actually have a look-good glow. But don't take my word for it; get started and see for yourself.

It's often easier to go on a journey with a companion. Don't go it alone; bring along a friend. By sharing the "new you" with others, you will be helping to stop the obesity epidemic. On this street, you can use your mirror more to admire the changes that are happening, not only outside, but on the inside as well. Keep in mind that even exercise alone builds self-esteem.

Ask yourself this question: Isn't it better to add years to your life than to add inches to your waist? So set goals, be realistic, and start slowly. If you slip one day, so what? Just get back on track. It's not a reason to give up.

> *DID YOU KNOW that it takes about twenty minutes for the stomach to signal the brain that you are full?*

So eat slowly and stretch out meals so that you will feel satisfied sooner. When you eat fast, you end up eating more than your body needs, so go slow and enjoy the flavors. Eat wisely and exercise regularly (3-4 times a week). Remember thin is not in. Healthy living is not all about diet and looking like a model. This whole chapter is about living a longer, healthier life.

Eating Disorders

Before we part, I would like to talk to you about eating disorders. It is estimated that one percent of American teens have an eating disorder. Think about it! This means that out of a class of 400 students, there is a great chance that four of them have anorexia or bulimia.

People with anorexia have a fear of being fat and have an altered perception about their bodies. They usually do not eat and often exercise all the time to lose weight. When a person with anorexia looks in the mirror, she will actually see a fat person. Is this condition dangerous? Yes!

A person with this disorder can cause damage to the heart, liver, and kidneys, as she is literally starving herself to death.

The next disorder, bulimia, is different, for this person doesn't avoid eating. She will actually eat everything in sight and then try to get rid of it by vomiting or taking laxatives. Such behavior is known as "binge and purge." This is not healthy, for there can be damage to the stomach and the increased acidity can cause tooth decay. Bulimia can also damage the heart, for the body of a person with bulimia is not able to absorb required nutrients. Bulimia can be serious enough to cause death as well.

Learn the warning signs and help anyone you feel is suffering from either of these disorders. If you have any of these signs or know of someone who does, please seek help.

The Warning Signs of Anorexia and Bulimia

A person with anorexia:

• Drops weight about twenty percent below normal

• Claims to never be hungry

• Feels fat

• Does not participate in social activities

A person with bulimia:

• Makes excuses to go to the bathroom right after meals

• Eats large amounts of food, but doesn't gain weight

• Uses laxatives or water pills

• Does not participate in social activities

It's time for our journey to end. Before we do so, however, I'd like you to answer the questions I asked at the beginning of this chapter once again. Look at your answers and compare them to your earlier answers.

1. What does healthy living mean to you?

_____

2. What is a balanced meal?

_____

Before starting a diet or heavy exercise program, seek the advice of a professional—a doctor, trainer, or physical therapist. So get off the couch, get out of the bed, put down your book, and get moving. Twenty minutes of continuous activity is better than none. Call a friend and take a walk. Sing, dance, or maybe surprise yourself and pull out the vacuum. Turn on some music and move. Get the family involved and you all will benefit from this journey by feeling good. So enjoy! Make it fun! Try new things. Don't overdo it, make one small change at a time. You can do it!

Notes:

ABOUT THE AUTHOR

STARLA JACKSON

Starla Jackson is Founder and President of the Personal Empowerment Institute, a personal and professional development firm specializing in seminars, business consulting, life coaching, and corporate training. She is a member of The Professional Woman Network, Toastmaster's International, and the National Association of Female Executives.

Starla is a highly sought-after and dynamic keynote speaker and facilitator. Ms. Jackson's mission is to inspire, empower, and motivate all who cross her life's path to not only survive life's struggles and tragedies, but to thrive in spite of it all. Starla Jackson is a "serial entrepreneur" and uses her personal and professional experience to empower others in moving beyond a life of mediocrity to a life filled with infinite possibilities.

Contact:
The Personal Empowerment Institute
P.O. Box 712
Corona, CA 92878
(951) 738-0626
starlamotivates@yahoo.com
www.protrain.net

FIVE

NO MORE! ELIMINATING TOXIC RELATIONSHIPS

By Starla Jackson

Have you ever found yourself in a situation with a friend, boyfriend, or family member when you just felt terrible every time you were in their presence? If you answered yes to this question, you are not alone. Almost everyone at one time or another has had the unfortunate displeasure of experiencing what is called a toxic relationship. The following is a list of behaviors that will help you to identify whether you are involved in a toxic relationship with friends, family or any interpersonal male/female love relationship. I would suggest that you invest in a journal or notebook and take notes while reading this chapter and following the recommended exercises.

Toxic relationships consist of friends, family, or anyone else who consistently does one or more of the following:

- Constantly puts you down or criticizes you. Nothing you do is ever good enough.

- Ignores what you say or do.

- Acts as though you do not exist.

- Takes up more than a fair share of attention, conversation, or physical space.

- Talks about you, rather than to you.

- Spreads gossip or rumors that undermine you.

- Expresses in actions, words, and tone of voice or body language that you are stupid, ignorant, incompetent, or defective.

- Makes undermining comments about your past errors or shortcomings.

- Gives constant reminders that diminish and deny you a "fresh start," or acknowledge your efforts, intentions, or progress toward change.

- Bullies, manipulates, pressures you, or encourages you to have feelings of guilt, inadequacy, or inferiority.

- Makes poisonous remarks that leave you feeling guilty, wounded, or traumatized.

- Inflicts physical abuse.

- Lies, deceives, or steals from you.

- Damages things that you value: possessions, relationships, your ethical or spiritual values.

- Does not allow you to live your own life your own way, with your own beliefs.

Eliminating relationships is never an easy thing to do, even when the relationship is no longer serving you positively. The way in which you can decipher whether or not a relationship is toxic is by asking yourself the following questions:

EXERCISE

1. How do I feel when I'm around this person? Am I happy or uncomfortable? Explain:_____
_____
_____

2. Is this person emotionally draining? Am I happy and full of life after I leave his/her presence?
Explain:_____
_____
_____

3. Does this person add value to my life? Am I motivated to be all that I can be? Explain:_____
_____
_____

4. Is this person truly supportive of me? Is he/she truly happy for me? Explain:
_____
_____
_____

5. Is this person critical of me? Is he/she always negative? Explain:
_____
_____
_____

6. Is this person judgmental? Does he/she always find something wrong with me or what I am doing? Explain:_____
_____
_____

7) Is this person happy for my successes? Does he/she seem jealous of me? Explain:
_____
_____
_____

Take a moment to review the previous questions and answers. You must be very honest with yourself concerning the people you allow into your inner space. It's important that you only allow those people into your life who are indeed positive, supportive, loving, caring, giving, and truly want the best for you.

I've discovered in my own life that whenever I set really high goals for myself and, if my friends feel uncomfortable with what I am doing, they might exhibit very critical and judgmental behavior. For instance, several years ago I went on a personal mission to lose weight. I hired a personal trainer and sought the counsel of a nutritionist. I shared my goals with all of my friends and family. However, some friends would make sly remarks as to my progress and tell me that I probably would never get to where I wanted to be. As the weight began to come off and my body became just as slim or slimmer than theirs, they would act as if I were invisible. All of a sudden the invitations to parties and social events ceased. Needless to say, I never had to eliminate any of those relationships, as they fizzled on their own! Some of these friends were actually uncomfortable with me after I reached my weight loss goal.

I met an awesome new guy I was ecstatic about! I immediately called my friend Sheryl to share the news of my new love interest. I eagerly shared with her the details of my first date. Her reaction was the total opposite of mine. She didn't seem to be very happy for me at all! She began to belittle my choice of this new boyfriend because of my past failure in relationships. I ended the call with Sheryl feeling wounded, bewildered, and insecure about my choices. After thinking about it for a while, I realized that this wasn't the first time Sheryl had treated me this way. Whenever I shared happy news with her about a new date or new job, she always seemed to become upset and belittle me in some way. I realized that Sheryl was not happy in her own life and would probably not be supportive of me. I eventually became true to myself and ended my friendship with Sheryl.

Friends will reveal their true selves and whether indeed they are supportive friends when you reach such milestones as making the honor roll, acing a test, receiving an academic or sports scholarship, graduating from college, buying a new car, purchasing your first home, or giving birth to your first child. Unfortunately, jealousy is usually the culprit behind someone not celebrating your personal successes. It is sometimes difficult for people to separate from their failures in order to rejoice in your happiness. If someone is not happy with themselves, they will probably not be happy for you. Please don't be alarmed if you discover that you only have one or two "real" friends.

Renee, a recent high school graduate, was very popular in high school. By the time college started, Renee no longer had any girlfriends. Her friends had started participating in lewd sexual acts, experimenting with drugs and alcohol, and living lifestyles that conflicted with where Renee saw herself. Fortunately, Renee had very high self-esteem. Instead of following the "in" crowd, Renee stood by her principles and moral beliefs and removed these friends from her life. What can be learned from Renee's story? You must set boundaries in your life, know who you are and where you are going. If the people in your life who are occupying your space are not in alignment with who you are and where you are going, then this is potentially a toxic relationship and you must remove yourself from the relationship. Remember that Renee found new friends once she started college and these friends shared similar positive life goals and they had many things in common with Renee. You can find new positive and supportive friends, too.

There are also the friends that simply want to be YOU. They want everything that you have: your clothes, your shoes, even your bedroom furniture and the same color paint that is on your bedroom walls. I know that sometimes you can be close to your girlfriend and automatically like the same things. That is to be expected. However, it is a completely different story when you both have the same quality things but she always thinks that whatever you have is better than hers. She is always comparing herself to you and trying to emulate you in every way. Some may consider this to be a compliment, and yes, in the beginning it comes across as such. However, eventually it becomes annoying. Inevitably, things between you become strained and you begin to separate yourself. There is a fine line between what is healthy and what is not. If your friend's competition against you becomes so extreme that it makes you uncomfortable, talk to her about this. If she continues her constant comparison, you may consider that this relationship is simply not healthy. As close as best friends can be, it is important to keep your individuality. Your friend should accept that you have certain gifts and talents (and material things) and that whoever she is just fine. She needs to have her own identity and not be a carbon copy of you.

Male and Female Relationships
April and Marcus had been dating for two years. April was sixteen and Marcus was eighteen. They were really "in love," but Marcus always wanted to know where April was going, what time she would return, what she was wearing, and who she was going with. April was just tickled pink because Marcus really loved her. One day April spent a girl's day out with her mom and a couple of her girlfriends. They started out having breakfast, then they went for manicures and pedicures. They

followed up with shopping at the mall and lunch. It was really late by the time April returned home. When April checked her voicemail messages, Marcus had left fourteen messages. By the time she listened to the last few messages Marcus had become completely enraged.

April proceeded to call Marcus. He was so irate by the time April got him on the phone, that she immediately started to cry because she didn't know why he was so angry with her. Marcus asked April to sneak out of the house so that they could see each other and April agreed. They met at the park around the corner at 1 o'clock in the morning and when April arrived, Marcus was already there waiting for her. He immediately rushed toward her, grabbed her and pinned her up against the lamp post in the park. This was the first time that April was afraid of Marcus. He began to rant and rave about how April must be cheating on him. April protested but Marcus became so enraged that he couldn't hear her. He became physically violent with April, but she managed to get away and run back home. When she awoke the next day, she had bruises all over her body and a black eye. Needless to say, when April's mother saw the bruises, she made April confess to what had taken place and she lovingly advised April to break things off with Marcus. This had become a toxic relationship. But it wasn't as simple as that.

Marcus was obsessed with controlling April and harassed her almost daily at school. April's family eventually decided to send April to live with her aunt in another state to get her away from Marcus. Situations similar to this happen daily amongst young women and men. If any of this sounds familiar to you, perhaps you are in a situation such as April and Marcus. Please find an adult that you can confide in and get help getting out of this relationship. Love shouldn't hurt. If any romantic relationship causes you pain, it's a clear indication that this is a situation you may want to reconsider. Love edifies, strengthens, builds, encourages, inspires, empowers, heals, and brings you a great job and happiness. Love should not tear you apart.

EXERCISE
Male and Female Relationships
The following is a series of yes or no questions that will help you to determine whether or not the relationship with your boyfriend is healthy or toxic. It would be most helpful to get a journal and review this material; really go into depth when answering these questions. By journaling you will become crystal-clear as to what type of relationship you are involved in and start to understand what a healthy, loving relationship is and is not.

1. Is my boyfriend possessive and controlling of me?_____

2. Does my boyfriend tell me who I can and cannot hang out with? _____

3. Does my boyfriend love me?_____

4. Does my boyfriend want to know where I am 24 hours a day?_____

5. Does my boyfriend like my family and friends?_____

6. Does my boyfriend tell me what clothes to wear to school?_____

7. Do my friends think we make a good couple?_____

8. Is my boyfriend physically abusive towards me?_____

9. Does my boyfriend sometimes hit me when he is upset?_____

10. Is my boyfriend supportive of the goals I have set for myself?_____

11. Do my parents like my boyfriend?_____

12. Does my boyfriend sometimes tell me that I'm stupid or fat?_____

13. Is my boyfriend emotionally abusive towards me?_____

14. Does my boyfriend cheat on me and tell me that it's my fault?_____

15. Does my boyfriend have positive goals for his life?_____

16. Does my boyfriend drink liquor and/or experiment with drugs?_____

17. Does my boyfriend encourage me to try liquor or drugs?_____

18. Does my boyfriend sometimes ask me to ditch school?_____

19. Does my boyfriend encourage me to get good grades?_____

20. Do my boyfriend's friends think that I'm "the one" for him?_____

21. Does my boyfriend pressure me to have sex even though I've told him I'm not ready for that yet?_____

22. Does my boyfriend respect my feelings and thoughts?_____

23. Is my boyfriend a responsible person?_____

Family Relationships

With regard to toxic relationships within a family, there is not a family on the planet without some level or dysfunction. Your family is your family and there is nothing that you can do to change that. What you can change, is the way you are treated. You should be treated with respect.

Sometimes constructive criticism from parents can be viewed as disrespectful or critical. But there is a fine line between offering constructive criticism and being downright judgmental. One sure way to tell the difference is to know whether or not your parent is coming from a place of love. Most parents love their children and want the absolute best for them. However, there are few extreme situations where that is simply not the case. In such situations (where there is real toxic behavior), you may choose to live with a grandparent or other family members, if possible.

> *Lisa was a very talented singer. All she ever talked about was being a superstar one day. She would sing around the house and keep her family entertained all day long, but when it came to performing live or singing in front of people, she could never bring herself to do it. Lisa's mother, Monica, could see that Lisa was gifted in a few other areas as well and decided to gently guide her in one of those directions. Lisa viewed her mom as being critical of her singing and her desire to become a superstar. In actuality, her mother was giving her constructive criticism and trying to support her in another area that seemed to come a little easier for her.*

As with Lisa's mom, sometimes parents steer you in another direction if they see that you are having difficulties overcoming fears and obstacles. It may sound like criticism or being judgmental, but your parent means well.

Dr. Phil says that "we teach others how to treat us." If this is true, you want to confront the person who is treating you with disrespect and tell them how you want to be treated in the future. This relates to your family members, friends, and boyfriend. There is no need for toxic relationships which poison you and hold you back. If a person is not willing to respect your wishes, you must let that relationship go. With regard to family, cruel or toxic behavior may have to be mediated by a counselor. There is no reason that you must tolerate deliberate cruelty.

In closing, you always want to pay attention to your innermost gut feelings. If you are miserable while in the company of a toxic person, immediately leave their presence. Stand up for yourself and don't tolerate that kind of environment. You deserve to have supportive and emotionally healthy people in your life and only you can set the limits of keeping toxic relationships out of your life. You can make it happen!

Notes:

_____

_____

_____

_____

_____

_____

_____

_____

_____

_____

_____

_____

_____

_____

_____

_____

_____

_____

_____

_____

_____

_____

ABOUT THE AUTHOR

DOLORES O. ROBINSON

Dolores O. Robinson is a career educator who has served more than twenty-five years in the Palm Beach County Florida School District. Ms. Robinson's service spans the entire gamut from classroom teacher/guidance coordinator to accreditator of Florida schools with the Southern Association of Colleges and Schools. She has written county curriculum and school grants for over a quarter million dollars.

Ms. Robinson is certified by the Florida Department of Education in the following areas: Educational Leadership, Vocational Director, Guidance and Counseling, and Vocational Adult Home Economics. She acquired her Master's Degree from Nova Southeastern University and Palm Beach Atlantic University.

For the past thirteen years, Ms. Robinson has been a licensed Business and Education Consultant in Palm Beach County, where she assists community organizations and churches in obtaining state and federal 501(c)(3) non-profit status. She also assists businesses with start-ups, business plans, marketing, and grant resources, as well as designing after-school programs and teaching grant-writing.

Because her entire career is involved with youth and people empowerment, she recently incorporated a new component into her enterprise, "Community-N-Crisis," which focuses on youth violence interventions and youth entrepreneurial training.

Contact:
867 Azalea Drive
Royal Palm Beach, FL 33411
(561) 312-2185
Robinsond867@aol.com
www.protrain.net

SIX

PREPARING FOR COLLEGE OR A CAREER

By Dolores O. Robinson

Who knows better than you what inspires, excites, and motivates you? So, become a designer—not of clothing or machines or systems—but of your own future! Think about what makes you happy! Think about what really excites you! Envision yourself in a career that makes you happy and gives you a sense of accomplishment. That might be difficult if you don't have broad-based knowledge of various occupations. To gather such information, you might talk to school counselors, occupational specialists, teachers, parents, and various employers for advice.

Now, let's start at the beginning of your search! You must know the kind of student you are. What best describes you: a student with good grades, a student with average grades, a student who could do better, or a student who is, by choice, a complete disaster.

When you're preparing for college or a career, you start by getting good grades! There are ten easy steps:

1. Believe in Yourself

"To succeed, we must first believe that we can"! You must believe in yourself and your abilities, whether you're an athlete preparing for competition or a student tackling a difficult subject. You must recognize the talents and abilities that you possess. You must know and believe that you can succeed.

2. Get Organized

If you are organized, you have what you need, when you need it! Get a notebook or three-ring binder. Write assignments, get classmates or mentor phone numbers, design a list of helpful resources, and organize your daily schedule nightly. Complete all assignments on time.

3. Manage Your Time Well

With good time management, you'll have time to complete all projects immediate and future. Create your own study plan, use class time, study halls, and the library. Prepare to handle sabotages such as TV, phone calls, friends, added chores, or extra-curricular activities.

4. Become a Classroom Success

Adapt to each of your teachers; they are all different with different expectations and rules. Be prepared for each class. Come ready to learn, be on time, bring all resources, remain interested, be respectful, ask questions if in doubt, and get your parents involved in school activities.

5. Take Good Notes for Tests

Tests cover information discussed during class time. Therefore, it is important that you become an active listener, pay attention, recognize important information, take accurate notes, and review notes nightly.

6. Read and Understand Your Text

First, scan: read subtitles, bold print, italics, summaries, charts, and review questions. Then read with a purpose and review to see if you understand the information.

7. Study! Study! Study!

Find a good study place, start on time, understand your learning style, learn how to study for tests, memorize information, tape record, write a paper using informational notes, learn word processing, learn and practice oral presentations.

8. Test-taking Strategies

To perform well on any kind of test, you must study hard and be well prepared. Some of these strategies may help you do well on your test:

- Bring all of your resources—pen, pencil, calculator, etc.

- Look over the test and develop a plan to answer each section. Mark difficult questions and return to them later.

- Use a method of elimination on answering multiple choice questions.

- Look for key words in true/false questions (the answers "all, never, every, none and always" used in questions are usually false).

- Before answering essay questions, read and understand the entire question, brainstorm, write down words, ideas, points, and facts that you want to cover, then organize in the order of presentation. Write legibly, read through your answer, re-read, then read again.

- Find a partner, tutor, or after-school program to assist in any subject you feel weak in for grade improvement.

- Review all returned tests and correct for finals.

9. Test Anxiety

A little anxiety improves concentration and alertness. Reduce high anxiety by preparing early: mentally practice taking the exam, visualize yourself coming in a little early and confidently passing the exam. (When you need help: There may be times when you need the intervention of a teacher, guidance counselor, administrator, principal, or a parent. When this is necessary, DO NOT hesitate to seek their help to solve your problem.)

10. Parent Involvement

Children need their parents to be interested and involved in their academic progress. Though you as a student must be responsible for your own grades, attendance, and behavior, ask your parents to be involved with your school progress. Discuss classes, grades, progress, teachers, and educational goals with them. Ask for assistance with homework assignments, but don't ask your parents to do your work for you. Don't think it is "uncool" to have your parents involved in your schooling and education. The more involved they are, the better your grades will be!

We are what we repeatedly do.
Excellence, then, is not an act, but a habit.
– Aristotle

What Colleges, Universities and Technical Schools Look for in Potential Candidates:

• Challenging high school classes with AP, Honors, or IB classes.

• GPA and ACT / SAT test scores (see below).

• Your essay: It paints a picture of you, reveals who you are, what you have learned, and how this influences your goals.

• Your interview: Prepare like you would for a job! Learn all you can about the school. Dress appropriately and arrive early.

Types of Schools

- State universities

- Independent colleges

- Private institutions

- Religious institutions

- Community colleges

- Technical schools

Living Arrangements for College

Compare these factors when it comes to deciding where you are going to live:

1. Mom and Dad's House

Cost factor – Free

People factor – Low

Fun factor – Low

Comfort factor – Medium

Safety factor – High

2. Dorm

Cost factor – Usually cheaper than an apartment

People factor – High

Fun factor – Medium to High

Comfort factor – Low

Safety factor – Medium to High

3. Apartment

Cost factor – From $500 to $1,500 per month (varies with number of roommates)

People factor – High

Fun factor – High

Comfort factor – Varies

Safety factor – Medium

Hot Jobs for Grads

Engineering

1. Mechanical

2. Agricultural

3. Civil

4. Electrical / Electronic

Computer

1. Information technology

2. Network administrator

3. Computer support specialist

4. Systems analyst

5. Computer programmer

Health Care

1. Licensed practical nurse (LPN)

2. Medical assistant

3. Dental hygienist

4. Registered nurse (RN)

5. Occupational therapist

6. Physician assistant

7. Physician

Education

1. Teacher's aide

2. Elementary school teacher

3. Secondary school teacher

4. Special education teacher

5. Guidance counselor

6. Resource teacher

7. School security /police

8. Behavior intervention assistant

9. District specialist

10. District supervisor

11. District administrator

12. Superintendent

13. Community college /college /university professor

14. Financial aid specialist

15. Coach

16. Band director

Public Service

1. Emergency vehicles dispatcher

2. Correctional officer

3. Firefighter

4. Police patrol officer

5. Sheriff and deputy sheriff

6. Postal worker

Construction Trades

1. Carpenter

2. Drafter

3. Electrician

4. Heating, A/C, refrigeration mechanic

5. Plumber

6. Construction supervisor

7. Contractor

8. Architect

SAT and ACT Test Information

SAT (Scholastic Aptitude Test)
The SAT test consists of SAT I: Reasoning Test,
and the SAT II: Subject test.

The SAT:

- Measures verbal and mathematical reasoning abilities that are important to college success

- Score scale: 200-800

- Format: 3 hours, primarily multiple choice

- *Verbal:* 78 questions/75 minutes, emphasis on critical reading

- Question types: Sentence completion, analogies, critical thinking

- *Mathematical:* 60 questions/75 minutes (Two 30-minute sections; one 15-minute section)

- Emphasis on data interpretation and applied math questions

- Ten questions require your own student response

- Calculator permitted but not required

- Question type: quantitative comparison, grid-ins, multiple choice

- Test dates: 10/13, 11/3, 12/1, 1/26, 3/16, 5/4, 6/1

- Fees: Basic registration – $14.00; Reasoning – $25.00

- Contact information: Tel: (609) 771-7600 or www.collegeboard.com for ACT information

ACT Guides
How to prepare for the ACT – Barron's
Getting into the ACT – Harcourt Brace

Where to Go to School

1. Select a college, university, technical school, or private institution that meets your needs ranging from culinary arts to computers. Many state institutions, community colleges and technical centers have virtual tours on their web sites.

2. A personal on-site tour is an excellent idea because parents can come along for a personal inspection/question answer/approval.

3. Once you have selected a school, you may need to look into financial aid. The cost of some universities can be excessive and well beyond your means. Therefore, you may need to check out available financial aid and scholarship opportunities.

Financial Aid

Federal Financial Aid: FAFSA, website: www.fafsa.ed.gov

What you need to complete the application:

1. Social security number

2. Driver's license number

3. W-2 form

4. Most recent income tax return

5. Current bank statement, stocks, bonds, other investments

6. Other untaxed income, such as social security, veteran's benefits, welfare

7. Business farm records, if applicable

8. Alien registration, if applicable

If you are a dependent student:

1. Parents' income

2. Parents' financial records

3. Parents' latest W-2 documents (Use income records the calendar year before application.)

Getting a FASFA "PIN" Number for Financial Aid:

1. Apply for a U.S. Department of Education PIN at www.pin.ed.gov.

2. Print your pre-application.

3. Save your FASFA as you go using the "save" button. (If connection is lost, you can regain your FASFA connection.)

4. Get help. The "need help" button is at the bottom of every online FAFSA page.

5. Sign your application. If you have a PIN, you can sign electronically.

6. Submit your application: Click the submit button located on the last page of FAFSA.

What can you do with a Financial Aid PIN number:

1. Sign your FAFSA electronically.

2. Review your FAFSA if necessary.

3. Sign loan promissory notes.

4. View information about your federal loans and grants.

5. Reapply for financial aid in the future.

6. Conduct other online business with the U.S. Department of Education.

College Resource Information

Barron's Profiles of American Colleges

The College Handbook

Peterson's Four-year Colleges

College Admissions Index

Resources with College Rankings and Ratings:

The Insiders Guide to Colleges

Barron's Best Buys in College Education

The Fiske Guide to Colleges

The College Finder

Competitive Colleges

Guide to the Best Colleges in the United States

Daystar Guide to Colleges for African American Students, Kaplan

The Best 331 Colleges, Princeton Review

Financial aid and scholarship resources:

College Cost and Financial Aid Handbook, Prentice Hall

Paying for College, Princeton Review

The Scholarship Book, Prentice Hall

College Money Handbook, Peterson's

Scholarships, Grants and Prizes:

The A's, B's, and C's of Academic Scholarships

The Big Book of Minority Opportunities

(Check your State Department of Education for state grants.)

The Best and Most Popular Web Sites for Financial Aid Information and Scholarship Searches:

www.fastweb.com

www.finaid.com

www.salliemae.com

www.ne-epc.com/aid.htm

www.fasfa.ed.gov

www.cashe.com

www.edgov/inits/hope (Life-long learning credit information)

Web Sites for Testing Tips and Information:

www.cts.org

www.review.com/college

www.act.org

www.collegeboard.org

Websites for College Testing Information:

www.collegeboard.org

www.collegenet.com

www.collegequest.com

www.petersons.com

www.collegeview.com

www.kaplan.com

How to Get Good Grades in College:

• Write down your courses.

• Be organized. Use an assignment book.

• Get instructor conference hours, contact phone numbers

and email addresses.

• Form a study group; get phone numbers and email addresses.

• Manage your time. Create a daily study plan.

• Realize that there will be sabotage—prepare for it.

• Learn to adapt to different instructors.

• Come to class on time and prepared.

• Participate in class.

• Treat others with respect and dignity.

• Get lecture notes if you are absent.

Checklist for Your Journey from High School to College, Career and Beyond:

Check with your guidance counselor early.

Take appropriate classes –AP/IB/Honor's.

☐ Prepare for SAT/ACT test.

☐ Check out dual enrollment courses with community colleges.

☐ Check out colleges on line. Take virtual tours.

☐ Start financial aid search.

☐ Get high school academic evaluations.

☐ Search for and investigate state and private colleges.

☐ Send admission and financial aid applications online.

☐ Check college degree requirements.

☐ Get high school or college transcripts and grades.

☐ Evaluate progress towards degree.

☐ Use transfer applications and credits.

☐ Log on to www.facts.org for more information.

Remember that your journey toward college begins now! Become serious about your classes in high school! Be prepared on a daily basis to give 100% to your studies and you will find the road to college much smoother and your chances of getting accepted into your first choice of schools much better! You have the tools! Now get started and GOOD LUCK!

ABOUT THE AUTHOR

JANET BURNS HOLLIDAY

Janet Burns Holliday values genuine self-reflection for optimal personal and professional growth. Her childhood transitioned full circle, taking her from the south to the north and back to the south. Her late mother, Shula B. Matthews Burns, instilled in Ms. Holliday many seeds of perseverance and determination before her sudden death. From the age of ten on, Janet was raised by her late grandmother, Alma Wilson, along a dirt road in Mississippi. The events along this dirt road gave her the premonition of bigger and better things.

Janet Burns Holliday holds a Master's Degree in Management, is a Certified Professional Development Trainer, and also a Certified Self-Care Consultant with Warm Spirit: www.warmspirit.org/janetholliday. She is a member of the American Nurses Association, National Black Nurses Association, and is listed in the Manchester Who's Who Among Executive and Professional Women in Healthcare.

She completed her formal education after marrying Frankie Holliday, who has given her continual support in achieving her personal and professional goals. As the mother of two, Stacey and Ashley Holliday, she appreciates being a role model and mentor to shape others' lives. She credits her father, Raymond Burns, and his vision and words of wisdom, for her accomplishments and efforts to build a legacy.

A special thank you to Frankie Holliday for seeing the big picture.

Contact:
INSPIRE 3°
2503 E. Alberson Drive
Albany, GA 31721
(229) 439-0177
janetholliday@mchsi.com
www.protrain.net

SEVEN

TWENTY STRATEGIES FOR INCREASED SELF-ESTEEM

By Janet Burns Holliday

As your life begins to unfold and evolve into something great, these twenty strategies will guide you to a higher level of self-esteem. To fully embrace the twenty strategies outlined in this chapter, you must have a clear understanding of the meaning of self-esteem. According to the *American Heritage Dictionary*, 2nd Edition, self-esteem is "self-pride or self-respect." As you read this chapter, it's imperative that you understand the depth of self-pride. Let us begin the journey!

Now, let's start at the beginning of your search! You must know the kind of student you are. What best describes you: a student with good grades, a student with average grades, a student who could do better, or a student who is by choice a complete disaster?

Strategy 1: Have Self-Respect
Stand approximately 6 to 8 feet in front of a full-length mirror. Look at yourself from your head to your toes and from side to side. Looking into

your eyes, ask yourself, "Who am I?" Do you like the person that's looking back at you?

EXERCISE
Use the table below to complete the following exercise. Start by writing down the physical characteristics you like about yourself. Next, write the physical attributes and characteristics that you dislike.

Physical Attributes   **Personal Traits**

Likes   Likes

_____   _____
_____   _____
_____   _____
_____   _____
_____   _____
_____   _____
_____   _____
_____   _____

Dislikes   Dislikes

_____   _____
_____   _____
_____   _____
_____   _____
_____   _____
_____   _____
_____   _____
_____   _____

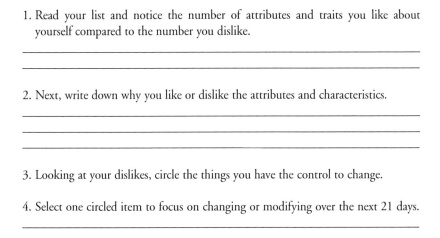

1. Read your list and notice the number of attributes and traits you like about yourself compared to the number you dislike.

2. Next, write down why you like or dislike the attributes and characteristics.

3. Looking at your dislikes, circle the things you have the control to change.

4. Select one circled item to focus on changing or modifying over the next 21 days.

To respect yourself, you must like who you see in the mirror. You must understand why you like yourself (or why not!). When you begin to have self-respect, you will learn to accept those things you cannot change (e.g, height, race, gender) and set goals for changing things that you don't like about yourself which you CAN control and change. Remember, there is no greater love than self-love! So let's start the journey into finding out what you like and don't like about yourself. Pick up a pencil and let's go!

Strategy 2: Practice Self-Love
The portrait of self-love is a reflection of whom you see when you look into the mirror. Are you able to look into the mirror and accept those things you cannot change? Can you love yourself unconditionally, knowing that no one is perfect? Can you love yourself enough to make changes to yourself that would enhance your self-esteem?

Your self-image is a direct reflection of how you feel about yourself. The person you portray externally is the person the world will see and society will meet. "How do I love thee? Let me count the ways," is a famous quote by poet Elizabeth Barrett Brown. Just think if she would have said, "How do I love thyself let me count the ways; for in order to give thee true love, I must first love myself." How can you give love to someone, if you don't have love for yourself? Complete the following exercise to gain an understanding of what you expect to give and receive when it comes to love.

EXERCISE
Love List
Make a list of the ways you love yourself:

1._____
2._____
3._____
4._____
5._____

Make a list of the things or treatments you receive from others that make you feel loved:

1._____   6._____
2._____   7._____
3._____   8._____
4._____   9._____
5._____   10._____

Make a list of the things or treatments you give others to express love:

1._____   6._____
2._____   7._____
3._____   8._____
4._____   9._____
5._____   10._____

Strategy 3: Live a Spiritual Life

Throughout your life, you will experience the good, the bad, and the ugly. No matter what you experience, it's important to keep your spirituality central to your life. This essential strategy will help increase your self-value and aid you during times of need. If you are of the Christian faith, being Christ-focused will help guide you. If you are

Muslim, Buddhist, Jewish, or of any other faith, your spirituality will play a big role in making decisions and life choices. When you have a relationship with God, all things are possible.

Strategy 4: Learn to Forgive

This strategy will help sustain an increased self-esteem, because to forgive is to move forward. If you allow the bitter emotions of anger to weigh you down, your self-esteem will begin to diminish. Forgiveness gives you strength to release and proceed! You live in an imperfect world and are surrounded by imperfect people who make mistakes and hurt you.

If you hold your resentment within and never forgive them for their mistakes, it really only hurts you! Holding onto grudges and anger truly only hurts you in the end. It's equally as important to forgive yourself as it is to forgive others. You are your own worst critic, but you must learn from your mistakes and forgive the past. Start increasing your self-esteem today by forgiving yourself and accepting that you are not perfect.

Strategy 5: Do an Attitude Check

How is your attitude today? How was it yesterday? Your attitude directly impacts your self-esteem. By practicing a positive outlook, you will continuously increase your self-esteem by believing in your own personal power. You will begin to believe that there is an answer to every problem, and not always feel like the victim in life.

A positive outlook takes continuous effort. Your attitude determines how you interact and react to circumstances. A key to success is sharpening the skill of having a positive attitude. Your attitude is a reflection of how you see or feel about yourself. Keep in mind that a positive attitude attracts positive people and turns lemons into lemonade!

Strategy 6: Set Goals

This strategy involves the ability to set and adhere to your goals. Goals give you focus and purpose. The following steps will assist you with establishing your goals and developing an action plan to achieve success:

EXERCISE

1. List your values and beliefs:

_____

_____

_____

_____

2. List your strengths:

_____

_____

_____

_____

3. List your strengths identified by others (these may or may not match your list):

_____

_____

_____

_____

4. Where do you want to be in the next five years, three years, and one year in your life?

Five-year goal:_____

Three-year goal:_____

One-year goal:_____

5. List the steps and resources needed to accomplish your goal. Complete the following "Goal Sheet":

My goal:

_____

Accomplish by _____ (date)

Objectives (steps)   Needed Resources

_____   _____
_____   _____
_____   _____
_____   _____
_____   _____

Closely monitoring and evaluating your progress in achieving your goal increases your self-esteem. Observe and record all the small (and LARGE) successes in achieving this goal. The steps for an effective goal evaluation are:

1. Determine your frequency of follow-up.(How often do you want to complete a progress report? Daily? Weekly?)

2. Mark the dates in your day-planner, calendar, or palm pilot.

3. Make a journal entry of how you feel each time you follow up on your goals and see achievement.

It's important to write down how you feel when you accomplish a goal, when you almost achieve a goal, and when your attempts are unsuccessful.

During your journey toward completing a goal, you might need to repeat some steps, change some steps, or take a different course of action. The emotions you experience will impact your attitude and self-esteem. Achieving your predetermined goals and objectives increases your self-esteem.

Strategy 7: Face New Challenges

A friend of mine always says, "Change is good." A practice to live by is, "if it's not broken, strive to make it better." Personal improvement increases your self-esteem, so be open to new ideas, different concepts, and skills. The following is a list of examples of new challenges:

1. Volunteer to be a part of a project that's new for you.

2. Learn a new dance.

3. Join a book club.

4. Prepare a new gourmet dish every week for a month.

5. Memorize a poem and recite it to a group.

6. Participate in a play.

7. Travel someplace you have never been.

The ability to face new challenges develops flexibility and supports positive growth, which increases your self-esteem.

Strategy 8: Learn the Lessons of Life

The "University of Life" is never ending. Life is full of lessons and trial by error. Just think what would happen if you could apply for the University of Life and major in "Life's Lessons." What would be the focus of your degree? A Bachelor's degree in "Keep Living," a Master of Science in "Life" or a Doctorate in "Hope"? Your life would be outlined in a syllabus, supported by research papers of whose life and destiny would be predetermined. You would pay for your lessons in Life or apply for a grant or loan to learn about living. Your professors would be of all ages to teach you across a life span. The campus would represent different stages of life or different parts of your life. It's not about the buildings; it's about what occurs within you during your time in each building or stage of life!

Experiencing life's lessons will result in an increased self-esteem, when you learn something from each lesson. Life is not something you can register for or learn about over a semester, a quarter or four years. Life is full of daily lessons. Live and learn!

Strategy 9: Stand on the Balcony
Write down the names of the five people you are around the most.

1. _____
2. _____
3. _____
4. _____
5. _____

Look at each name and make a + (positive), - (negative), = (neutral) mark next to each name, noting how each individual makes you feel or impacts your life. The names with a positive symbol are the balcony people and these are the individuals you want to surround yourself with. They are supportive and encourage you to become the best you that you can be. The names with a negative symbol are known as basement people and these individuals bring you down and are not supportive of your goals.

This strategy will increase your self-esteem, because balcony people positively impact your emotions, which impact your attitude, which reflects your self-worth. (Keep your eye out for the basement people because they can really drag you down!)

Balcony people:

1._____   6._____
2._____   7._____
3._____   8._____
4._____   9._____
5._____   10._____

Basement people:

1._____   6._____
2._____   7._____
3._____   8._____
4._____   9._____
5._____   10._____

Strategy 10: Take Time for You

You hear a lot about managing your time effectively, doing more with less, and working smarter not harder. The focus of this next strategy is to master the time you spend with your inner self. This is the time spent in a manner that allows you to relax and have deep thoughts. It's the time of inner synergy, when each thought builds off the last one, and ideas are evolving with creativity. It's when you smile internally and externally.

Look at your daily and weekly schedules and complete the following steps:

1. Mark off the times you work, attend school, and church.

2. Mark off the times of routine activities.

3. With the remaining time, schedule time for yourself on a daily basis. Take the time to reflect and be at peace. You owe it to yourself to take at least ten minutes a day just to let your mind wander and contemplate.

Strategy 11: Take Care of Yourself

Taking care of yourself is a definite motivator. Look in the mirror again and this time, take a survey of what you would like to change (or enhance) about yourself. A great way to increase your self-esteem is to take good care of your body. Look like you love yourself!

Hair: Don't do what you are not trained to do! Have your hair trimmed and styled by a professional. Have you received a compliment on your hair lately? Remember, if you have not received a compliment on a new hair style within the last week, it's time for a different look!

Face: Do you use a skin care regimen that meets your skin type and needs? Do you know how to apply make-up? If you answered no to either of these questions, then schedule a facial with a trained skin care consultant. (Go to a cosmetic counter at any department store. The makeover is free!)

Body: Are you satisfied with your body's appearance, dressed and undressed? Do you exercise regularly? Invest in your health by exercising regularly and learning how to prepare and eat healthy foods.

Nails: Are your fingernails manicured? Do you know how to trim and file your nails? Schedule a manicure! (Watch the manicurist and learn the correct way to trim and file nails).

Clothes: Do you have a sense of style? Do you know what styles enhance your body? Schedule an appointment with a fashion expert. (Department stores have fashion consultants who would love to show you the latest colors and fashions, and they are free!)

Strategy 12: Maintain Healthy Relationships

How do you relate to others? How are your interpersonal skills? Increasing your self-esteem is directly related to your relationships with others. The following tips will assist you in building healthy relationships in all areas of your life:

1. Understand who you are.

2. Know what you value in personal and professional relationships.

3. Learn to communicate effectively. Master the ability to express yourself verbally and nonverbally.

4. Learn how to manage conflict. When you relate with people there will be disagreements. All conflict cannot be resolved; however, conflict can be managed.

5. Learn how to listen. Giving others your undivided attention builds solid relationships through communication and understanding.

These five tips will help build healthy relationships, which support an increased self-esteem.

Strategy 13: Be a Mentor

Mentoring increases your self-esteem and well-being because you are sharing yourself in a positive way and positively impacting someone's life. The following are ways to be a mentor:

1. Volunteer to read to a kindergarten or preschool class.

2. Volunteer to assist with a Brownie/Girl Scout or Boy Scout Troop.

3. Participate in a Big Brother/Big Sister Program.

4. Volunteer in a nursing home.

5. Teach someone your job.

Giving of yourself, time, and expertise increases your self-esteem without focusing on you.

Strategy 14: Manage Your Money Wisely
Having your finances in order will determine the breadth of your self-esteem. Money doesn't make a person! However, it does gives you choices. Learn the following:

1. How to manage your checking account

2. How to budget your money

3. How to understand a 401(k) plan

4. How to develop a savings plan

5. Don't spend impulsively. Learn to save for what you want
   and pay in cash.

6. Avoid credit card debt like the plague!

Strategy 15: Discover the Power of Networking
Building strong networking circles is a key for strengthening your self-esteem. The stronger your circle, the stronger your information sharing opportunities will be. Learn the art of networking. As a young person, it is important to learn this art now. How can you begin? Consider what you want to have as a career and begin asking people who are already employed in this field if they might mentor you or share information. Keep the business cards of these people, as they may be perfect contacts when you are actually interviewing for a job.

Strategy 16: Be Innovative
What better way to increase your self-esteem and confidence than putting your ideas into action? Being creative without taking action is like a merchant vessel that remains on shore full of valuables for no one

to purchase or enjoy. The ability to have an idea and put it into action is the ability to be creative. The vision of seeing your ideas put into action is self-fulfilling. Make a list of your ideas. What's keeping your ideas from becoming reality? Is it because you need feedback from others? Start with the "balcony people" in your life, your mentor, or your networking circle. Is it because you don't have a plan? Then set a goal and develop your plan. The vision of seeing your ideas turn into reality is a definite self-esteem booster!

Strategy 17: Occupy Your Space

I recently heard a speaker share a story about a supervisor who gave him some words of wisdom early in his career. She told him to occupy his space, because if he didn't, someone else would!

In order to occupy your space in a meaningful and effective manner, you must respect yourself. Self-respect requires you to know what you will and will not accept in your space. In short, it's having personal standards of excellence.

Are you occupying your space? Let others know your standards and boundaries and be the keeper of the "gates" as to whom and what you will allow into your private space. Remember: you are worthy of a healthy space!

Strategy 18: Be of Community Service

Your community consists of the environment outside your personal space. The significance of building relationships is that they will strengthen your community involvement. Community service will increase your self-esteem, especially when it involves helping others. Use your expertise, passion, and needs of the community to identify ways you can assist.

Strategy 19: Practice Self-Validation

Each of the previous strategies supports the importance of self-validation in increasing your self-esteem. Your self-worth or value is your responsibility. You can't attain validation for who you are from anyone else. Your feeling of self-worth comes from within YOU. When you have self-awareness and validate who you are:

1. You can allow others into your space without losing who you are and compromising your values.

2. You can give of yourself and time.

3. You know your boundaries.

4. You are not an attention seeker.

Understanding yourself and knowing your purpose becomes your way of life! Your way of life becomes your legacy, and your legacy flourishes in the future. Remind yourself of how important you are. Validate yourself on a daily basis. Remind yourself of your purpose.

Strategy 20: Follow Your Passion

The ability to turn your passion into fuel, your heart's desires into reality, and to have a vision of the end result will increase your self-esteem and help sustain a higher level of self-pride during the peaks and valleys of your life's journey.

Passion gives you the fuel to ignite your heart's desires. Your passion is found in your heart and in the things that you look forward to. What are your passions?

EXERCISE

My passions:

1._____   6._____
2._____   7._____
3._____   8._____
4._____   9._____
5._____   10._____

The things you have a deep burning for are your heart's desires. It might be a concept, a value, or something tangible. It's critical to understand the desires of your heart. What is your heart's desire? What do you want more than anything else in the whole world?

My heart's desire:

_____
_____
_____
_____

When you live your life in a direction that is passion-driven, you will find that you are living a life of purpose. And when you feel that you are living a purposeful life, your self-esteem will soar! The foundation of your self-esteem has evolved over your lifetime and regardless of your past, your self-esteem can be strengthened. You are a young woman of value.

I hope that this chapter has given you the chance to look within yourself and see your strengths. I want you to be patient with yourself, but set your sights on always growing and improving. Remember always just how valuable you are. Love yourself.

Notes:

ABOUT THE AUTHOR

DR. CAROL ANN RYSER

Carol Ann Ryser, M.D. is a Board Certified Pediatrician (FAAP), Board Certified Clinical Analyst, member of: F.A.A.P.; AMA, OHM (Orthomolecular Health Medicine); and The American Academy of Anti-Aging Medicine. The primary focus of Dr. Ryser's medical practice is on the prevention of illness and disease. As a physician, analyst, and practitioner of preventative medicine, Carol Ann Ryser has a broad background of experience, training, and knowledge to meet the demands of the 22nd century.

Dr. Ryser has published and presented a number of papers in her area of expertise, appearing in such publications as *American Journal of Diseases of Children; Journal of Neurology, Neurosurgery and Psychology;* and *Pediatrics.* She has most recently published a chapter in the *Anti-Aging Medical Therapeutics,* Volume 5 entitled "Innovative Diagnosis and Treatment of Chronic Illness," and "The Role of Growth Hormone Deficiency in Chronic Illness,"*Anti-Aging Medical News,* as well as several articles in alternative medical magazines.

Dr. Ryser has been a pioneer in the field of medicine since her graduation from Kansas University Medical School in 1963. She was one of the first physicians to speak out against child abuse in Kansas and traveled throughout the state as a spokeswoman against child abuse. She also testified to help change child abuse laws in the state of Kansas.

Dr. Ryser provides workshops, training seminars, and is a popular speaker throughout the United States. She speaks on medical issues concerning chronic illness; focusing on Lymes disease, Chronic Fatigue Syndrome, and Fibromyalgia, autoimmune diseases and preventative medicine, as well as self-esteem, psychotherapy, children, and child development.

Dr. Carol Ann Ryser is a co-author of *Becoming the Professional Woman* in the PWN book library.

Contact:
Health Centers of America
5308 E. 115th St., Kansas City
MO 64137-2731
(816) 763-9165
www.carolannrysermd.net
www.protrain.net

EIGHT

EMOTIONAL WELLNESS

By Dr. Carol Ann Ryser

We live in a day and age when people wear their feelings on their shirtsleeves and their emotions are running and ruining their lives. This has always been a critical issue for teenagers. It is during the teenage years when emotions seem to be all over the place and teens have a tendency to "do what they feel like."

To better understand emotional wellness, the first task is to put in perspective a developmental overview of "growing up" as a teenager. It is important for you as a teenager to have a better understanding of your emotions, your body, and what you need. It is then that you will have a better chance to create emotional wellness for yourself. A good support system helps you in this process.

Developmental Stage: Recycling Ages 12 Through 18 Years
The general needs and behaviors of this developmental stage include:

• To achieve a clearer separation from family

• To take more steps toward independence

• To understand and explore male/female differences

• To stay at home vs. leave home

- What do I want to do when I grow up?
- At times independent, at times dependent and regressive
- To explore new ideas and definitions of self
- To achieve levels of competency: work, emotions, sexuality, thinking, relationships
- Needs to eat and sleep excessively from time to time
- Requires explanation and reassurances by parents about changes that occur at puberty
- Privacy–own room if possible or place for prized possessions
- Tolerance of sloppiness and untidiness within limits when not affecting others
- "Freshness" ignored, unless it goes beyond bounds of adult tolerance
- Reassurances about differences in size and development
- Skills: mending, cooking, carpentry, sewing, baby care, etc.
- Opportunity to learn social dancing
- Rules around privileges/responsibility
- Sex education and counseling
- Affirmation for being alive
- Parental involvement in activities
- Nutrition: Food, sleep, health information
- Less involvement with family, more with peers (time on phone, gossiping with friends)
- Involvement with other adults, teachers, parents
- Being responsible with parents' backing

- Trying out new roles

- Exploring new information, concepts

- Unify beliefs and values

- Integrates personal identity

- Being responsible for own needs, feelings, and behaviors

- Integrates sexuality

- Gains new information, skills

- Contact with peers

- Self-esteem building – working accomplishing goals.

- Dating

- Reaffirm saying "No"

- Be like peers in dress, etc.

- Father involvement: males need nurturing and good modeling of how to relate to the mother and women.

- Girls need support for being assertive, especially by the father and making contact with the world, learning to deal with conflict.

General Challenges for this Developmental Stage
Sometimes adolescents act reasonable and competent, and at other times rebellious.

- Conflict with parents, friends, sex, and sex roles

- Confuse sex and nurturing

- Fragile, low self-esteem

- Act out:
  - drugs
  - grade failure
  - sexual
  - alcohol
  - lying and/or stealing

- Belong to gangs

- Act irresponsibly

- Hostile, reject parents

- Ambivalent about needs

- Break rules to get limits and protection

- Vulnerable to peer pressure

- Trouble keeping commitments

- Unsure of maleness and femaleness

- Depression, risk of suicide

- Shame

- Difficulty with responsibility

- Regressive behavior, e.g., failing with school, work, and peers

- Girls have conflict with mother due to separation problems and needs the father's support to solve problems with the mother.

- Increasingly modest–trying to defend self, is critical to self

- Critical of others' failures to measure up to ideals

- Increased interest in religion, anxious about own shortcomings

- Easily embarrassed

- Apt to be fresh with adults the adolescent knows well

- May be sloppy and untidy

General Characteristics for this Developmental Stage

• Increasingly modest

• Trying to defend self, is critical of self

• Has favorite friend of same sex

• Discusses abstract age ideas, (i.e., honesty, justice)

• Critical of others' failures to measure up to ideals

• Increased interest in religion

• Anxious about own shortcomings

• Easily embarrassed

• Apt to be fresh with adults that the adolescent knows well

• Wants to be like others in dress, mannerisms, and privileges, and to be popular. Peer influence is critical

• May be sloppy and untidy

• Girls begin to primp more and are more apt to be spectators in sports

• Boys acquire skills in sports, are interested in vehicles (wheels), may explore drugs, alcohol, sex, being own boss

EXERCISE

Identity Status Questionnaire

It is critical in the development of the human personality that a person establishes a personal identity, a "Who I am" from within. It is from this internal definition of self that we make additions and subtractions to our personality. The following is an "identity-status" questionnaire that will help to increase your understanding of "Who I am."

Ask yourself these questions. Write them down in a notebook or on your computer:

Introduction

1. Where are you from? Where are you living now?

2. Did your father go to college? What does he do now?

3. Did your mother go to college? What does she do now?

4. How much education do you need?

Occupation

1. What are your plans for a career, occupation, college?

2. What do you want to major in? What are you doing with that subject?

3. What do you love to do?

4. Will this career give you satisfaction and contribute to the betterment of society?

5. Most parents have plans for their children, things they would like them to go into or do. Do your parents have any plans like that for you?

6. How do your parents feel about your plans now?

7. How willing do you think you'd be to change if something better came along? (What might be "better" in your terms?)

Future Family

1. What are your plans for marriage? Do you plan to work after you are married? Why or why not?

2. Do you plan to have children? Work after you have children? Why or why not?

3. How do you plan to have sufficient income to care for your children?

4. Do you expect to take time off from work when you have children?

5. How do you think you'll combine work and marriage and child rearing? What problems do you think might exist? How do you feel these might be solved? Have you ever felt differently about this? How important would it be that your prospective spouse agree about these things?

Money

1. What is your value of money? Your parents'?

2. What is "enough" money? How do your parents define "enough" money?

3. Will you learn how to manage money? From whom?

4. What is "enough" money if you plan to have children?

5. Is it important that your prospective spouse agree on your value of money?

6. What type of life style do you want?

Religion

1. Do you have any particular religious affiliation or preference?

2. Is your religious preference like your family's?

3. Are you active in church/synagogue/temple, etc.? Do you get into many religious discussions?

4. How do your parents feel about your beliefs? Do you agree or disagree with your parents?

5. Was there any time when you came to doubt your religious beliefs.

6. How did it happen? How did you resolve your questions? How are things for you now?

Politics

1. Do you have any particular political preference? How about your parents?

2. Do you ever take any kind of political action—join groups, write letters, participate in demonstrations, etc.?

3. Are there any issues you feel pretty strongly about?

4. Was there a particular time when you decided your political beliefs?

Sex

1. What are your views on premarital intercourse? What criteria do you use to determine your actions?

2. How do you feel about your sexuality? Have you ever had any doubts? How did you resolve them?

3. What would your parents think about your sexual standards and behaviors?

Conflict Resolution

1. Do you feel there is ever any conflict between your ideas, emotions, and behavior?

2. Could you give an example? How do you handle the conflicts? How frequently do they occur?

Your Beliefs

1. What is your belief about the value of your life, your health, relationships, and contributions to society?

2. What is your work ethic?

3. What value do you place on your life?

4. What are your beliefs about your rights to be protected, set limits, and be treated with respect?

5. What is your belief about what the world owes you? Why?

Negative Memories

Negative memories reinforce negative beliefs in ourselves. Adolescents are not free to develop their own personalities if they are preoccupied with worry and fear. Here are some concerns most adolescents have that influence their identity:

1. Worry about health of parents; adolescent may become a caretaker.

2. May be upset or angry about the behavior of parents (inconsistency of a parent and lack of parental support). The adolescent may become a caretaker or a rebel.

3. Worry about fights between parents; adolescents feel they have to take sides.

4. Worry about violence or potential violence; adolescents feel unsafe and fearful.

5. Worry about inappropriate behavior, may even include criminal or sexual behavior; adolescents feel shame and fear.

6. Are disappointed by broken promises; adolescents may feel unloved.

7. Feel responsible for parents drinking, smoking, gambling, lack of working.

8. Miss being nurtured unconditionally if parents are withdrawn.

9. May be violent; adolescent misses learning without fear.

10. If ridiculed, adolescent may miss acceptance.

11. May focus all energy on parent(s); adolescent may miss being l loved.

Adaptive Behavior to Reduce Anxiety in a Stressed Adolescent

Adolescents may develop negative patterns, such as being isolated, people-pleasers or caretakers, become withdrawn or dependent, exhibit out-of-control behavior or act out with sex, drugs, or regress (act like a little child).

Adolescents may develop strengths or positive behaviors because of the crisis, although these may be learned in a painful way. Adolescents learn to take care of themselves, become survivors.

Boys and girls task with equal competency, respect, and will maintain gender identity.

Adolescents may blame others and show lack of empathy.

Adolescents may exhibit perfectionistic behavior, becoming tense or anxious if things are out of order.

Critical Belief Systems that are Myths

☐ These belief systems are based on fear of rejection, and can be carried forward into adulthood. Which of the following are myths that you are carrying around?

☐ If I please everyone, everyone will be happy.

☐ If I control everything, I can keep people from being upset.

☐ Those who love you cause the most pain.

☐ Take care of others first.

☐ Something is missing in me, i.e., I am not good enough.

☐ If I am good, everything will be fine.

☐ If I love enough, he/she or they will change.

☐ If I get too close, someone will leave me or die and I will be left alone.

☐ He can/She can't be powerful. (cultural/sexual differences)

☐ Make others happy first, please myself second.

☐ Something catastrophic will happen if I live my own life.

☐ Happiness only comes with sacrifice, hard work, and misery.

☐ Work is hard, unpleasant, and never done.

☐ Bad things happen to people who deserve it.

☐ Strong women are bitches.

☐ No one will like me if I'm responsible.

☐ Having fun is a waste of time or even sinful.

Positive Thinking that Confronts the Myths

To overcome these powerful messages from childhood into adolescence, and even into adulthood, the following affirmations or messages can be used:

• I'm a survivor.

• I can handle a crisis.

• I have a good sense of empathy.

• I can take care of myself.

• I'm not easily discouraged.

• I find alternatives to problems.

• I'm not afraid to rely on my abilities.

• I do have choices.

• I can be depended upon.

• I appreciate my inner strength.

• I know what I want.

• I am a good person.

• I may not be perfect, but parts of me are great.

EXERCISE

The following are guidelines to help you handle your feelings and achieve emotional wellness. It would be a good idea to invest in a small journal and answer the following questions:

ANGER			
In your journal, write down:	It is best to:	It is OK to:	Try not to:
How do you handle your anger?	• Tell someone you're angry	• Cry • Scream	• Hurt other people or yourself
What do you do when you get angry?	• Explain why you are angry	• Yell • Jump up and down	• Mistreat other people's things or your own
Do you know it's OK to get angry?	• Solve anger feelings and behavior	• Hit a mat with a tennis racket or baseball bat	• Act it out by driving fast, doing poorly in school, drinking
	• Decide to get over the anger	• Use a punching bag • Hit or kick things that cannot be damaged as long as you don't bother others • Leave the room	• Be vengeful • Be too critical or aggressive • Blame others for your behavior or mistakes

JEALOUSY			
In your journal:	It is best to:	It is normal to:	Try not to:
List people you feel jealous of.	• Tell someone about your jealousy	• Be jealous of your brothers and sisters	• Say mean things about the person/ people you're jealous of
How do you handle your jealousy?	• Ask for help or attention	• Want to be the best at everything	• Gossip about the person/people you're jealous of
What do you do when you're jealous?	• Think about the fact that you're a special person • Think about the fact that you have many things no one else does	• Want to have the most	• Hurt the other person/people in any way • Compete with the person/people you're jealous of

GRIEF/SADNESS			
In your journal, write down:	It is best to:	What you may do or want to do:	Try not to:
When was the last time you felt sad?	• Admit that you're sad • Tell someone about your grief	• Cry • Want to be alone • Wish whatever caused your sadness or grief hadn't happened.	• Pretend that nothing is wrong • Get angry • Hide your grief
How do you handle your grief/ sadness?	• Write about your sadness • Watch a sad movie	• Get physically ill • Want to forget or deny what made you sad	
What did you do?	• Listen to a sad song		

GUILT			
In your journal, write down:	It is best to:	It is understandable if you:	Try not to:
What do you / did you do that makes you feel guilty? How do you handle your guilt? What do you do?	• Admit that you did something wrong • Say you're sorry and correct whatever it was you did wrong • If possible, apologize and make up for what you did • Change your behavior • Think about how your actions affected the other person/ people	• Cry • Feel ashamed or embarrassed • Don't want others to know	• Lie • Pretend that nothing has happened • Hide what you have done • Avoid the person/ people you might have wronged • Avoid admitting you were wrong
REJECTION			
In your journal:	It is best to:	It is understandable if you:	Try not to:
When did you last feel rejected? How do you handle rejection? What do you do?	• Remember that no one is liked by everyone • Remember that no one can be good at everything • Remember that not everyone can do all the things you do well • Hang with people who like and accept you • Avoid people who don't appreciate you	• Wonder about yourself and your abilities • Don't want to be around those who reject you • Want to prove yourself to those who reject you	• Believe that you're no good • Give up or give in • Stop trying • Hurt yourself with negative behavior, smoking, drinking, etc.
LONELINESS			
In your journal, write down:	It is best to:	It is understandable if you feel:	Try not to:
List the times you have felt lonely. How did you handle your loneliness? What do you do?	• Admit you're lonely • Remember that no one can be good at everything • Make friends • Call a friend • Be creative	• Bored • Rejected • A need to be noticed	• Refuse to make friends or reach out • Get someone to notice you by acting out • Believe that no one likes you

ANXIETY

In your journal:	It is best to:	You may worry about:	Try not to:
List the things or people who make you anxious. How do you handle your anxiety? What do you do?	• Take ownership of being anxious • Get information • Talk about your anxiety • Let others comfort you	• The unknown • Getting hurt • Money, other people, etc.	• Stress out (get stressed) • Over worry • Over-think things

HUMILIATION / EMBARASSMENT / SHAME

In your journal:	It is best to:	You may:	Try not to:
List times you felt humiliated or embarrassed. How do you handle humiliation or embarrassment? What do you do?	• Ignore a put-down • Walk away • Tell people to stop • Ask for help • If possible, find humor in the situation • Get information • Talk about your anxiety • Let others comfort you	• Not want to be around people who humiliate or embarrass you • Not want to remember or think about the embarrassing moment	• Put anyone else down • Shame another person • Get back at the people who your shamed you • Hurt the people who shamed you

FEAR

In your journal:	It is best to:	You may:	Try not to:
What scares you? How do you handle your fear? What do you do?	• Pay attention to your fears • Remember that fear is a signal that you may be in danger • Admit you're afraid • Be cautious • Get information • Ask for a hug or reassurance • Tell someone about your fears • Ask questions and find out what scares you	• Want to be with other people • Learn more about the unknown things that frighten you or that you fear might hurt you • Get away from things that scare you	• Hide • Act as if you aren't afraid • Bully others to hide your fear

FRUSTRATION			
In your journal:	It is best to:	It's OK to:	Try not to:
List things that frustrate you. How do you handle your frustration? What do you do?	• Slow down • Try again at another time • Read the instructions	• Cry • Scream or yell • Jump up and down • Hit or kick things that cannot be damaged and won't bother others	• Break things • Mistreat things or other people • Take your frustration out on someone else
DISAPPOINTMENT			
In your journal:	It is best to:	You may:	Try not to:
List times you were disappointed. How do you handle your disappointment? What do you do?	• Tell someone you are disappointed • Explain why you're disappointed • Find out why you were let down	• Need to cry • Want to be alone • Be angry at the person who disappointed you • Wonder if the person would let you down again or not • Be afraid to trust the other person	• Say mean things to the other person • Get back at the other person • Pretend you weren't disappointed
DEFEAT			
In your journal:	It is best to:	You may:	Try not to:
List the times you have felt defeated. How do you handle defeat? What do you do?	• Remember that everyone loses every once in a while • Remember that no one wins all the time • Set goals and work toward them • Practice • Don't give up • Express your feelings • Get help or coaching	• Not want to fail • Feel embarrassed about losing • Not want others to know about your loss or failure • Get discouraged • Want to give up	• Be vengeful or get back at people • Believe you're a loser • Believe you'll never win • Give up • Stop trying

"Don't Grow Up" Behavior

Sometimes adolescents just don't want to grow up. There are some adults who exhibit the following behaviors as well. As you get older, you may want to work on overcoming these:

• Is undependable, unreliable

• Withdraws

• Is rebellious, may exhibit passive-aggressive behavior

• Is angry. Has temper outbursts when frustrated; sets up arguments to express anger. Acts out with alcohol, drugs, etc.

• Acts helpless. Life overwhelms such people, who feel compelled to let others be the caretakers.

• Acts pitiful. Pouts, sulks, suffers, but is unwilling to do anything other than complain.

• Acts guilt-ridden; feels regret and ruminates.

• Feels dependent and waits for someone else to initiate activities.

• Can be manipulative. Can't be trusted to be real with others or exploits others.

• Is secretive, withholds self. Is unable to be in close or vulnerable situations.

• Exhibits lack of empathy for others; stays self-focused all the time.

• Exhibits grandiosity; feels superior; feels invincible.

Learn to express yourself in a way that you are able to keep your own dignity and self-esteem. The following are some general guidelines to check in with yourself about your decisions and your behaviors. Ask yourself: "If I make this decision and take the action I am thinking about, does it accomplish the following?"

- Keep me on track with my values, goals, and the direction I want my life to go.

- Is it respectful and considerate of others, not intentionally harmful, vengeful or hurtful to someone?

- Is it legal?

- Is it moral?

- It is ethical and within the guidelines of how I would like to be treated?

If these questions check out, it is then that you can move forward with action and a confidence within yourself. You will know that you have made the right decision, even if others disagree with you or think you should be someone different or do something different.

It isn't easy being a teenager, I realize that. But if you learn to express yourself in a healthy way and understand that you are going through some powerful emotional and physical changes as a young woman, then perhaps you can be patient and loving with yourself. Remember too, all adults have been teenagers once in their lives! When you think that you are the only person in the world who is feeling lonely or different, know that the majority of people in the world go through these same difficult changes. Follow the guidelines in this chapter for open communication with others, and be proud of the person you are today and the woman you are about to become.

ABOUT THE AUTHOR

SHARVA HAMPTON-CAMPBELL

Sharva Hampton-Campbell, a native of Louisiana, resides in Champaign, Illinois with her husband, Marshall, and her mother, Patricia. She received a Bachelor's and Master's degree in Social Work from the University of Illinois at Champaign–Urbana. Ms. Hampton-Campbell also completed paralegal training at Roosevelt University and conflict resolution and mediation training from Aurora University in Chicago, Illinois. She is employed full-time as an academic advisor at Parkland College and is an independent social work consultant and counselor. Currently, Ms. Hampton-Campbell is working on her clinical social work license.

Ms. Hampton-Campbell provides staff development training and workshops for public and private social service agencies, as well as youth seminars for churches and community based youth organizations. She has developed and conducted the following workshops: "Becoming a Competent Case Manager," "It's all About the Attitude," "Engaging African American Youth: A Strength's Perspective," and "Show Me the Money Financial Planning for Teens." She is also a Certified Trainer on women's issues, diversity and multiculturalism, and youth issues. Her latest projects are the development of Sista Circle, a Christian youth program that focuses on studying the word of God, giving back to the community and academic excellence, as well as Youth Empowered for Success (Y.E.S.), a therapeutic mentoring program for youth aged 11 to 18 years old.

Ms. Hampton-Campbell is a member of The Professional Woman Network International Advisory Board, and has received national recognition in *Who's Who Among America's Teachers*. She is a co-author of *Becoming the Professional Woman* in the PWN Library.

Contact:
Sharva Hampton-Campbell
Post Office Box 135
Champaign, IL 61824
(217) 202-5498
shamcamp@hotmail.com
www.protrain.net

NINE

VOLUNTEERING: REACHING OUT

By Sharva Hampton-Campbell

"Our American tradition of neighbor helping neighbor has always been one of our greatest strengths and most notable traditions."
– Ronald Reagan

Our country was built on the notion of helping people. America's history is rich with information regarding the volunteer efforts of people and communities. Volunteerism was a means of survival during the colonial period. The Revolutionary War was fought and won through the organized volunteer efforts. The anti-slavery movement and the Underground Railroad were notable efforts of many people who volunteered their time and sacrificed their lives for a cause they believed in. The Underground Railroad has been noted by many researchers as one of the largest and strongest collective efforts in this country's history. The Civil War followed the anti-slavery movement; the efforts of this war ended slavery but our country was left torn apart. The Reconstruction period was a time of rebuilding and restructuring with volunteers playing an active role in rebuilding and industrializing our nation.

In the 20th century, volunteerism continued as Americans lived through two world wars, the Depression Era, the Civil Rights movement and the Vietnam War. President Kennedy's appeal to America for service became famous when he made the following statement: "And so, my fellow Americans: ask not what your country can do for you, ask what you can do for your country." The Peace Corps was developed during the Kennedy administration and was the first federal program that promoted volunteerism. Many programs followed thereafter, all of which were led by a presidential plea for civic duty and service among the American people. As we continue through the new millennium, volunteerism continues to positively impact the citizens of this great nation.

According to the United States Department of Labor, in 2004, about 64.5 million persons or 28.8 percent of the population age 16 and over volunteered through or for organizations at least once from September 2003 to September 2004. Women volunteered at a higher rate than men across age groups, education levels, and other major characteristics. Teenagers had a relatively high volunteer rate, 29.4 percent, although the volunteer rates were lowest among persons in their early twenties (20 percent). Volunteers spent about 52 hours on volunteer activities during the reporting period.

Volunteers worked the most hours for religious (34.4 percent) and educational/youth services related (27 percent) organizations. Another 12.4 percent of volunteers performed activities mainly for social or community service organizations and 7.5 percent volunteered most of their hours for hospitals or other health organizations. Two in five volunteers became involved on their own accord, whereas 42 percent were asked to become volunteers most often by someone in the organization. Among those who volunteered at some point in the past, the most common reason for not volunteering during the reporting period was lack of time (45 percent), followed by health or medical problems (14.4 percent) and family responsibility or childcare problems (9.1 percent).

Now that you have been briefed on the history of volunteerism, let's discuss what it means to you. I believe that volunteerism generates an overwhelming feeling of contentment, especially when you make a difference in someone's life. I have developed a list of characteristics that are promoted by volunteerism. Please complete the following and feel free to add words of your own.

EXERCISE
Volunteerism promotes:

1. Self-esteem	6. Unity	11. _____
2. Commitment	7. Giving	12. _____
3. Leadership	8. Caring	13. _____
4. Stability	9. _____	14. _____
5. Connectedness	10._____	15. _____

I have developed three assessment tools (Personal Interest Questionnaire, Plus and Minus Responses, and I.S.C.E.) that I believe are important for all potential volunteers to complete. These assessment tools will assist you with taking a closer look at yourself as a person. This is important because you have to know who you are and understand your own value system before you can determine in which capacity you could best serve.

For instance, if you are a strongly opinionated person, your skills would be greatly utilized as an advocate for better health care for senior citizens. If you are a very passive but organized person, you could also volunteer at the advocacy agency, but in a different capacity. Perhaps your organization skills could be utilized as an office assistant. I challenge you to complete the following questionnaire and analyze your responses to determine your personal areas of interest. This self-assessment will help you to make an informed decision about what may be your most rewarding volunteer experience.

EXERCISE
Personal Interest Questionnaire
Complete the following statements:

1. What I like most about myself is_____
_____.

2. What I like least about myself is_____
_____.

3. I am good at doing the following things:_____
_____.

4. I don't like doing the following things:_____
_____.

5. I have been successful in the following positions or activities
   (list the position title and briefly; describe your responsibilities):
   a.
   b.
   c.

6. I have been unsuccessful in the following positions or activities
   (list the position title and describe your job responsibilities):
   a.
   b.
   c.

7. My hobbies or things I enjoy doing are_____
_____
_____

8. I am proud of the following achievements:
   a.
   b.
   c.

9. I like working with people   True   False

10. I prefer to work alone   True   False

11. I have transportation or access to transportation   True   False

12. I am willing to travel   True   False

13. I prefer to work in my neighborhood   True   False

14. I prefer to work directly with clients   True   False

15. I prefer to work "behind the scenes"   True   False

16. What societal issues are of importance or interest to you?

_____

_____

17. Is there an agency or group that is currently trying to address any of the issues you listed in number 16?   Yes   No
      If you answered Yes, list the agencies below:
      a.
      b.
      c.

18. I have to overcome the following obstacles before I can commit to a volunteer experience:_____

_____

_____

I strongly believe that all potential volunteers should assess who they are as people, examine their values and beliefs, and be familiar with their strengths and weaknesses. The next assessment requires you to determine your assets and liabilities and how they will impact your ability to provide a needed service. This assessment is called "Plus and Minus Responses." What do you perceive to be your strengths? What do the people who matter the most in your life perceive to be your strengths? If you have never asked them, I challenge you to do so.

EXERCISE

Plus and Minus Responses

Start by asking the following people to share with you a strength (a "plus") you possess:

PERSONAL	RESPONSE
1. Mother or Father	_____
2. Grandparent	_____
3. Significant Other	_____
4. Best Friend	_____
5. Previous Employer	_____
6. Current Employer	_____
7. Spiritual Advisor	_____
8. High School Teacher	_____
9. YOU	_____

Then, ask each of them to share with you a weakness (a "minus") that you possess:

PERSONAL	RESPONSE
1. Mother or Father	_____
2. Grandparent	_____
3. Significant Other	_____
4. Best Friend	_____
5. Previous Employer	_____
6. Current Employer	_____
7. Spiritual Advisor	_____
8. High School Teacher	_____
9. YOU	_____

When I approached the above individuals, I was told exactly what I already knew to be my strengths and weaknesses. My perceived strengths are that I am kind-hearted, easy to get along with, compassionate, very focused, goal driven, honest, and forthright. My perceived weaknesses are that I analyze "things" too much, I'm a "workaholic," and my expectations of others are often too high. I received this feedback early in life; and it helped me decide on a career path. I knew that I was destined to work in a helping profession and that I had strong leadership skills. I sought out volunteer experiences that would improve and strengthen my leadership skills and allow me to gain valuable experience helping children and families.

Also, all of my volunteer experiences provided me the opportunity to give back to my community and "sharpen my saw." Stephen Covey provides tips in his book *Seven Habits of Highly Effective People* that helped me to become more productive in life. He refers to productivity as "sharpening your saw." Volunteering helped me sharpen the saw of life. I was able to help others during their times of need; and in the process, I learned more about myself and about career fields that were of interest to me.

I knew how I felt about volunteerism but I had never captured anyone else's viewpoint about the subject matter. My friend Katherine told me that she received her first "Volunteer of the Year" award when she was only sixteen years old. Since then, she has received numerous awards for volunteering. She shared that there is nothing more rewarding than to see a smile on someone's face who hasn't smiled in years.

Katherine's comments sparked my interest in knowing how the people who impacted my life on a daily basis felt about volunteerism. My quest for information began. I interviewed my husband, mother, sister, best friends, co-workers, spiritual advisors, and other relatives. I developed a questionnaire that asked each person to share information about his or her volunteer experiences or desire to engage in a volunteer experience. The questionnaire focused on the following four areas: Interest, Skills, Commitment, and Expectations (I.S.C.E. – pronounced "I see"). I wanted to know what type of cause they would like to volunteer for or why they already volunteered for a particular cause. I wanted to know what type of skills they had to offer, their level of commitment, and what they expected to gain from the experience. You will have an opportunity to evaluate your I.S.C.E. in the next exercise.

I received an array of responses from my interviewees. My mother remembered helping a local radio station sort toys and wrap gifts for needy children during the holiday season. She stated that she wanted to make a difference in someone's life but was not able to make a long-term commitment due to her work schedule and family obligations. She remembered hearing the announcement on the radio and immediately thought that this would be the perfect opportunity to give back to her community. She stated that she gained compassion and understanding from this experience. She remembers reading the wish lists that some of the children had sent in to the radio station and saying to herself that "we (her family) should never take things for granted and we should cherish the simple things in life." The children's list consisted of items such as socks, coats, gloves, hats, and boots. One child asked for some Old Maid cards. My mother reflected back on the lists that her youngest daughter and her grandchildren had given her. It consisted of items like Cabbage Patch dolls, bicycles, remote control cars, and expensive video games. At that moment, she decided that she needed to remind us about the true meaning of Christmas and help us focus more on giving than receiving.

My twenty-five-year old sister shared her experience of volunteering at a nursing home when she was sixteen years old. She stated that she volunteered at the nursing home because she had always been fond of "old people." She offered them kindness, compassion, and laughter. She loved making them laugh. She stated that she made a six-month commitment and went into the experience hoping to make someone's day by showing that person she cared. She remembered the experience to be very rewarding and fulfilling.

One of my girlfriends shared that she participated in several volunteer experiences while in college. One of her experiences came about as a result of her wanting to gain hands-on knowledge about group facilitation. She was able to volunteer for a program that worked with children who were at risk of being physically and sexually abused. She developed and co-facilitated a 16-week abuse awareness group. My friend stated that the organization utilized her creative and interpersonal skills and in the process, she learned valuable facilitation skills. She also commented that this was a rewarding experience because by the end of the group, she had developed a solid rapport with the participants. This alone boosted her self-confidence about working with groups.

Everyone else I interviewed gave similar responses. They had specific interest, felt as though they were competent to do the job, knew their level of commitment, and expected to gain something from the experience. I would like you to evaluate your I.S.C.E. Please answer the following questions:

EXERCISE
Interest, Skills, Commitment, and Expectations (I.S.C.E.) Questionnaire
Have you ever volunteered?   No   Yes
If you answered No, please respond to the following questions:

1) If you had the opportunity to volunteer, what would you like to do? (Interest)
_____
_____

2) What do you have to offer? (Skills)
_____
_____

3) How much time do you have to give? (Commitment)
_____
_____

4) What would you hope to gain from the experience? (Expectations)
_____
_____

If you answered Yes, please respond to the following questions:

1. Why did you volunteer? (Interest)

_____

_____

2. What did you have to offer? (Skills)

_____

_____

3. How much time did you have to give? (Commitment)

_____

_____

4. What did you expect to gain from the experience? (Expectations)

_____

_____

If you have never engaged in a volunteer experience, your I.S.C.E. will provide you with information that will help you determine whether or not a particular volunteer experience would be beneficial to you and the person or persons needing the help. If you have previously engaged in a successful volunteer experience, perhaps your I.S.C.E. will aid you in engaging in another rewarding opportunity.

After you complete your I.S.C.E, you must be able to agree with at least two of the following statements:

1. "I see" that I am going to make a difference because my interest, skills, commitment, and expectations are in alignment with the needs of this volunteer experience.

2. "I see" that I will be an effective change agent.

3. "I see" that I will be an asset and not a liability by volunteering for this cause.

4. "I see" how the person or persons will benefit from what I have to offer.

I hope that I have inspired you to join the ranks of many Americans offering a helping hand for a worthy cause. I would like to share with you one of my favorite quotes, written by Mahatma Gandhi: "The best way to find yourself is to lose yourself in the service of others."

ABOUT THE AUTHOR

SUZETTE SALANDY

Suzette Salandy, a native of the beautiful island of Trinidad, has been working in public relations and human resources for over eleven years. Also, since 1997, Suzette has been working as a Professional Image Consultant specializing in multi-occasion make-up artistry. Suzette's philanthropic interests have enabled her to donate her time and talents to many charitable organizations, including Dress for Success, a not-for-profit organization dedicated to helping under-privileged women succeed in the work force. As an image consultant, She conducts individual con-sultation sessions helping women improve their self-presentation and makeup/grooming habits, and has successfully led several workshops helping teen mothers enhance their image and professionalism in the workplace.

Suzette, a member of the Society of Human Resource Management and the National Association for Female Executives, has recently been appointed to the International Advisory Board for the Professional Woman Network. Suzette loves to travel and her philosophy is dream it, do it!

Suzette Salandy is a co-author of *Customer Service & Professionalism for Women* in the PWN library.

Contact:
Salandy Consulting
590 Edbridge Road
Morrisville, PA 19067
(215) 313-0242
S90971@aol.com
www.protrain.net

TEN

YOU'RE ON STAGE!

By Suzette Salandy

Stepping out on stage requires preparation and good fashion insight. Whether your stage is trendy, career or formal, it's important for a young woman to be aware of her environment and the effects of her wardrobe within the environment. By now we have all heard of the term "wardrobe malfunction." For women, especially young women, the key is to know the setting when applying your sense of style. Also, each of us comes in a different shape and size; knowing our bodies and embracing the fact that not every style is a fit for us is important. This is what gives us the ability to enhance our look as we get older. It's what separates the fashion "do" from the fashion "don't." Remember when it comes to style, the look must fit the body and the setting. Dressing for any occasion requires some key elements in your wardrobe: color, fabric and accessories.

Color

Color, in conjunction with style, is a great way to express yourself. When choosing colors, make sure they blend with your undertone. Your undertone is determined by the color of your eyes and your natural hair color. If you're uncertain of your undertone, you can visit any cosmetic counter and they will provide you with a free color analysis. However, if you are less daring, neutral or darker colors such as black, navy, or camel can be used; these are more easily accessorized, and blend well with other colors.

EXERCISE
Visit a department store cosmetic counter and have your colors analyzed. Now list the colors that best complement your skin tone and hair color.

Colors that compliment me:

1._____

2._____

3._____

4._____

5._____

Fabric

Take the time to become familiar with the "feel" of various fabrics. Visit a department or consignment shop and allow your fingers to explore the "give" or "stretch" of fabrics. This familiarity will enable you to target your true fit, which may require purchasing a larger size, particularly if a garment contains Lycra. This knowledge becomes especially useful if you prefer ordering clothing from catalogs where your perception of fabrics might otherwise be skewed.

As you build your wardrobe, you should invest in clothing with fabrics that are all seasonal. Such fabrics as silk, light wool, gabardine and rayon work well in your wardrobe. If you're budget conscious with your dry-cleaning bill, some fabrics are washable and may work best for you. During the warmer months, silk blends will provide more comfort. Although linen is a good fabric for the summer, choose linen blends, as pure linen tends to wrinkle.

EXERCISE

Visit a department store. What fabrics are you drawn to? Which ones make you feel good?

My favorite fabrics for casual wear:

1._____

2._____

3._____

4._____

My favorite fabrics for dressy wear:

1._____

2._____

3._____

4._____

Shoes

The next critical feature to any wardrobe is shoes. Whether you decide on sandals, pumps, or boots, the shoes and handbag serve as the principal complement to the outfit. Ladies, if you love to wear those wonderful sandals, jazz them up by getting a pedicure. Nail polish for both the feet and hands are fantastic, especially for the summer. Always maintain stylish footwear with dressy outfits. High sandals or strapless shoes looks great for those sexy skirts or evening dresses. For a more casual look, opt for some comfortable loafers or even a sandal with lower heels; these shoes go well with jeans. If you're choosing a more professional look, then it's very important to keep a pair of pumps with a medium heel or a square-toed shoe with a tapered heel. Boots are not just for the winter; whether they are ankle or knee high, they look terrific with a long skirt or knee-length skirts. Boots are also the perfect complement for jeans and dress slacks.

Some helpful tips with regard to shoes are:

• Wear shoes with ankle straps if you have long legs. The straps give a nice look to the leg without making the legs seem longer.

• When shopping for shoes to match an outfit, bring the article of clothing.

• Ladies, please avoid shoes that are uncomfortable, as they will cause major foot problems.

• Always be careful with heels and platform shoes as a misstep may cause you to twist your ankle.

• Finally, while your shoes may not necessarily match the color of your outfit, they should match your handbag or purse.

EXERCISE
Visit a shoe store or a department store.
What are your favorite shoes for casual/school?

1._____

2._____

3._____

What are your favorite shoes for dressy?

1._____

2._____

3._____

Accessories

Fashion has emerged to such high levels that not only do we have clothing designers but jewelry designers who have also capitalized on the market as well. Depending on the occasion, your accessories can be limited or limitless. Be careful when using accessories for your professional wardrobe; too much jewelry or other accessories, especially for those business-related meetings, can be extremely distracting. Keep those accessories to a minimum.

If you are going to a more formal occasion such as prom, keep your accessories to more gemstones or gold and silver pieces. Faux diamonds or cubic zirconia are always suitable for such occasions and faux diamond studs work well in a formal setting and even with casual wear. They simply epitomize that classic look. Choose accessories that have a naturally rich and exquisite feel to them, like turquoise, shell or wooden types of jewelry. Scarves are wonderful accessories and can be quite versatile; worn as headbands or around the neck; they can bring a lot of vibrancy to a wardrobe.

Career Chic

Many of you may be just starting your career and are attending job fairs and job interviews. The job interview process is a two-part process. The resume serves as a quick scan of your achievements, but the actual face-to-face interaction is truly where the challenge lies. Oftentimes its how you're dressed that sets the tone of the interview. Conservative attire is always the safest route for any job interview.

Your "professional" wardrobe should be different from your "fun" wardrobe. Clothing in the office should not be too tight as it might be deemed unprofessional. For example, when wearing suits in the office or even for a job interview, your jacket should be smooth and sit well on the shoulders. It should also be able to button without a pull or tug across the bust area. The same applies to your blouses and shirts; maintain a neckline at least two inches above your cleavage. Always wear the proper undergarment, i.e., a camisole under blouses made of lighter fabrics. Remember, for those white pants, beige/nude or black underwear is a must! Skirts should never be more than two inches above the knee.

Other tips for career chic are being able to mix and match your wardrobe, especially if you are on a tight budget and want to maintain a look that's versatile. Suits that have jackets without lapels can accommodate a variety of necklines. Also, a classic black or navy suit can be accessorized with a variety of styles and colors. When it comes to style, classic suits can be worn in any business setting.

Trendy Chic

It's truly fun to spice up your wardrobe, especially one that's trendy. There is nothing like a fabulous pair of comfortable jeans. The growing popularity of jeans is thanks in part to those modern designers and celebrities, who not only wear them but also maintain their signature trademark, like Jennifer Lopez, has her JLO trademark and designs her jeans for a more full-figured woman. Clothing stores such as the Gap have labeled their jeans with the intent of accommodating as many diverse shapes as possible. The popularity of jeans has transitioned from simply casual to a lot more flair. Designers are using such features as Swarovski crystals to jazz up the denim. A pair of jeans can now range from $80-$200. Paige Adams Geller from Paige Denim recommends the following tips when shopping for jeans:

1. If you want a flatter tummy , then a wide waistband or a high-waisted pair of jeans will help to hold the midsection.

2. For smaller hips, a slight flair in the jeans will work.

3. Darker jeans will make thighs look slimmer and overall will make the legs look more slender. These tips also pertain to regular dress slacks.

Trendy can be fun and sexy but can have a short style life. Oftentimes, the look does recycle but keeping up with the latest styles can be quite expensive. Most people tend to shop at vintage clothing stores to obtain their trendy looks. Sometimes we can get the fashion runway look for a lot less in vintage and department stores. A major fashion tip for trendy looks is to be very conscious of the fabrics and how they hug and drape on your body. (Also consider consignment stores!)

Formal Chic

When it comes to formal attire, one should pay attention to the invitation or event announcement. If it says black tie, that means the men are expected to appear in tuxedos and the women in long gowns. However, if black tie is optional, then an evening dress can vary in length. Everyone loves that wonderful "black dress." This can be a very sexy look and be worn for many formal occasions.

When shopping for formalwear, look for details that flatter your shape such as strapless to show off great shoulders and waist details to optimize an hourglass shape. Pick a length anywhere from mini to below the knee for the most versatile look. Everyone should have at least two black dresses in her wardrobe.

Sometimes events require us to change straight from the office. Some helpful tips for a day to evening look is changing your shirt or blouse to a sequined blouse or lace camisole. This is a nice transition with a black skirt or pantsuit. Also replace your jacket with a pashmina (a beautifully designed shawl or wrap) and you have an excellent look for a cocktail party.

Ladies, don't forget the shoes; replace those pumps with some stiletto heels and you're ready for the evening. Finally, there has been an ongoing debate about wearing black to a wedding. I would recommend a black cocktail dress for an evening wedding, pastel colors are great for summer weddings, and in keeping with proper color etiquette, you should never wear white to a wedding unless you're the bride.

Perfect Prom Night

With such great fashion trends and new waves in technology, shopping online has become extremely popular. With such great buys as designer jeans for less, it was just a matter of time before shopping for prom dresses would be available online as well. Your Prom Night is a very important night so buying a prom dress is a major decision. Buying prom dresses online can be helpful as you can choose from a larger variety, from designer dresses to plus-size dresses. However, whether you are shopping online or in a traditional store, the key to fitting into any prom dress is body type.

As you shop for your dress, select a dress that accentuates your best features. Don't choose a dressed based upon only a designer name or price. Young women come in many different shapes and sizes: hourglass, straight, rounded, or pear-shaped. Each body type is different and in some cases, prom dresses do not always reflect your true size. For example, you may be a size 12, but based upon the cut and style of the dress, a size 14 would be your perfect fit. Sizing can be different and it's important to review the size charts for all dresses. Let's review the body types and styles of dresses that would be appropriate.

Hourglass Shape

The hourglass shape is classified as large bust, small waist, and curvy hips. Hourglass shapes are very curvy and strapless or halter dresses would be flattering. Dresses may have a sash or cinched waist.

Straight Shape

The straight shape is described as straight waist, narrow hips, and smaller bust. Dresses that are flattering for a straight shape are A-line dresses and styles with open shoulders. Straight-shaped ladies should avoid any body-fitting dresses.

Rounded Shape

The rounded shape is typically a rounded look at the top and bottom. Dresses that work for a rounded shape are styles with drop waist and low neckline. A low neckline enhances the bust and the drop waist lengthens your torso.

Pear Shape

A pear shape is a figure that is significantly larger on the bottom than on the top. A-line dresses with a straight cut and empire waist are good choices for this figure.

Accessorizing your prom dress is important. If your dress has a lot of shimmer, your jewelry should be simple and elegant. Strapless sandals are great for evening wear and if you opt to use or purse or handbag, it should match your shoes.

Finishing Touches

It's time to step out for your big night, but your dress is only part of your look. Make-up and hair are also important components to your overall look.

1. Hair

Stylish pony tails and updos are always an elegant look for evening wear. If you choose to keep the length, then long waves and curls are just as nice.

2. Foundation

Light powders and bronzing powders are great. They give your skin a very natural and radiant glow without the look of heavy foundation. If there is a need to apply foundation, then use a foundation stick and apply directly to cover any acne or blemish followed by a slight application of powder. You can use a concealer for dark circles under the eyes, and again apply powder.

3. Make-up Colors

Choose colors that work best with your skin tones instead of choosing colors that blend with your dress. Beauty expert Bobby Brown suggests that for darker complexions, colors such as deep plums and chocolates would be ideal. Medium skin tones require roses and tawny shades, and light skin tones require more pinks or pastel colors.

Eyeliners are great for prom or evening events, but not for every day. Sheer colors for eyes and lips are great. Keep in mind that when you do smokey eyes or choose to accentuate the eyes with more color, keep the lips natural by using a light gloss or sheer lipstick.

Makeup Dos and Don'ts

• Do wash your makeup brushes once a month to avoid
  bacteria buildup.
• Do wash your face after every makeup application to avoid clogged
  pores and acne build-up.
• Do wear more sheer shades of lipsticks and lip gloss.
• Do keep a consistent skincare regimen.
• Don't wear deep red lipsticks; it tends to look like you're wearing
  your mother's or grandmother's makeup. If using red, use a gloss or
  sheer lipstick.
• Don't wear dark or black lipliners, as they tend to overpower the
  lip color.
• Don't apply shimmer makeup to both the eyes and lips as it can
  be overkill.

Conclusion

Wardrobe is important. Having the right accessories, shoes, handbag, and jewelry can be fun, but your hair and makeup seal the entire look. I have always maintained the motto that "less is best," so when it comes to makeup and hair, aim for a soft look and enhance those wonderful features. Whether it's a little mascara or a touch of lipstick, make-up can be fun and sexy.

Shopping for the right body shape can be challenging, but price, quality, and comfort are important. Remember, no matter how great a bargain, if it's too tight and you are unable to reach with ease, or too loose where it's unflattering, then it's not worth your investment. Let your sense of style exude confidence without any wardrobe malfunctions.

ABOUT THE AUTHOR

HANNAH CRUTCHER

Hannah Crutcher, President and CEO of Hannah Crutcher & Associates, is an educator with over twenty years of experience in higher education. Most of that experience is in career counseling and job placement at six colleges and universities. Her passion for education extends to K-12 students as well; she has served as a Brownie Girl Scout troop leader, and president, treasurer, and secretary in the Parent/Teachers Association. Hannah is also a member of the Professional Women's Network International Advisory Board.

Ms. Crutcher received a Bachelor's degree in Speech Education with a minor in drama; she loves live theater and has appeared in such classics as *The Amen Corner, The Women,* and *The Merry Widow.* She has a Master's degree in Management and is a certified seminar trainer with particular interest in leadership skills, sales, and customer service.

She and her husband Melvin have been married for thirty years and have two adult children.

Contact:
Hannah Crutcher & Associates
1994 Steeplebrook Drive
Cordova, TN 38016
(901) 757-4203
crutcherf@bellsouth.net
www.protrain.net

ELEVEN

YES, I CAN! DEVELOPING A POSITIVE ATTITUDE

By Hannah Crutcher

Projecting that "Yes, I can!" attitude is within everyone's power. How firmly you believe this to be the case and how strongly a positive attitude is projected has everything to do with your ability to take your life experiences to another level. Developing and keeping a positive attitude can be quite habit-forming.

Just as we learn our beliefs, habits, or customs from those closest to us (parents, siblings, teachers, religious leaders), the same people also provided the basis of our "Yes, I can!" attitude (or not). It is difficult to maintain a positive attitude (or for that matter, a negative attitude) toward any person or anything without somehow being persuaded to do so. What is important, though, is to be sure and keep an open mind. Always be willing to listen to others' views and compare them to yours and with what your instinct tells you is right.

Why is it important to develop and keep a positive attitude? A positive attitude is motivating! Whenever you meet people with a positive attitude, you can be sure that they first believed in themselves, which in turn allowed them to believe in others as well. A positive attitude lends itself to small private victories and leads to one to have more successes. Motivated people tend to surround themselves with like-minded, positive-thinking individuals. They get energy from each other by sharing ideas and always serving as a support system for one another.

EXERCISE

Think back to your earliest remembrances of your childhood memories. What positive feelings did you experience because someone spoke encouraging words and displayed kind acts toward you?

My feelings:

1._____

2._____

3._____

What positive, encouraging words were said to you by your mother, dad, sister, brother, or a teacher?

Encouraging words:

Person #1:_____

Person #2:_____

Person #3:_____

What kind acts were done by your mother, dad, sister, brother, or a teacher?

Kind acts:

Person #1:_____

Person #2:_____

Person #3:_____

Name three people whom you knew as a child who always had a positive attitude:

1._____

2._____

3._____

How did it feel to be around these positive people?

_____

Developing and keeping a positive attitude may be habit-forming, but it requires a certain amount of practice. Learn to devote time each day to remembering and re-living those special motivating moments that were a part of your day. Do not be afraid to embrace and hold onto whatever positive feedback you received or were able to pass on to another person.

One of the easiest ways to finding and keeping that "Yes, I can!" attitude is to deliberately and actively help others develop their own positive attitudes. It is impossible to help someone else achieve any degree of greatness without becoming a better person yourself.

Become Someone's Angel

Recently, I needed to coordinate appointments between several different offices, and for some reason, it seemed the people I was working with had little or no interest in helping me reach my goal. Every time I thought I had done exactly what was needed, I would be sent back to another office because the person I was speaking with would not take responsibility for a task. I usually am a pretty self-assured, confident person and can work with most people without any problems. Somehow I could not make this situation work and was becoming increasingly frustrated.

Then one day, I walked into an office and there was my angel. I explained to her what I was trying to do and what was happening. She immediately called the other offices and started working on my behalf. Apparently she knew what needed to be done, and was willing to share this information with me. She explained to me how things should work and that I had to politely and kindly (and with some degree of urgency) make sure that certain things were done. I took her advice and sure enough, the next day things started to happen. My angel has no idea how much strength she provided me with that day.

Sometimes things that seem small to you can mean a lot to someone else. Become someone's angel and help her develop a positive attitude. I know what it feels like to be around someone who helped me! Now I need to pass that on to others!

EXERCISE

1. Think about a frustrating experience you have had and write it down:

_____

_____

2. List the feelings you experienced during that time:

a._____

b._____

c._____

3. What steps did you take to work through this situation?

Step #1:_____

Step #2:_____

Step #3:_____

4. Did you have an angel on your side? If so, what exactly did this person do to help?

Angel's name:_____

What he or she did:_____

_____

5. If you didn't have an angel to help in that frustrating situation, how would you have wanted an angel to help?

_____

_____

Find and Keep a Mentor

As a young woman, I am sure that at times it is hard to balance school and possibly work. There are days when you probably feel very overwhelmed, and this can impact your attitude! I recommend that you find mentors who may be a bit older (an aunt, teacher, youth minister) who may be able to share how they balance their lives. These people can serve as a sounding board and advise you on an array of topics.

Be proactive in seeking out a mentor. Do not be afraid to ask someone you admire and want to emulate to serve as your mentor; most people will be very flattered! If they are unable to mentor you for whatever reason, they probably will pass your name on to someone else they admire and believe you will work well with. They also may agree to speak with you whenever they are available and to serve as a reference if needed. The important point to remember is that it is imperative to develop relationships with people who you can trust and depend on (who have awesome, positive attitudes!). Whatever you do, make sure they can count on you to do your part! Also express your appreciation whenever people give of themselves on your behalf.

EXERCISE
1. Think about a time in your life when you needed a mentor. When was it?

_____

2. What were some of the problems you faced?

_____
_____
_____

3. What were some of the feelings you experienced?

_____
_____
_____

4. How do you think a mentor could have helped?

_____
_____
_____

Be a Mentor

Later on, once you have established yourself in your career, make sure you take time to be a mentor to someone else. What might seem like "simple rules to live by" to a seasoned professional might serve as life-changing events to a young, up-and-coming person. You are a young person now and know the value of having a mentor, so be keenly aware of the power of speaking from experience! Having lived through and learned from situations makes one incredibly able to share, advise, and mentor others.

To lift your attitude, consider serving as a volunteer! I know that life can get you down, but it is good for society and good for the soul, and it is an especially good opportunity to serve as a volunteer. There are numerous volunteer positions available. First, concentrate on things you enjoy doing, whether it is helping someone learn to read, assisting at a non-profit, or visiting someone who would enjoy your time and company (i.e., a children's hospital, animal rescue shelter, or nursing home). Secondly, think of things you would like to learn more about; this can be especially exciting and invigorating because you get the added bonus of learning a new skill and helping others.

A Positive Attitude Keeps a Body Healthy

Have you ever tried getting on the tread mill or stair-climber for a vigorous workout when you are in a not-so-good mood? It takes great motivation and determination to follow through, doesn't it? The end result is worth a few minutes of suffering, though. Amazingly, it is hard not to feel better after you exercise! Positive thinking allows one to think clearly and stay focused, making it much easier to make the right decisions. The mind and the body react to your disposition, whether it is positive or negative. Therefore, it is very important to train your mind to have positive thoughts. Think about it! If you are in a great mood, it is reflected in how you feel and your body reacts in a positive way, not only in your facial expression, but in your overall feeling of well-being!

EXERCISE

1. Think about your workout schedule. Is it consistent? Was your last workout session enjoyable and relaxing or a time of torture? Share your thoughts:

_____

_____

2. Now remember and list what thoughts you experienced right before you exercised:

_____

_____

_____

3. What feelings did you have immediately following your session? Were they positive, life-affirming feelings?

_____

_____

4. Think about people you know who are committed to an exercise regimen. Do these people usually exhibit happy and healthy attitudes? Write down their names:

_____

_____

Never Underestimate the Power of a Positive Attitude

The subconscious mind is powerful and within everyone's reach. Many people have developed the ability to chart much of their life's course by tapping into their subconscious mind.

Remember what you were taught at a very early age: to think before you speak? Now add to that: "Think positive thoughts before you speak and act." It is really amazing how siblings, childhood friends, and close acquaintances can practically have the same start in life, but end up living very different lives. One young woman could be very happy with the way her life is going, and the other could be quite miserable, constantly questioning why she can't seem to do anything right! The subconscious mind plays a significant role in these two very different lives and attitudes.

Many of us know (or know of) people with very humble beginnings who have done incredible things. If you spend time with them, you will find that they have mastered the art of using positive thinking and maintaining a positive attitude. Whether they are widely known by a large number of people or perhaps only familiar to a close-knit community of family and friends, they have made a big impact on the lives of others because of their positive attitudes.

My father lived to be 96 years old; he lived a rather simple, but very gratifying life. One of the most poignant statements at his memorial service came from a grandson who said, "One of the things I learned from him was that he taught me to always make time for others." My father always had time for other people, was always ready to engage in a lively, spirited, one-on-one conversation—and he did it in such a way that made it special.

EXERCISE
1. Make a list of famous people who you believe exhibit a positive attitude:

a._____

b._____

c._____

d._____

2. What is it about these people that make you feel they are positive-thinkers?

a._____

b._____

c._____

d._____

3. List similar qualities that you possess:

a._____

b._____

c._____

4. Observe others for a couple of days and list those whom you believe have a positive attitude:

a._____

b._____

c._____

5. Who do you know in your life who exhibits a negative attitude?

a._____

b._____

c._____

6. Now list what changes you would like to make in your life in order to develop a more positive attitude:

a._____

b._____

c._____

Allow the wondrous power of your subconscious mind to work for you. It is really quite a natural process to think positively! However, many of us are trained to think and to believe otherwise. Choose to think and act in a very positive way! Thinking positive thoughts and speaking positively will affect and program your subconscious. Surround yourself with people you admire and want to model your life after, and never, ever underestimate the power of positive thinking!

Recommended Reading

Emotional Intelligence by Daniel Goleman.

I Could do Anything If I Only Knew What It Was by Barbara Sher.

The Power of Your Subconscious Mind by David Murphy.

Principle-Centered Leadership by Stephen Covey.

The 7 Habits of Highly Effective People by Stephen Covey.

Notes:

ABOUT THE AUTHOR

VERDONDA ALEXANDER WRIGHT

Verdonda A. Wright is a native of Norfolk, VA and President of Family Empowerment Solutions, an organization specializing in personal development workshops and professional training seminars. She graduated *magna cum laude* from Norfolk State University with a Bachelor's degree in Consumer Services and Family Studies Education. She has taught in both middle and high schools and is a certified secondary culinary educator and safety and sanitation instructor and currently teaches culinary arts at Phoebus High School in Hampton, VA. She loves working with teenagers and sponsors one school club, Family, Career and Community Leaders of America (FCCLA) and also sponsors the Class of 2007. As a teacher, she is proudest of the nomination by her students for five consecutive years to Who's Who Among American High School Teachers.

She is passionate about the family, women's issues, and parenting. She has presented at numerous workshops and conferences at churches, college campuses, and school divisions. Verdonda and her husband Timothy are certified to conduct interactive marriage enrichment classes through Family Dynamic, Inc. Workshop topics include "Me, Myself & I," "Building Resili-ency in Children," "Women: Stepping Into Excellence," "Know Your Ministry Gift," "The Phenomenal Family," "Temple Care," "Professional Etiqutte and Protocol," "The Balancing Act: Family & Career," and "Aging with Dignity and Grace."

Professional affiliations include American Association of Family and Consumer Sciences; Virginia Association of Teachers of Family and Consumer Sciences, Associations for Supervision and Cirriculum Development, National Restaurant Association; National Council on Family Relations and The Professional Woman Network.

Wright, a liscensed evangelist, serves as Director of Women's Ministries and Christian Education at Victorious Living Ministries COGIC, where her husband is pastor. She married Elder Timothy E. Wright in 1979 and three children were added to this family by birth and one by marriage, Kimberly and her husband Bobby, Dedra, and Timothy. Verdonda is the proud "Mema" to two beautiful grandchildren, Xavier and Brianna.

Contact:
Family Empowerment Solutions
4221 Pleasant Valley Road
Suite 125 #123
Virginia Beach, VA 23464
(757) 343-5070
www.protrain.net
www.missiontransition.org
vwright@missiontransition.org

TWELVE

GETTING ALONG WITH FAMILY AND FRIENDS

By Verdonda A. Wright

When we come to the end of our lives, it won't matter how big our house was or what the balance in our savings account has grown to. We won't regret not having one more degree or concern ourselves about the business meeting scheduled for next week. We most likely will regret that brother, sister, or even father we have lost touch with. We will think about that old friend we haven't spoken to in years and have long forgotten why. Relationships are far more important than acquisitions. There is an old adage that says: "Things are temporal; people are eternal. Invest, therefore, in the latter."

When looking at strategies for getting along with family and friends, consider first being friends with yourself, and then understanding the family culture. How can you be friends with yourself? First, you need to know yourself. In his book *All I Ever Really Needed to Know I Learned in Kindergarten,* Robert Fulghum penned what has become quite profound.

"Play fair. Don't hit people. Don't take things that are not yours.
Live a balanced life..."

If we understood the importance of transferring the things we learned when we were young to the next stages in life, we would avoid much heartache and disappointment. The concept of living a balanced life eludes far too many people. Until we exercise balance in our own lives, it will be difficult to experience the best situations in other relationships. Until we become "real" with ourselves, it will be futile to try to establish true and lasting relationships.

First, we must have an understanding of the word balanced. An Indian proverb speaks of a person as being a house with four rooms, to reflect the fact that we are complex beings with several dimensions. The four rooms are directly related to our being physical, mental, emotional, and spiritual aspects. How "well-kept" are your rooms? Do you visit each one regularly?

Ideas for Mental "Housekeeping"

• Listen to good music.

• Read an exciting book.

• Learn a new skill or hobby.

• Retreat to a spot for a quiet time of meditating and reflecting.

• Build yourself up with positive affirmations.

• Slow down.

• Say "no" to good things and save your "yes" for the best things.

Ideas for Physical "Housekeeping"

• Exercise regularly by walking, jogging, doing Jazzercise, etc.

• Eat foods that promote health and energy.

• Take a stress management class.

• Investigate food combining.

• Take a stroll on the beach or near a quiet stream.

• Take a quiet bubble bath by candlelight with the phone turned off and soft music on.

Ideas for Spiritual "Housekeeping"

• Read a chapter of *Proverbs* every day.

• Write your worries in the sand at the beach and watch them wash away.

• Examine your motives. (Are they self-serving?)

• Join a young women's fellowship.

• Keep a journal about your spiritual journey.

Ideas for Emotional "Housekeeping"

• Have a good cry.

• Have breakfast or lunch with a friend.

• Spend a day doing anything you want.

• Serve a friend in need.

• Buy flowers for yourself.

• Write a letter to your parent(s) informing them of the things they did right.

There are two children's books that cause me to cry every time I read them: *The Velveteen Rabbit* by Margery Williams and the somewhat controversial book *Love You Forever, Like You for Always* by Robert Munsch. There are tremendous life lessons to be learned in these books.

In *The Velveteen Rabbit*, the old Skin Horse, who has been around for a long time, befriends the newest toy in the playroom, the little rabbit. The focus of the entire book is the concept of "being real." What a novel idea! The Skin Horse tells the rabbit exactly what takes place in the progression to becoming real. Progression is such a reassuring word. It gives permission to make mistakes because we have a complete understanding that growth, development, learning ourselves–becoming real–doesn't happen all at once. It takes time, a long time. The Skin Horse also said that's why people who break easily don't usually become real. He warned the rabbit that before one becomes real, "Your eyes may fall out, your hair loved off, and you become loose in the joints and shabby."

When we become real, we realize that we live for ourselves and are not manipulated by others. We learn to keep the main thing the main thing: to be true to our God-given purpose and direction. When we become real, we sell the shadow for the substance. We need not pretend to be anything or anybody we are not. We have such a love and appreciation for who we are that we are completely free to allow others to be who they are. When we become real–and it is progressive–we realize that not only should we not try to please everybody, but we can't do it anyway. When less becomes more, enough becomes more than enough.

- We must make self-care a priority.
- We must learn to "manage" life stressors.
- We must learn to rest, reflect, renew, and rejoice in the small things.

- We can't be too sensitive; we don't want to break.
- Our past should not ruin our future.
- We must know our limitations in time and energy.
- Striving for realistic goals is medicinal.
- Expressing love each and every day opens the door for love to return.
- It is necessary to continue to search for and refine the authenticity in ourselves.
- We should never make a promise that we can't keep.
- Whatever the ending, it will give birth to a new beginning.
- Some days are full of questions, and others hold the answers.
- A heart's desire delayed is not always a heart's desire denied.
- To travel the distance with excellence, we must keep it simple!

Are You a Thermometer or a Thermostat?

A thermometer is a device which measures temperature. The glass-enclosed medium rises or falls as it expands or contracts from changes in temperature. A thermostat, on the other hand, is an instrument that automatically regulates temperature. This device allows you to control the temperature in a room by telling the heating or cooling unit how much air to produce. Are you controlled by circumstances and go up and down as the situation dictates or are you the controlling factor? Do you set the standard and the circumstances have to get in line with you? Circumstances should not control our attitudes or behaviors. We must maintain control of our own responses and reactions at all times. We regulate!

Munsch's *Love You Forever, Like You For Always* contains a powerful illustration of unconditional love of a mother for her son. This book is controversial because many people find it "creepy" and feel that it illustrates a dysfunctional family. One of the many reviews I have read about this book echoes my sentiments: "It is about the internal feelings that this mother has for her son and we should not consider literal the actions contained in the book. The story tells of a mother who rocks her son to sleep each night and sings him a song, *I love you forever, I like you for always, and as long as I live, my baby you'll be.*"

These demonstrations of love go on throughout his childhood and into adulthood. Regardless of how mad he made her or how frustrated she became, her love was constant. When her son became an adult, he in turn rocked and sang to his daughter. The book ends with a picture of the grown man rocking and singing to his elderly mother. The point is this: your family of origin has instilled in you a "family culture." There are written and unwritten rules that families follow and understand. When we understand that our family culture is not like that of any other family, we will experience better relationships. Family culture, beliefs, or practices may include:

• Children do not speak unless spoken to.
• Never question your parents.
• You don't jump on the bed.
• Wherever you are, you know that dinner is at 6 p.m. and you must be at home.
• Daddy's word is the last word (or the only word).
• Siblings never fight each other.
• Blood is thicker than water.
• The views of a woman are not important.
• Marriage is not important.
• Divorce is not an option.
• You don't call an older person by his/her first name.

As you can see, family practices can vary from trivial to extremely important. Depending on the relationship, disagreement on any of these topics could cause a myriad of problems in friendships. If a friendship turns into a dating situation, it is crucial to learn the family culture as much as possible to be proactive.

I remember when I first heard my brother share with his son details about our family culture. Father told son that he had to do exactly what his older cousin told him to do, because in our family, the oldest tells the youngest what to do and it is done. Although I had never heard it verbalized, the accuracy of that statement took me aback. It was one of those unspoken rules. I realized that I had seen this done and had followed that rule all of my life. It was just understood by all of the family members. I was never told, but it was modeled and I understood.

Such unspoken or spoken rules may become problems when someone wants to "buck" or challenge them. We may become the family outcast, or at least the topic of much discussion. I was shunned by family members when I exercised authority and refused to do what I was told because I didn't feel that it was right or fair. We must decide what behaviors we will not accept and those we will. Disrespect of any kind, cursing, or yelling are behaviors I will not tolerate. It does not matter who the individual is; older or younger, he or she will be told that the behavior is not acceptable and to refrain from doing it.

We teach people how to treat us. If anyone treats us in a disrespectful manner, it is because we have taught them it is permissible. There are some basic principles to follow when attempting to establish lasting relationships and get along with anyone:

• When dealing with a behavior, use "I" statements rather than "You" statements. Defenses don't show themselves as quickly as when we say "I felt bad when you raised your voice while talking to me" instead of "You made me feel bad when you raised your voice at me."

- Regardless of our age, we may all be faced with peer pressure. Once again, sell the shadow for the substance. Don't allow yourself to be compromised or lose your integrity. Just because you have the family name, doesn't mean you are required to play the family game.

- Embrace healthy friendships. Avoid friendships that constantly drain you and don't pour energy back into you. Realize that there comes a time when we outgrow some relationships.

- Squash gossip.

- Association leads to assimilation. We become more like those we spend time with. Consider the character of those you are close to.

- Have well-rooted support systems. Understand that not everyone is your best friend and confidant. Choose carefully whom you share your heart with. Be selective in those from whom you receive guidance and counsel. Choose people who honor and support your aspirations.

- Let your compliments exceed your criticism. It is not a good thing to be known as a critic. Find ways to genuinely compliment someone every day. Look for the positive; the negative stands out by itself.

- Observe with your eyes and your heart. Be concerned enough to feel the hurt, joy, or doubt beyond what you see. Wouldn't it be wonderful to have friends who care enough about us that when we cried, they tasted salt? Listen with care.

- There is never a good excuse to demonstrate bad manners.

- Never give "a piece of your mind." Exercise tact in all you say and do. We don't have to give "a tit for a tat." Be the mature one.

- "NO" is an acceptable answer. You cannot do everything and be all things to all people. For every "yes," let there be a "no." Don't overschedule. Instead of always "doing," learn to "be."

• Don't allow anyone to take advantage of your precious resources: time, creative energy, and emotions.

• Continue to plug yourself into healthy choices for mind, heart, body, and spirit.

Shakespeare's words "To thine own self be true" are priceless. Remember, becoming real is progressive. Don't stop the journey. We want to always have respect for the young woman looking back at us in the mirror. Family members or friends may attempt to tell you how to live your life. Sweetly remind them that it is your life.

Let's not get to the end of life with regrets for what could have, should have, or would have happened, if only…. "Love your neighbor as yourself" is a commandment in the Bible. However, it is impossible to give what you do not have. How can we show love to another when we don't show love to ourselves? Value your family and your friends. Invest in them your time and your love, but never neglect to demonstrate love for yourself.

ABOUT THE AUTHOR

MYRTLE LOOBY

Myrtle Looby is the President and Primary Consultant of LEAP Training Consultants, based in Antigua and Barbuda. Having enjoyed a successful career as a trained educator of English and Communication Skills, she now makes keynote presentations, and designs and conducts outstanding workshops and training seminars throughout the Caribbean. Some of her most sought after workshops are on Customer Care, Communication Skills, Leadership, Effective Supervision, Team Building and Women's Issues.

In addition, Ms. Looby is an advocate for lifelong learning. She owns and manages the Guidance and Learning Centre, which offers educational opportunities to persons seeking to become more self-sufficient

Myrtle's background and expertise have contributed to the passion and dynamism that she brings to all aspects of her life including community service. She is a founding member of the Professional Organisation for Women in Antigua/Barbuda (P.O.W.A.), a member of the Advisory Committee of the Directorate of Gender Affairs in Antigua and Barbuda and a member of the Antigua Lions Club. As a Lion, she has held the position of Zone Chairperson, Region Chairperson, and District Trainer for District 60B. She is also an active member of her church community where she uses her expertise to conduct seminars with the Young Adults Group. Internationally, she serves on the Board of Advisors of the Professional Woman Network and is a member of the Professional Woman Speakers Bureau

In fulfilling one of her lifelong dreams she has co-authored the recently published best-seller, "Becoming the Professional Woman," and is currently working on her fifth publication.

Myrtle holds a Bachelor of Arts in English and History, a Diploma in Education, a Certificate in Guidance and Counseling and a Diploma in Gender and Development Studies.

Contact:
LEAP Training Consultants
P.O.Box W704 Woods Centre, St. John's, Antigua
(268) 460-5504
guidance@candw.ag
www.protrain.net

THIRTEEN

OVERCOMING HURT AND SADNESS

By Myrtle Looby

Surmounting difficulty is the crucible that forms character.
– Anthony Robbins

Listening to music on a Sunday afternoon has often been my pastime, but the music on that Sunday struck a chord! They were playing "Oldies and Goldies" and I realized that there was no end to songs about sadness and hurt—songs that chronicled the brokenness of the human spirit. My mind was flooded with memories when in times past, I was in a similar place of emotional brokenness.

Grief is indeed stressful and can take a toll on you emotionally and physically. There were those lonely days and long, sleepless nights. Time has erased the details and I can now look back and laugh at myself. Don't get me wrong. I felt dejected and alone. I even thought my life would end. The first stanza of John Keats' poem *Ode to a Nightingale* stuck to my mind:

"My heart aches, and a drowsy numbness pains
My sense, as though of hemlock I had drunk,
Or emptied some dull opiate to the drains
One minute past, and Lethe-wards had sunk."

Let me ask you:
• Have you ever lost someone near and dear to you through death or illness?
• Have you ever been rejected or disappointed in love?
• Have you ever experienced the pain of humiliation?
• Have you experienced a sudden, devastating life change?

These are a few of the occasions that send us into a tailspin. If you have experienced hurt or sadness caused by personal crisis or any other form of adversity, you are not alone. Most young women can cite an example of when they have been emotionally wounded. We all have different ways of responding. Some of us never get over it and others only do so partially. For some, the hurt surfaces around holidays and special days. A friend of mine whose mother disappeared under strange circumstances never closed that chapter in her life. She always felt that her mother would return, and for years was consumed by depression around Mother's Day.

Let me share with you parts of letters written by young women like you, who were desperately looking for answers and healing for their pain. Perhaps you can see yourself or someone you know in one of these letters.

Dear Myrtle:

How can God take away someone's mother in the prime of her life? They lied to me and said that He knows best. Is this the best? Why did she have to suffer? Who will take care of my little sister? Who will be there for me, no matter what? Can anyone provide the answers to heal this pain? I did not have the chance to speak to her and hear her last words. I wanted to tell her one last time that I love her. –Rochelle

Dear Myrtle:

My best friend has done the unthinkable. She has gone off with my boyfriend, whom I thought would have been my husband some day. To think that I was betrayed all along into telling her all our secrets, when she was sneaking off with him behind my back! Now I am without a boyfriend and a best friend. I feel so angry and humiliated. I was deceived big time. How can I trust anyone again? –Valerie

Everyone has problems, and each problem is unique and personal. Some are more devastating than others and you may even think life is not fair. You are right! But who said life was fair anyway? What I know for sure is that the human spirit is stronger than anything that happens to it, and hurt shall eventually pass! In the search for life's meaning, some of us become more spiritual and connected to a Higher Being. It is in that connection that we find healing, happiness, peace, and love.

A sister-friend once told me that life is a series of ups and downs, and that valleys and mountains are a natural part of life's terrain. She said to get to the mountains, we must go through the valleys, some darker, deeper, longer, and more treacherous than others, and that it is in those valleys that we grow. It is in crossing those valleys that we become resilient and stronger, wiser and more resolute to succeed, that is, to get to the mountain tops. She said if we do not go through these valleys, we do not become our best selves and reach new heights.

But you know what? I found out that she was only partly right. Life is really a journey along two roads that crisscross each other. They lead us along valleys and up hills, and at any time, we can be on both high and low ground. More often than not, we have good and bad experiences at the same time. What matters most is how we respond to those experiences; and that, my friend, is left to us.

Character cannot be developed in ease and quiet.
Only through experience of trial and suffering
can the soul be strengthened, ambition
inspired, and success achieved.
–Helen Keller

So come, Sister, read on. If you are going through one of your valleys, I may not be able to walk with you but there is a ray of light that would bring hope. Look for it and let it guide you through. May this chapter bring some light to start a healing in your life through these tried and tested strategies. I have included some interactive sections to assist you.

Honor Your Feelings
It's OK to feel hurt, because you are human. Allow no one to tell you that you ought not feel that way. The hurt is emotional but it may manifest itself physically. Listen to your body. You may be experiencing unexplained aches and pains, loss of appetite, or sleeplessness. Your emotions may run the gamut from hurt, anger, anxiety, fear, confusion, hopelessness, emptiness, self-pity, or

numbness. It will help if you can identify and label how you feel and recognize what triggers these emotions.

EXERCISE
I feel:

_____

_____

_____

_____

Is the source of your pain internal or external to you? Be honest now. Sometimes we mistakenly blame others when the problem lies within us.

Completing the statements below may help you move through the process.
I feel this way because:

_____

_____

_____

_____

I experience _____ (the emotion) most when

_____

_____

_____

_____

Give Vent to Your Feelings

Let yourself grieve. It's normal and you cannot cheat the process. Bottling up feelings can lead to physical illness, depression, as well as unproductive or destructive behavior. Let these feelings out so that you can be open to healing. Tears cleanse and bring relief so let the tears flow, without apology. Punch a pillow, yell, scream, or write notes on your mirror with lipstick. As long as you do not deny or suppress those feelings, or channel them into negative behavior, you are on the right path.

Use Lessons from Past Experiences

One of the tenets I live by is: "Whatever situation you are in, let it add value to your life." When we choose to learn from sad experiences, we become empowered to grow. Try to remember a past experience that you have overcome. Find meaning in the situation and congratulate yourself on your growth.

EXERCISE
Something that made me feel hurt was:

_____

_____

_____

What helped me cope?
Knowledge:

_____

_____

_____

Attitude:

_____

_____

_____

Actions:

_____

_____

_____

What healthy lessons did I take away from the experience?

_____

_____

_____

Believe in Yourself

Sister, you have been blessed with emotional strength and resilience to overcome. Allow yourself to reclaim your value. Remember that you have successfully overcome other problems. We do not have all the answers as to why "stuff happens." You cannot change anyone nor do you have control over everything in life, but you can change how you view the situation. Accept yourself as being already complete and able so you need not look to others to make you complete.

Bolster Yourself

Women often lower their expectations to avoid being disappointed. We tend to compromise our values and accept other people's behavior because we fear rejection. We also passively accept mediocrity because we believe that it is a part of "a woman's lot." Is it that you are disappointed in love? Why would you want to be with someone who does not want to be with you? Sister, examine your sense of self-worth and seek to improve your self-esteem. How you think of yourself and your life is important for change and growth.

Sadness and hurt can sometimes keep us pegged to feelings of unworthiness. We may see ourselves as losers or hapless maidens waiting to be saved by the handsome prince. An important step to healing is to become aware of how we view ourselves and the negative thoughts and words that reinforce the poor self-perception. When you replace the negatives with those positive qualities with which you have been endowed, you will notice a positive difference in your outlook.

Close your eyes and think of positive descriptions of yourself. Have you been told that you are a wonderful person, talented, bright? You may not have thought of yourself this way for a long time. Ask your close friends. You may be pleasantly surprised. Now, jot down some of those positive descriptions and repeat them daily for reinforcement.

EXERCISE
My positive points are:

I am:

_____
_____
_____

I can:

_____
_____
_____

I know how to:

_____
_____
_____

I am good at:

_____
_____
_____

I excel in:

_____
_____
_____

Let It Go

Learn to live with the hurt and sadness for a while until they dissipate, but you must be prepared to let it go! This is the key to releasing your hurt. You need to gain freedom to grow and to think clearly enough to make rational decisions, but you've got to work at it. At some point, sooner or later, you must face reality, so do not become a prisoner of your own pain. It is said that when you harbor bitterness, happiness will dock elsewhere. This means that you must free yourself of guilt and resentment in order to be happy. If you made a mistake, don't berate yourself and destroy your self-confidence.

There is an English saying: "To err is human, to forgive divine." So just as you learn to forgive yourself, be prepared to forgive others. Remember that forgiveness is a choice you make for your own happiness, not for the other person's. Yes, feel the hurt, but forgive anyway. When you cling to feelings of resentment, you place walls between yourself and your healing. You become bitter and lose your joy for life. Let go of your resentment and get on with living.

If there is something holding you back and you experience difficulty in forgiving, your religious practices like reading the Bible, prayer, meditation, or consulting with your spiritual leader may help.

Sometimes we say we let it go and "throw it into the garbage," but in a moment of weakness, we go back to the dump heap and retrieve it. Then we hold a pity party alone or with friends, and gloat over the problem, as we would a prized possession. Remember, those old emotions can become toxic, so you don't want to keep them around. Toss them back in the garbage, and when you have the urge to reclaim them, check yourself and say "Stop, don't go there!"

Start a Journal
Journaling is a simple way to let the feelings and thoughts flow and ease your pain. Studies prove that there are emotional and physical health benefits to be derived from writing. Your pain is reduced; your immune system becomes stronger; you are more resistant to colds and flu; and you manage stress more efficiently and effectively.

You can give yourself unfettered permission to express your entire range of emotions when they occur, either on paper or on the computer. Your writing is private and you have to account to no one. Make a date with your journal every day and pour your heart out using your favorite pen, book, time, and location that help you relax when writing. Journal entries can be poetry, prayers, letters, memories, blessings, or lists of things to do to aid your healing. If words fail, you can make a collage or draw.

In one of my journal entries, I drew a line down the middle of the page. On one side I wrote all the disempowering experiences I had endured. On the other side, I wrote all the empowering things I could do since the relationship ended. After that, whenever I thought of pitying myself, I remembered my lists and thanked my lucky stars!

This is one of the poems I wrote in my journal back then, when I was consumed by grief.

Untitled

Alone, alone,
in my own head,
in my own room.
I feel so hurt,
and numb inside.
There must be things I need to do
but don't know how
to climb outside myself and to move on.
Can someone help?

This pain, it would not go away
and hurts too much.
Life makes no sense
right now!

They say this too shall pass.
They say…they say,
I'm so confused.
Can s-o-m-e-o-n-e help!

But I know
one day I shall rise up
and fortify myself.
I shall be strong,
no matter what,
and I shall no longer be alone!
– Myrtle Looby

Sister, I have risen up and have come a long way. Like a ship, I sailed out of that harbor of hurt and disappointment. I have moved on. With time, you, too, will eventually come to terms with your grief and gain control of your life. Try to think of setbacks in life as gifts; opportunities to make us stop and re-examine who we are, explore our values, recognize our strengths and weaknesses, and learn from our mistakes.

At times, journaling can cause us to become overwhelmed by our emotions, so we need to know when to vent and when to distract ourselves with some self-soothing activities. If you find that you have become stuck or are regurgitating the same old pain and hurt, give up journaling a while and try other options. This is a good time to examine where you are in the process and determine where you want to go.

Here are some questions you can answer to get yourself unstuck and to nudge yourself on:

EXERCISE
What would I like to change in my life now?

_____
_____
_____
_____

How would I like to spend my time?

_____
_____
_____
_____

Whom would I prefer to have around me?

_____
_____
_____
_____

What activities would bring me joy?

_____
_____
_____
_____

What simple things can I do now to make a positive difference?

_____
_____
_____
_____

Pamper Yourself

You deserve to give yourself some TLC–Tender Loving Care! Take a hot bath with fragrances and candles. Have a soothing massage, manicure, pedicure, or treat yourself to a new hair-style. Eat well, exercise, and drink plenty of water. Avoid mood-altering substances. Get enough rest and relaxation. You will feel lighter and less encumbered. Your body will respond by saying "Thank you!" and you're less likely to suffer from physical aches and pains, sleeplessness, and other problems.

Create a Support Network

When we are hurting, we often seclude ourselves from others. Such behavior is counter-productive. Don't suffer in silence. You need to create a network of support comprised of trusted friends, relatives, or persons who are willing to listen. They may not understand what you are going through but they will be there for you. You may just need a physical hug or a gentle squeeze of your hand. Tell them where you want to get and how you want to feel, so they can chart your course with you.

Is there someone who has been an inspiration to you at some time? An author, speaker, person in the community? Can you find someone who might give you an objective view of the situation and help you to understand what has happened? You may know someone who has overcome obstacles, one who would hold your hand, or allow you to climb onto her shoulders during the rougher parts of your journey. She will not take the pain away but she can show you ways to minimize the hurt.

There may be support groups within your community where you can be around persons who understand your pain. There are also wonderful support groups online, but a word of caution here. Be guided by personal referrals. The internet is replete with persons who wish to prey on the insecurities and vulnerability of others.

Seek Professional Help

If it becomes necessary, seek professional help, especially in the areas in which you need greater support. Don't be ashamed or embarrassed. Seeking help is not a sign of weakness but an act of empowerment! You may also want to include in your support network an attorney, a medical practitioner, a counselor or therapist, a minister, rabbi, or another spiritual counselor. If you are not comfortable contacting them, your friends can assist you. There is power in teamwork!

EXERCISE
The list of persons on my support team would be:

_____

_____

_____

_____

_____

Get a Life!

Go out with your friends and have fun. Find things to laugh about. Getting involved in a sport or physical exercise is not only a form of distraction, but a way to use up energy as well. Some people take up a new hobby. Some walk, do yoga, or meditate. Whatever you choose, do so in moderation. Oversleeping, overeating, or excessive drinking are a cause for concern. Monitor your thoughts, moods, and behaviors and take steps to get help or feel better.

Take up a Hobby

Disappointment often causes us to unleash our creativity. Many persons channel that creativity into music, dancing, painting, drawing, or writing poetry. One woman recognized she possessed a talent in painting when her husband died. By the time she was fifty, she had become a renowned artist.

Clean Out the Clutter

Cleaning out clutter is both an act of self-care and the clearing of space for new beginnings. We have already dealt with clearing the negative thoughts that clutter your mind. Now we deal with clearing your physical space of material clutter; for example, your desk, cupboard, room, garage, or home. A good place to start is your clothes closet, where you have been saving those items that you know you will never wear. Then there are those trinkets that have been dust collectors and the memorabilia from times past that you would prefer not to remember. There are several organizations or persons who would welcome them. This is a good opportunity to assist someone in need and that, too, can aid the healing process.

Make a start to free up your living space for happiness, peace, tranquility, and the free flow of life, and help others at the same time!

Create an Action Plan

Finally, have a vision of your destination on your journey to wholeness and design a plan of action. Then commit yourself to work your plan. There may be days when you encounter setbacks but keep at it. Either in your journal, a separate book or on note cards, write down the small steps that you plan to take daily. For example: "Today, I shall (not "hope to") make the appointment to _____(volunteer to read to the blind/clean out my drawer/write a letter to)_____ " Review your progress and make the necessary adjustments.

Sister, as I leave you, don't forget to have big dreams for yourself. Eleanor Roosevelt once said, "The future belongs to those who believe in the beauty of their dreams." If you can find the words for the song "I Have a Dream" by ABBA, they may give you courage to cross your many streams. May you have a future full of hope and may all your dreams bring happiness.

ABOUT THE AUTHOR

HAZEL BLAKE PARKER

Hazel Blake Parker is Chief Executive Officer of The Parker Institute for Excellence, LLP and Director of Staff Development and Training for the South Carolina Department of Social Services (DSS). She has gained extensive knowledge and experience in management, training and family life issues through these positions. She has developed, coordinated, facilitated and evaluated training sessions for groups that have included all levels of staff from administrative assistants to executive staff.

Ms. Parker established The Parker Institute for Excellence, LLP in 2001 to provide personal and professional development training seminars to all types of organizations. Topics include Conflict, Time and Stress Management, Parenting, Effective Supervision, Leadership, Enhancing Family Strengths, and Self-Esteem. She also conducts grant-writing workshops, writes and reviews proposals for nonprofit organizations, and assists organizations in obtaining nonprofit status. She has been a Certified Grant Writer since 1998.

As Training Director, Ms. Parker develops and monitors over $9 million in training contracts and manages over 20 staff responsible for training about 4,000 DSS employees statewide. Ms. Parker has worked for the agency for over 17 years in various capacities, from frontline caseworker to manager. She is also involved in many organizations and a member of the International Board of Advisors for the Professional Woman Network. She resides in Orangeburg, South Carolina with her husband, Terry and son, Taurean.

Hazel Blake Parker is a co-author of *Becoming the Professional Woman* in the PWN library.

Contact:
The Parker Institute for Excellence, LLP
P.O. Box 2438
Orangeburg, SC 29116
(803) 347-5627
parkerinstitute@oburg,net
www.parkerinstitute.com
www.protrain.net

FOURTEEN

SHOULD I? HANDLING PEER PRESSURE

By Hazel Blake Parker

Black, white, rich, or poor—no teen is exempt from peer pressure. What should you do? Many of you have asked yourself this question numerous times. Peer pressure is simply a fact of life for teenagers. Whether or not you fall prey to it depends upon several factors. Your personality, personal values, and decision-making skills are very important as you try to take a positive path through your teenage years. This chapter will discuss how these important factors can help you resist peer pressure. It also includes areas of self-reflection, so that you can determine where you stand with regard to handling peer pressure. The chapter closes with a look at your personal goals.

What exactly is peer pressure? It's when others in your age group attempt to influence how you think and/or act. It's especially important to be aware of peer pressure during your teen years because you're at a critical point in life when important decisions are being made that will affect your future. You're also becoming more independent and taking on more responsibilities. Many of you may have drivers' licenses or a part-time job. If peer pressure is not handled appropriately, it can cause you to make decisions that have negative consequences.

EXERCISE

Before we begin discussing peer pressure in detail, think of a situation when your friends tried to talk you into doing something that you didn't want to do and briefly describe it below.

_____

_____

_____

_____

Answer the following questions about the situation.

1. Was the situation negative or positive?

_____

2. What were your personal feelings about the situation?

_____

_____

_____

3. What were the potential consequences of the action?

_____

_____

_____

4. What did you do (went along, didn't participate, etc.)?

_____

_____

_____

5. How did you reach your decision?

_____

_____

_____

_____

There are several things you need to know to effectively handle peer pressure:

- **Personal values.** Values are principles or standards you set for yourself that guide the way you live your life. They are things that are important to you.

- **Self-esteem.** This is how you feel about yourself. You need to accept and respect yourself just as you are and have confidence in your abilities. High self-esteem will help you to make your own decisions.

- **Decision-making skills.** This involves how you solve problems and make choices. Developing good decision-making skills will help you achieve your goals.

Let's take a closer look at each of these and how they impact the way you handle peer pressure. Personal values are things that you deem important. They often reflect your character traits and how you would like to be viewed by others. Values are important in helping you deal with peer pressure in that they help guide your thoughts and decision-making processes. The following chart lists some common values.

VALUES	
Being honest	Being popular
Respecting others	Being healthy
Doing your best	Helping others
Having a sense of humor	Following your religious beliefs
Being with family	Developing your talents

EXERCISE

Think about your own values for a moment. Then list your five most important values, with the most important being number one:

1._____
2._____
3._____
4._____
5._____

When faced with tough decisions, keep these values at the forefront of your mind, as they will guide you in all that you do. Paying attention to your values will give you the confidence you need to walk away from peer pressure.

Next, let's examine the role of your self-esteem in handling peer pressure. Remember, self-esteem is how you view yourself. People who have positive views of themselves are generally more confident about their looks, style, and abilities. They accept themselves for who they are, without trying to be perfect or like someone else. Those with low self-esteem are less accepting of themselves, less confident, and more likely to give in to peer pressure to feel liked and accepted by others, which in turn gives them a temporary boost in their self-esteem. This boost, however, is usually false and short-lived, as the low self-esteem returns when their "friends" are no longer around. Like values, high self-esteem helps you to make better decisions because you aren't dependent upon others to validate yourself.

EXERCISE
How does your self-esteem rate? Check "Agree" or "Disagree" for each statement below.

STATEMENT	AGREE	DISAGREE
1. I accept the way I look.		
2. I feel good about myself most of the time.		
3. I set goals for myself and believe I can reach them.		
4. I'm not overly discouraged if I'm not successful at a task.		
5. I am true to myself and my values.		
6. I can be alone without feeling lonely.		
7. I feel that I have control of my destiny.		
8. I take responsibility for my actions.		
9. I'm able to say 'no' to others without feeling guilty.		
10. I'm proud of my accomplishments.		
TOTALS		

If you checked "Agree" for six or more of the statements, your self-esteem is good. If you checked fewer than six, look for ways you can improve your self-image. Talk to a parent, teacher, counselor, or other trusted adult about your feelings. No matter what your score, always work on self-improvement. We can all improve ourselves in some manner. The following list provides ways you can enhance your self-esteem:

• Know your values and be true to them.

• Find friends who have similar interests.

• Set personal goals and work towards them.

• Take care of yourself—physically and emotionally.

• Engage in activities you like and are good at.

• Stay away from people who treat you badly.

• Reward yourself when you're successful.

• Make choices that are best for you.

• Do things that make you feel good.

• Focus on positive things about yourself—your skills, talents, accomplishments, etc.

• Have a support system to help you when you have problems.

• Don't blame yourself for mistakes. Learn from them.

EXERCISE

Before we leave the topic of self-esteem, take a few minutes to list five things you like about yourself.

1._____

2._____

3._____

4._____

5._____

Another important factor in how you handle peer pressure is your decision-making skills. Making choices is an important part of life, especially during your teenage years. As mentioned earlier, the values you embody play a critical role in the decisions you make. Decisions may be as easy as deciding what to order at your favorite fast-food restaurant or as difficult as deciding whether or not to cut school or smoke with your friends. You won't always make the right choices, but improving your decision-making skills will help you make more informed choices. Making decisions that are in your best interest can help you resist pressure to engage in activities that make you uncomfortable, such as smoking, drinking, having sex, or using drugs.

EXERCISE
Let's talk about some decisions that you've made. List ten decisions you have made in the last three to six months:
1._____
2._____
3._____
4._____
5._____
6._____
7._____
8._____
9._____
10._____

Which three would you consider the most important?
1._____
2._____
3._____

Write a brief explanation of how you reached one of these three decisions.
_____
_____
_____
_____
_____

If you felt that you could have handled this situation better, don't feel bad. Just make a better decision next time.

When faced with difficult or important decisions, there are steps you can take to help you make a better decision. Keep the following steps in mind the next time you're faced with making a choice:

1. What is the situation? What exactly is involved? Find out what you're dealing with, what you'll be doing, where it will take place, etc.

2. Find out the details. Who will be involved? What will happen if you participate? What are the consequences? Are there risks involved? Talk to someone you trust or research the topic, if possible, before making your decision.

3. What are your options? Determine what solutions are available.

4. What are the pros and cons? Weigh the advantages and disadvantages of each of the available options. Be sure you consider any safety issues that may come into play.

5. Make an informed decision. Choose the option that has the most positive outcome for you. The option should be a good fit for your values and personality, and have consequences you can accept.

6. Take necessary action. Once you've decided, stick to your decision, even if it means going against your friends. When your decision is contrary to the group, they may try to persuade you to change your mind. This is where high self-esteem and values can help you stand your ground.

While this may seem like a lot of things to consider, all these steps are necessary in making good decisions. Remember, some decisions will not require much thought before acting. Once you've made your decision, take responsibility for the outcome. At times, the result may be different than you expected, but think it through, learn from the misjudgment, and try to make a better choice next time.

EXERCISE

Name a decision you made recently that didn't turn out the way you expected:

_____
_____
_____

What did you do to resolve the situation?

_____
_____
_____

If faced with the same situation again, what will you do differently?

_____
_____
_____

Although we hear a lot about the negative impact of peer pressure, it isn't all bad. Peers can also encourage you to do things that have positive outcomes, such as getting good grades, taking part in sports or other positive extracurricular activities, and staying away from troublemakers, drugs, and alcohol. When peer pressure is positive, everybody in the group is a winner. The friendly competition to achieve helps all to try harder to reach their goals. You're more likely to stay out of trouble and avoid risky behaviors when involved with positive activities.

EXERCISE

Think about some of the peer pressure to which you've been subjected. Name three positive peer pressure situations in which you were involved:

1._____
2._____
3._____

Was it difficult to think of three positive situations? _____ If so, why?

If you had a difficult time thinking of any positive situations, you may need to take some time to reflect upon your values, friends and goals. You may need to make some changes in your life to avoid trouble.

Before we end, let's discuss goals and their importance in dealing with peer pressure. Goals are things you'd like to do or achieve. When faced with peer pressure, your goals can help guide your decision-making. Any activities that don't help you move forward toward attaining your goals should be examined carefully to determine if they are worth your time.

Goals may be short-term or long-term. Short-term goals are things you'd like to do in the next year and should help you reach your long-term goals. Long-term goals span up to ten years. You may even set intermediate goals for two to three years from the present to help you meet your long-term goals. When setting your goals, make sure that they are far-reaching, yet realistic. If you set your goals too high, you may become frustrated by constant failures. If they're too easy, you won't be challenged to improve yourself.

EXERCISE
List five of your short-term goals below. Short-term goals may involve improving your average in science this year, making the baseball team, or getting a summer job.

1._____
2._____
3._____
4._____
5._____

Now, list five long-term goals. These may include going to college or choosing a career.

1._____

2._____

3._____

4._____

5._____

Think about what you need to do to reach these goals. Do you need to make some lifestyle changes? If so, the time is now. Don't let peer pressure keep you from having the kind of future you desire and deserve.

Finally, remember the old saying "If it is to be, then it's up to me." Prepare yourself for the battles you'll face as a teen. Hold fast to your values, believe in yourself, keep your goals in mind, and think before you act. Know that you won't always make the right choice, but take responsibility and learn from your mistakes. Be willing to seek advice and assistance when necessary. Don't be unduly influenced by others. For when it's all said and done, the only person who can make up your mind is YOU!

Recommended Reading

The Complete Idiot's Guide to Surviving Peer Pressure for Teens by Hilary Cherniss.

How to Say No and Keep Your Friends: Peer Pressure Reversal for Teens and Preteens by Sharon Scott.

The 7 Habits of Highly Effective Teens by Sean Covey.

Notes:

_____

_____

_____

_____

_____

_____

_____

_____

_____

_____

_____

_____

_____

_____

_____

_____

_____

_____

_____

_____

_____

_____

ABOUT THE AUTHOR

DR. KAREN B. WASSERMAN

Dr. Karen B. Wasserman is a licensed Clinical Psychologist (Indiana and Ohio), a Registered Nurse (Missouri and Ohio), an experienced consultant, and Life Success Coach. Whether working with special populations such as adults abused as children, people with bariatric concerns or individuals with chronic illnesses, Dr. Wasserman's focus has been on teaching others to find personal empowerment, to feel good about themselves, and most importantly, how to maintain positive self-esteem! Her goal throughout her career has been to help others to be about the business of enjoying life and finding the joy around them.

Born and raised in the Midwest, Dr. Wasserman received her Doctor of Psychology (Psy.D.) degree from Wright State University, School of Professional Psychology in Dayton, Ohio. As an Air Force spouse, she has lived in Texas, Germany, and along the Gulf of Mexico. She is a founder, and co-owner for nine years, of Fairhaven Clinic, Inc., (Private Mental Health) in Biloxi, Mississippi. She and her spouse also owned and operated a small book and gift shop nearby. Besides enjoying visiting her two children and collecting antiques (especially McCoy Pottery), she is an avid gardener. With her husband and a very small cat, she now makes her home in Olde Worthington, a suburb of Columbus, Ohio. This is house number fifteen!

Contact:
Dr. Karen Wasserman
696 Oxford St
Columbus, OH 43085
(614) 296-3522
drKarenB@columbus.rr.com
www.protrain.net

FIFTEEN

DIVORCE, DEATH, AND GRIEF

By Dr. Karen B. Wasserman

I measure every grief I meet
With narrow probing eyes.
I wonder if it weighs like mine
Or has an easier size.
– Emily Dickinson, 1862

"Bummer!" "Downer!" "Catch you later!" might be some common responses we have to the topic of losses and our feelings about loss. This may be the first chapter you read, or the last chapter you want to read. Yet we all recognize that we have had various losses in our lives. When a pet died, your best friend moved away, your sister or brother got married, or when a grandparent died–these are all losses we may have experienced. Another frequent loss is that of divorce. No matter what age you are when you hear the news, it will likely be a shock. Even if your parents did not "get along well," you were recognizable as a family. If Mom or Dad goes out the door, we feel heartbroken. "Why couldn't they just work things out? After all, they are adults. Why does it have to be so hard?"

Losses are not just about the present, but also about the future. When parents divorce, you are losing ideals and dreams, plans and hopes. No other person can describe this experience for you; your experience is your own and must be lived and lived through in order to be understood by you. Onlookers may make inappropriate comments about the events: "You must be brave now, for your brother and sisters." "This will make you stronger." "I know just how you feel." These statements are non-supportive of our feelings, unhelpful and often hurtful.

Differences in the experience of loss can create tension in a family or a friendship, depending upon what age we are at the time, the nature of our relationship with the person (close and loving, abusive, or conflicted, ambivalent, or detached) and the social support systems available to us. To know that one may feel sad after a loss, while another feels a sense of relief, or that some people just feel numb, and all of these are "normal feelings," does not really help us handle them!

We may eat, sleep, go about the business at hand, but we may be experiencing a type of psychic shock, as we are still trying to absorb the impact of our loss and accommodate our changed life experience. You may have a feeling of being on auto-pilot, just feeling empty, or perhaps feeling mechanical. You can only process so much emotional information at a time. "What do you mean Dad or Mom moved out?" or "I'm getting married in three weeks!"

Change is rarely easy and always risky, as we trade the known for the unknown (no matter what you have heard about multi-tasking). We have developed certain expectations over time. When a relationship ends, we do not know what to say; what to do now; how to respond. Sensitive to changes in our environment, we may, as Dr. Shari Butler noted in *Becoming Myself*, "come to view some stages of life as being more about one [gain/loss] than the other." Often we find we are holding on to certain things as we are letting go of others. We release high school, the friends, the setting, and the activities, as we embrace college or employment. We release being primarily a daughter as we also become a wife. Indeed, some items need to be released in order to make room for new experiences and different meaningful events. Even though we are making good and necessary changes, growing and developing into who we are meant to be, there are emotional growing pains to be felt! No one else can go through these emotional ups and downs for another—these are our solos.

With a significant loss, you may first feel very vulnerable and maybe afraid.

You may also feel:

Irritable	Impatient	Tearful
Over-reacting	Under-reacting	Totally exhausted
"Hyped-up"	Wanting to talk	Wanting to be alone
So very hungry	Not hungry at all	Dumbfounded
Absolutely sure of what comes next	Absolutely lost	

As we encounter life transitions, we can find that our emotions intrude when we least expect. We cry for no apparent reason. We are angry, with or without a focus. We are so upset we are shaking or suddenly feeling at fault and do not know why. We may think we have been processing our feelings fairly well and suddenly we are caught off guard with longing, sadness, yearning, or dread. Just because an event may have occurred in our past, does not mean we have forgotten it. That memory can be triggered again. It is now an experience that is part of who we are, how we endured it and where we are now. Expecting oneself not to be reminded of a life-changing event is implausible and unrealistic.

We, then, just do not want to deal with grief, in any shape or form. In particular, as a culture, we do not want to deal with death. We have become a death-phobic society and see ourselves distanced from life's losses, even as the news' reports that soldiers are killed in a distant land or gang members are gunned down–somebody's son or daughter, mother or father, sister or brother.

So what to we do if a loved one dies? What if your grandparent has died or the mother of your best friend or one of your own parent(s)? In Victorian times and the early 1900s, mourning or grieving was an integral part of one's daily life experience. People died at home and the body remained there until burial. Children saw the dead, and parents frequently expected to outlive their children. *Harper's Bazaar*, in 1876, specified eighteen months of mourning for a spouse; a year for a parent; twelve months for a brother or sister, and only nine months for a child. There was an expectation that the bereaved would wear clothing of "dull black crape"[sic]; even a floor-length veil of this material for women! These were signs to alert the world that those involved were "showing respect for the memory of the dead." People were further advised to wear mourning for the relatives of one's spouse, and even the composition and type of jewelry was specified as to what was proper.

At least in these earlier times, the symbols and rituals were public signals for "Do Not Intrude—Grief in Process." Unreasonable social demands for participation at events were to be avoided and individuals' feelings were not to be intruded upon. Sympathy cards were not even to be responded to until the mourner felt ready to return to the world. While these customs may seem far from our societal patterns, they provided signals to others and bereaved alike of what was acceptable and expected. There was a sense of balance and symmetry. There was then permission to grieve. Grieving was essentially a "normal" process, rather than a negative or unusual undertaking.

Today, we hear people saying, "Aren't you over that yet? It's been six weeks, for goodness sake!" "You just need to get out; get on with it." "What do you mean you are not going to be in the wedding now?" All this, while you may be having the feeling of time being markedly slowed down, moving by at a snail's pace. In this slowed stream, you may be in such intense pain that it feels as though it will never lessen, never resolve. What can you do about this twisting of the insides, of feeling turned upside down and dangling? You may have a sense of double-consciousness, "It was just two weeks ago I talked to him at the house and now he is gone."

No, we most earnestly do not want to deal with grief! We do not want to feel this way and besides, it is messy with all the crying. Common feelings can be:

Anger	Sadness	Fear	Overwhelmed	Anxious
Rootless	Insecure	Restless	Relieved	Preoccupied
Disorganized	Aggressive	Orphaned	Exhausted	

Current findings indicate that normal grieving over a loved one can last three to five years. No, we are not talking about crying every day for five years, but rather we are speaking of a process that concerns a major event in our lives.

Be assured that no matter whether we are young or old, we will still have questions about death, questions about losses, and questions about changes in our lives. The flow of life is ever onward, but you can only absorb and deal with feelings at your own rate. There is no way to speed up this experience of adjustment. Some of us, in fact, are slower than others to reconcile our feelings.

So, what about you? What questions about this transition do you have? Perhaps these might reflect your pondering:

• Where do I belong now?
• Am I somehow responsible for what happened?
• If I had the power to change one thing, what would that be?
• How will I get my needs met now that 'X' is gone?
• Who can I talk to and just be myself?
• What are we going to do about the holidays?
• How AM I supposed to feel?

When we contemplate losses—of the intact family, of a special relationship, a beloved pet, of a place, our health (or someone else's) or loved one--we are in the experience of mourning and grieving. We can expect certain events, anniversaries, music, scents, or special foods and locations to trigger memories and feelings. Yes, there are various stages of grief as the pioneering work of Dr. Elizabeth Kubler-Ross has demonstrated. For instance, initially you might be angry. "How could Gramps leave this way? or "Mommy didn't even say goodbye." While it may not seem logical to be angry with the person who died, nevertheless, there the feeling might be.

Depressed? Yes, you may feel quite depressed for some period of time. You might even try to bargain your way out of the pain and anguish: "God, if you just bring Mom and Dad together again, I'll always do my chores on time" or "If I just act as if everything is all right, I can have calmer feelings." You can deny the event is real or try to minimize its importance in your life. "Well, she was old and she is bound to be better off now." You might even be aiming for early acceptance and thereby hoping to ensure, somehow, smooth sailing in the course of this particular journey.

In reality, our level of acceptance, denial, or anger will vary from day to day or maybe even from hour to hour. Remember, that is why they call it "grief work." So what if you are not feeling better "yet"?

Do a reality check! How long has it been since the death or divorce? Now do a second-stage reality check: What expectations have you focused on and how critical are these expectations to your well-being?

But wait, what about the sudden crying jags, or nightmares, or finding yourself wanting to scream at strangers and/or those closest to you? What about that urge to run and run and just keep on going? What about that? What about wanting to smoke or drink or eat or "use" to just not feel the pain anymore?

We would acknowledge that using drugs, gambling to excess, shopping our way into debt, sleeping all day every day, or eating until we are in a stupor are not particularly effective ways to cope with our pain and grief. Yes, denial has surfaced. Yes, we may yearn for an escape, however brief. It may even be tempting to convince ourselves that we are really doing the "right thing" by "getting on with our lives." But what does this self-injury or self-punishment accomplish? These are not only physically harmful activities, but emotionally destructive ones as well. What will your lessened self-esteem change about an event that has already occurred? Putting yourself down for having conflicting emotions is nonsensical. The good news is that as a human being, you can have two precisely opposite feelings at one and the same time. Yes, indeed, this is also the "bad news"!

How, then, do we handle these intrusive memories and feelings? Primarily be aware you are not grieving to impress anyone. Just because someone else affects a "tough" stance or acts "all stony-faced" does not mean he or she knows how to grieve any better than you. It also does not mean that those are the only right feelings to have! It is honorable and honest to remember what happened, what was done, or what could not be done. Authentically, these recollections and experiences, as well as your feelings about them, belong only to you.

Set yourself up for success by anticipating that there will be significant "triggers" for your emotions and that your feelings may be quite acute for some time. Have a plan for the "Toughest Times."

EXERCISE
For instance, ask yourself:
a) The hardest thing about spending Christmas (any holiday here) without Dad is_____.
b) The toughest part of cooking for the family now will be _____.
c) When I go to a bookstore, how wrenching will it be to pass the children's books?
d) How am I going to be able to go to the park without "X"?

You need not expect yourself to react as you always have. Every day, you create yourself anew. Allow for the unexpected, or better yet, plan for it. Be experimental and brave, even, in creating new ways to celebrate significant life events. You can weave new patterns with differing symbols and develop rituals that reflect what is meaningful for you. For instance, you might like to consider the examples in the movie or book *The Divine Secrets of the Ya-Ya Sisterhood.*

"Take the best and leave the rest," as they say in Twelve-Step Meetings, such as Al-Anon. Others may advise, can offer suggestions and alternatives, but remember to check-in with your own authentic internal monitor. If the statements resonate with you and "feel right," you will be aware of this. If what is shared or said to you does not fit for you, you do not have to make it fit!

Do go on swimming in your own life stream and accept your joy. Laugh, shout, be happy in your moments of excitement and wonder. Speak readily of the person or relationship that has passed. Honor what has happened and what is yet about to occur. Dream your dreams and speak them aloud if you wish. To think your own thoughts and feel your feelings, is, after all, about being a "real" person.

At these times of changes in your life, you may also wish to create a "God Box" or perhaps call it by another name, a "Give-Over" Box; "Ruler-of-the-Universe" Box, or "Letting-Go" Box. This is to be a most beautiful and worthy container, so choose your vessel (which, of course, might not be a box at all) carefully, or create one!

Now, on small pieces of paper (think fortune-cookie-sized slip), write down those things that you, as a human being, are powerless to change. These can include, but are not limited to, events that have already occurred, the actions of other people, future events and outcomes, other's feelings towards you, etc. These slips are then put into your special box/container. You are letting go of these things as being beyond the power of mere mortals. If you decide to worry or trouble yourself about these items, you must now go and remove the slip(s) from the box, because you are taking back that care or concern. You might find that in taking the concern back, you have begun anew to try to achieve the impossible–to affect that which only our Creator could accomplish!

If, after several struggles, you simply cannot leave the concern alone, write the concern on a (helium) balloon and let it go, or write the concern down one hundred times, then burn the paper and let the smoke carry the idea away from you. If you must, do this more than once; do it as often as you need to! This process is, above all, for you. No one else needs to know or be involved, unless you choose it to be so. The ashes generated can be scattered, buried in an appropriate spot, or used to mark symbols in ways that are helpful to your process.

Grieving, holding on, letting go, and moving on are all part of life, yours included. Be not afraid to honor yourself and honor your process. This is an important part of life and our growth as human beings. Be sad, but accept gladness when it comes. Being glad in the now does not mean you have forgotten the loved one or the loss–it does mean you are honoring your life as well.

Recommended Reading

A Time to Grieve by Carol Standacher.

Becoming Myself: Living Life to the Fullest After the Loss of Your Parents by Shari Butler.

Courage to be a Single Mother by Sheila Ellison.

Grieving a Suicide by Albert Hsu.

Healing Your Grieving Heart by Alan D. Wolfelt, Ph.D.

I Wasn't Ready to Say Goodbye by Brook Noel and Pamela D. Blair.

Living When a Loved One Has Died by Earl Grollman.

Losing Your Parents, Finding Yourself by Victoria Secunda.

Mom's House, Dad's House by Isolina Ricci.

Moving, and Other Losses by Russell Friedman.

Nobody's Child Anymore by Barbara Bartocci.

Talking to Your Children about Separation and Divorce by Risa Garon.

"The Club No One Wants to Join," by Donna Schuurman, National Director of the Doughy Center, in Grief Matters.

The Grief Recovery Handbook on Grief and Grieving by Elisabeth Kubler-Ross.

What about the Kids? by Judith Wallerstein and Sandra Blakeslee.

When Children Grieve by John W. James and Russell Friedman.

When Children Grieve: For Adults to Help Children Deal with Death, Divorce, Pet Loss, When Bad Things Happen to Good People by Harold Kushner.

Notes:

ABOUT THE AUTHOR

DR. MAMIE SHIELDS NORMAN

Dr. Mamie Shields Norman is the library media specialist and technology coordinator at Thomas Johnson Middle School in Lanham, Maryland, Prince George's County Public Schools. She serves as adjunct faculty at Sojourner-Douglass College in Annapolis, Maryland, and is the owner/CEO of The Shields Group, LLC, an educational and personal development consulting firm.

Dr. Shields Norman owns and operates a pre-K Montessori weekend school. She has presented various workshops on early childhood and independence in the very young child. During 2004 Dr. Norman was a presenter at the Professional Woman Network International Conference in Louisville, Kentucky, and served on the 2005 Woman Network International Advisory Board.

Before returning to the library profession, Dr. Shields Norman taught pre-K Montessori for eight years. She has been an educator for 38 years and is committed to the education of children, youth and adults, encouraging them to reach their highest potential and become all they can be.

Certification in the following areas qualifies Dr. Shields Norman to be of great service to many: Leadership Skills for Women, Becoming the Assertive Woman, Self-esteem and Self-empowerment, pre-K Montessori, and Anger Management for Young People.

Dr. Shields Norman is a native of Memphis, Tennessee and the sixth child of seven. She currently resides in Bowie, Maryland with her two sons, Yohance and Zikomo. Dr. Shields Norman holds a Bachelor's degree in Sociology from Tuskegee University, a Master's in Library Science from Atlanta University, a Master's in Elementary Education from American International College, a Master's in Guidance and Psychological Services from Springfield College, and is AMI-certified as pre-K Montessori. She is currently awaiting the conferment of her Doctorate of Education from NOVA Southeastern University.

Contact:
The Shields Group, LLC
3540 Crain Hwy.
Bowie, MD 20716
msnorman4@earthlink.net
www.protrain.net

SIXTEEN

BOUNDARIES: WHAT YOU WILL AND WON'T ACCEPT INTO YOUR LIFE

By Dr. Mamie Shields Norman

We were all created by God to be free and not to be controlled and manipulated by others! We were born to be free to love, and to be loved, free to become closer to God and to others, and to enjoy life with fulfillment. So why do we have to set boundaries if we are created by God to be free?

Why are Boundaries Necessary?
Boundaries are necessary because they help with your personal growth, settle differences, and increase caring in personal relationships. They are necessary to help bring about change in your life. It is very important to have boundaries in your relationships with others because boundaries will protect you from potential negative put-downs. Boundaries are

necessary to help you to get what you are looking for and get what you want. Boundaries also help you to take care of yourself and take ownership for what happens to you, to love yourself, and to respect yourself.

Boundaries are necessary because they will prevent the development of poor relationships in home, school, church, and social life. Without knowing how to set boundaries or why you need boundaries, you may be easily led by your peers or possibly blame others for your actions and mistakes or shortcomings. Setting boundaries is an essential part of learning how to take care of yourself!

What is a Boundary?
Whether you realize it or not, each of us has boundaries that are intangible and with us all of the time. Boundaries are both spoken and unspoken. Have you ever been on a crowded bus or subway train and a total stranger gets too close to you, but the person is not aware of how close he/she is to your physical presence? You immediately back away or say to the person, "You are in my space," "Please back up," or some other indicator to let the person know that your boundaries have been overstepped. If you can't move away in the crowded situation, you feel very uneasy or have strange feelings inside. Such a situation would be considered an intrusion on your physical boundary.

Boundaries are lines of division concerning what others can and cannot do to you or what others can or cannot say to you. Boundaries clearly point out what is acceptable or unacceptable behavior towards you. Boundaries also determine how you are treated by other people or what they say to you. Did you know that boundaries are already established? Well, yes they are! You can tell by the uncomfortable feeling you get when someone is too close or speaks to you in an unappreciative fashion. Your spirit or soul feels wounded. There is a strange sensation that settles in your stomach and your feelings are hurt. The unspoken boundaries must be communicated.

When someone crosses the line and you become upset or angry, this indicates that you have unspoken boundaries, which possibly have not been made known to those around you. Your personal boundaries are subjective; they are not seen. The mores and values of our society have set up expectations that basically determine personal boundaries. It is not nice to be rude to others, but when it happens, the person insulted becomes angry. If this happens to you, it is essential that you learn to identify your own boundaries and express them to others. If this is not done, they you set yourself up for hurt, pain, disappointment, and unhealthy relationships.

The following descriptive statements outline what a boundary is, according to Constance and James Messina, from their book, *Building Healthy Boundaries.* The information below was retrieved from their website at http://www.coping.org/innerhealing/boundary.htm.

- A boundary is a space between you and someone else. It is both physical and emotional.

- A boundary is a limit or how far you allow someone to go because of the negative impact on your life.

- A boundary is the point where you stop and the other person begins and where you begin and the other person ends.

- A boundary is a line of demarcation where you have established a line that others can not cross over and violate and/or invalidate you and your rights.

- A boundary is an established set of limits over your physical and emotional well-being, which you expect others to respect in their relationship with you.

- A boundary is emotional and physical space you need in order to be the real you without the pressure from others to be something that you are not.

- A boundary is an appropriate amount of emotional and physical closeness you need to maintain so that you and another do not become too detached and/or overly independent.

- A boundary is balanced emotional and physical limits set on interacting with another so that you can achieve an interdependent relationship of independent beings who do not lose their personal identity, uniqueness, and autonomy in the process.

- A boundary clearly defines limits within which you are free to be yourself with no restrictions placed on you by others as to how to think, feel, or act.

- A boundary is a set of parameters that make you a unique, autonomous, and free individual who has the freedom to be a creative, original, idiosyncratic problem solver.

EXERCISE

When you were a young child, your parents set boundaries for your protection and for discipline. Can you recall and list some of those boundaries? Example: "Don't touch the hot stove; you'll get burned." This was a boundary established for your protection and benefit.

Boundaries in my life as a young child:
1._____
2._____
3._____

As you become older, it's important to learn how to set and maintain healthy boundaries. Here are some ways to do this:

- Do a self-assessment. What hurts your feelings? When do you feel your space has been invaded?

- Keep a daily journal of healthy and unhealthy thoughts.

- Write positive affirmations.

EXERCISE
Ensure your healthy boundaries by clarifying the connection between what you feel and what you think.

My Feelings	My Thoughts
1. Do I feel unhappy or sad a great deal of the time?	1. Do I think life is awful and no one spends time with me?
2. Do I feel that there is no hope for my situation?	2. Do I ever think there is no way out of my situation?
3. Do I feel confused and unsure of how I should behave when someone is upset with me?	3. Do I think that what I did wrong might upset someone I'm close to?
4. Do I ever feel self-hatred?	4. Do I think that I am weak or selfish?
5. Do I feel frustrated?	5. Do I think people do not listen to me or take me seriously?

Ask yourself the above questions and give honest and thoughtful answers. They will help you to understand the connectedness between your thoughts and your feelings.

Learning how to set your boundaries in a relationship helps you to learn how to be in charge of yourself, as well as how to respect and love yourself. If you do not respect yourself, then start expressing and becoming aware of your right to be treated with respect and dignity! Don't become comfortable developing relationships with people who will abuse you rather than developing relationships with people who will treat you lovingly and with respect. Set those boundaries! Let others know that you are worth a lot and worthy of being loved.

The Three Aspects of Setting Boundaries

1. **Defining Unacceptable Behaviors:** The first aspect of setting boundaries is laying the foundation or the behaviors you will not accept from another person. You must be very clear about these behaviors so the person(s) with whom you are communicatingb will fully understand your position.

2. **Actions You'll Take:** The second aspect of setting boundaries is deciding what action(s) you will take to protect and take care of yourself if someone oversteps the boundaries that you have communicated.

3. **Consequences:** The third aspect of setting boundaries is that without reservation, you make it clear what you will do if the violator continues to overstep your established boundaries.

When you set boundaries of what you will and won't accept, you are well on the road to becoming self-empowered! You will be in control of what happens to you in a relationship. God did not place us here on planet earth to be abused, put down, and walked upon!

Setting Clear Boundaries

1. Be very clear about the limits you set in a relationship with someone who is not respecting you.

2. Don't give long explanations. Be very brief and to the point.

3. Make friends and keep company with safe, boundary-oriented people. It is easier to set limits with people you know well and who understand the importance of setting boundaries.

4. Ask your close friends and family if you can practice setting boundaries with them.

5. Do not set boundaries to please other people.

Here are some examples of brief statements to use when setting boundaries:

• "I cannot be in your presence if you prefer not to be in conversation with me."

• "Don't put your hands on me."

• "If you expect a wholesome and positive relationship, there must be honesty, equal grounds, open communication, and respect."

• "I prefer not to be disrespected. If you can't respect me, then stay away."

• "If we are going to have a healthy relationship, I need honesty, respect and equality."

• "When we have a misunderstanding, I need to have communication."

• "Withholding is making our relationship unsatisfying for me."

• "I will not accept belittling jokes, criticism, or your condescending attitude toward me."

• "If you have to swear at me and call me names, then stay away."

Positive Affirmations for Expressing Boundaries

Here are a few affirmations that you can repeat on a regular basis to stay in touch with yourself:

• No one has the right to influence my mind, thoughts, or tell me what to think, feel, do, or say.

• I have the only rights to my own thoughts, feelings, values, and beliefs.

• If I am disrespected or abused by other people, I have the right to let them know and ask them to stop. I also have the right to avoid them.

- I love, respect, and stand up for myself.
- I have the right to be who I am and live my own life.
- I accept myself and I am true to myself.
- I am my own best friend and co-creator of my life.

Setting boundaries helps you to communicate honestly and openly with others. To have a healthy relationship with another person, one must have boundaries. When you set boundaries, you are telling the other person that you care about yourself and what happens to you and that you have intentions of taking care of yourself and protecting yourself from invalidation and abuse. Setting boundaries also lets others know that you expect only respect from them and that you have the right to say "NO" to anything that is not right for you, what you believe is right for you, and what you deserve and deserve from someone else

EXERCISE
Learning How to Set Boundaries
The following exercises can help you learn how to set boundaries in your life:

What are your morals? List five.
1._____
2._____
3._____
4._____
5._____

What are some goals for your life? List five.
1._____
2._____
3._____
4._____
5._____

What are your values? List five.

1._____

2._____

3._____

4._____

5._____

What makes you feel good? List five.

1._____

2._____

3._____

4._____

5._____

What makes you not feel good? List five.

1._____

2._____

3._____

4._____

5._____

After you have reflected upon the above questions, realize that these are YOUR feelings, thoughts, and values. You don't have to have others dictating and invading your boundaries by having you do something you don't believe in. Be true to yourself.

Setting boundaries will allow you to become mentally healthy and create a safety zone for you and the people around you. Stating of boundaries will:

1. Increase your sense of self, self-esteem, and self-worth. Why? Because you will be letting others know that you are "worth a lot," that you like yourself, and are worthy to be loved for who you are.

2. Increase positive relationships with those around you by letting them know what you will and will not tolerate or allow in your life.

3. Increase your ability to clearly speak these boundaries to everyone around you. This will make others feel comfortable and know how to relate to you. You have made it clear what they can and cannot do around you.

When you do take the steps to communicate your boundaries, be sure and speak in a neutral tone of voice. If you speak too passively, you will be ignored. If you speak too aggressively, you will offend.

An example of raising awareness about how others may be treating you would be asking: "Do you know that you are being disrespectful to me?" Speaking in this manner will likely cause the person who has been rude to you stop and think what they are saying and/or doing that you perceive as being disrespectful and not acceptable. Be firm, be clear, and do not disrespect the other person's boundaries.

In essence, setting boundaries means that you like yourself and that you are worth a lot. No one deserves to be mistreated, ignored, or abused, because God created us out of His love for us and He has no desire for any of us to be hurt or mistreated.

How to Determine if You Are Developing Boundaries

An early sign that you are developing boundaries is that you become angry, frustrated, or resentful when someone has crossed your boundaries. At first, you might not notice this, but anger or frustration are indicators that people have violated you and your boundaries. You may become very upset on the inside, which should let you know that something is very uncomfortable and needs to be addressed. This anger or frustration is an okay signal to let you know that you don't like being controlled by others.

• Making friends and keeping company with safe and boundary-oriented people.

• Asking friends if you can practice setting some limits in your relationship with them.

• You may feel guilty as you begin to set boundaries. This is a good sign because you are now beginning to develop and listen to your own values, rather than basing your life on pleasing others. As you continue to set boundaries, the guilt feelings will disappear. You will begin to function on the basis of the values of truth, love, responsibilities, patience, kindness, and all the fruit of the spirit.

As you continue to set boundaries, values like love of God, honesty, compassion, forgiveness, and faithfulness will become the driving forces in your life.

Boundaries Needed for Healthy Relationships with Others and Yourself

EXERCISE

Answer the following questions:

1. How much time do you set aside each day for the following? What are the time boundaries in your relationships?

2. Your work: _____

3. Sleep or rest: _____

4. Self-nurturing activities _____

5. Family: _____

6. Friends: _____

7. Leisure, vacation, and time alone: _____

You cannot afford to allow relationships to pull you away from the above activities, which are essential to your well-being.

How do you limit the finances spent in your relationships? What are your financial boundaries with yourself and others?

1. How much money do you spend in the relationship with your significant other?

_____

2. How would you make it clear that you will not spend your money to rescue or save your significant other from financial irresponsibility?

_____
_____
_____

3. List all the financial areas that you are or will be clear about not spending money:

_____
_____
_____
_____

4. What boundaries to you place on external resources–your family, friends, and support systems–in your relationships?

_____
_____
_____
_____

5. What boundaries do you place on your internal resources–your talents, skills, and abilities–in your relationships?

_____
_____
_____
_____

Now that we have identified the areas of boundaries needed in healthy relationships, you can begin developing and/or identifying boundaries in your life to ensure wholesome and positive relationships with others.

Boundaries are key ingredients in our lives. Without boundaries, harmony would not be possible and constant chaos would happen. There are physical and personal boundaries, spoken and unspoken boundaries. We set boundaries for our physical and emotional safety. As you continue to set boundaries throughout your life, keep in mind that setting boundaries does not mean you must live in isolation and become self-centered. It means that you know who you are, what your values are, and how valuable a person you are. Setting boundaries means that people your life are not allowed to be rude, mean, unkind, hurtful, and abusive toward you. Practice setting your own clear boundaries and accepting other people's boundaries, and you'll progress toward living a more harmonious life.

Recommended Reading

Building Healthy Boundaries by Constance and James Messina. The information in this chapter was retrieved from http://www.coping.org/innerhealing/boundary.htm.

Feeding Your Soul: A Quiet Time Handbook by Jean Fleming.

The Key to Life: Unlock Your Personal Power by Aymen Fares.

The Power of You by Rav Berg.

ABOUT THE AUTHOR

DAWN HARRIS

Ms. Harris is President and CEO of The Harris Institute for Professional Excellence. She received her MBA from Woodbury University in Burbank, California and her undergraduate degree in Biochemistry at the Cal Poly State University in San Luis Obispo, California. Ms. Harris has worked in the Medical Device industry as a Manager of Regulatory Training. Prior to this capacity, she worked in the biotechnology industry for over nine years in a variety of departments such as Quality Assurance, Manufacturing, Internal Audit, and Corporate Finance.

As a Certified Customer Service Trainer, Dawn Harris is committed to teaching individuals the importance of a professional image, positive attitude development, and business etiquette. As a Certified Diversity Trainer, she is passionate about training companies and individuals regarding the importance of exclusivity vs. inclusivity, and building teams among diverse corporate cultures.

Contact:
The Harris Institute for Professional Excellence
(443) 266-4066
dharris@theharrisinstitute.com
www.protrain.net

SEVENTEEN

A BALANCING ACT! JUGGLING HOME, SCHOOL & WORK

By Dawn Harris

I was compelled to write this chapter not because I made "all the right moves" in college, at work and at home, but because I made a lot of bad decisions and had tons of ill-thought-out plans. Despite my obstacles, I was still victorious and you will be, too! Once the balancing act has been achieved, I believe you will have learned the skills to be able to keep your life simple, low in stress, and easier to manage in the future.

If you are going through a work/home/school life as I did, without kids, no roommates (for the most part), limited access to a car, and keeping one or two jobs at a time, I am positive that at some point in time, you asked yourself some of the following questions: "What is this all for?" "Why do I have to go through this just to get an education?" "How come nothing is ever easy for me?" "Why don't my parents give me money like they said they would?" STOP!!! Do not ask yourself these questions any more. The answers to these questions will never be good enough for you to move past them!

These questions all come from Victim Thinking. We all have been "victim thinkers" at some point in our lives. Winners do not have that mentality. If you're a victim thinker, you will be waiting for someone to pay your rent, pay for school, pay for daycare, buy you a car...and the list goes on.

If you honestly want to commit to making changes in your life and get things into balance, then this chapter is for you. (However, this chapter is not for the naysayer, the negativist, or the pessimist. You will see no value in this chapter at all.) So for all of you positive, excited, encouraged women, I am ever so grateful to pass on my "pearls of wisdom" to you, with the hope that you will be able to apply some of this material to your life to keep it in balance!

Sometimes you have to get down before you can get up.
– Unknown

Home

Between the ages of eighteen and twenty, I had a lot of responsibilities at home. (Nothing overwhelming, but enough to have to budget time and energy). I was living with my mother at the time, who decided to go to Washington D.C. to take care of her father. I was in charge of the house, which was easy because all I had to do was pay the bills using my mother's money. Before my mother left, she allowed my girlfriend from high school to stay with us. We had a ball together! We went to school, cheered, and studied together. I felt like I had someone who could truly understand my home life and help me put things into perspective. Additionally, she contributed to the household financially and helped keep the house clean. I think her best-selling attributes were her organizational skills. From paper work to personal belongings, she was the epitome of organization. So, let's explore the importance of organization!

In my opinion, organization is the key to being successful. How organized are you at home? Can you easily find things? It is important to not feel overloaded at home, even though you might feel that way at work or school. Home should be a place of peace and relaxation, even if you are living with people and have a child or children. Here are some organizational tips to keeping your home life functional and in check!

The Paper Chase

Organize all of your paperwork at home. Clear out a space for you to be able to read and do some light studying. Additionally, your bills, letters, and personal mail should not be kept in the same space you study. Whether you can pay the bills or not, keep them in view. Paying your bills on time is critical to keeping a good credit rating.

Establish Good Credit and Stay out of Debt

Now there is good debt and bad debt. If you are in debt because of school, that is considered good debt. If you are in debt to a department store, that is considered bad debt. I find that most purchases are made based upon emotions or feelings we have at the time. Not to say you're not going to wear the jacket or the shoes that you bought, but be mindful of the financial decision you are making. Always weigh Needs versus Wants. Spend money like you do time: wisely!

I encourage you to establish some form of credit so cars, homes, or furniture will be available to you when you are ready to make these big purchases. An excellent credit score will set you apart from other potential job candidates (because companies can run your credit report before hiring you). It can separate you from other consumers. Remember, this is not the time to have the awesome apartment, the top-of-the-line car, or wear the top designer fashions! You have an excuse!

You are building! You're not supposed to be "there" yet. So enjoy a more simple life for now and look forward to a future when you can afford a more expensive one. You don't need to go in debt for "things." And that is just what they are, things!

Take Control of Your Environment

Whether you have three roommates, a young child, or are living with family, you have to establish "quiet time." Not a time where people are tip-toeing around the house or apartment, but an agreed-upon time where there are few visitors, no parties are being thrown, most of the phone calls are going to voicemail, and there is peace in the house. This could be when your roommates are going out of town, your child is staying with a friend or family members, and you are able to find a quiet area to conduct business, catch up on school, work, or just plain relax.

If you are living with others, communication is imperative. Find out what and when they are planning so you will know what to expect and how to plan your schedule accordingly.

Do Not Be Afraid to Downsize

If you are living with too many people or maybe your roommates have different excuses as to why they are not able to contribute fully to the upkeep of your place, you may need to downsize. If your roommates have a different type of lifestyle than the one you'd like to follow (i.e., experimenting with drugs, excessive drinking), it might be time to reconsider your living arrangements. At this point in your life, you have a choice. It is very different from growing up in this type of environment, where you were dependent upon someone else to provide for you. However, that is not the case now. You are in the driver's seat. If you cannot be recharged with positive energy in your current living space, then you may have to leave.

> *You don't stumble on success, it is planned for.*
> *It takes hard work and lots of sacrifices.*
> – Unknown

School

As you enter school or continue through your academic process, keep the big picture in mind. School is an institution to help prepare you for life. It's not just about getting a degree. It will take a lot of personal sacrifice, hard work, and dedication, but you have to remember that you can do it!

My parents always told me, "Progress is not made in a straight line." And boy, do I have the track record to prove that. I went to three junior colleges and three universities to get my undergraduate degree. I felt like I had a black cloud over my head that would constantly pour out bigger storms the harder I tried to succeed in school. In my college career, I have been dismissed, on academic probation, and was denied grants, scholarships, and loans.

I began to ask the questions that I stated at the beginning of the chapter. The ones the Victim Thinkers ask: "Why me?" "Don't my parents care about me?" "Why can't I keep a high GPA!" "Why do I have to work and go to school?"

I vividly remember the last time I called my father for money. I was a sophomore at UC-Berkeley, in need of a tutor, and other resources that I could not afford. When he said, "Honey, I just don't have it," I made up in my mind that I would never ask for money from anyone again. I could not take the rejection and I did not want to put my father through the pain of having to say that to me over and over again.

Ladies: I don't care if your fund for college was misspent by you or someone in your family or if a friend or family member promised to send you money weekly and hasn't. Understand that it is your responsibility to get yourself through school if you want a degree. It will not be easy but it can be done.

Here are a few tips to set yourself up for success while you're in school, now that your home life is on a more even keel. Consider the following for school:

Do Your Homework Before You Enroll in Class

Treat your academic life like you do your job. Find out how many different teachers are teaching the classes you need to take. Then find out about their teaching styles. Are they lenient with late work, multiple choice test-givers or are their tests mostly essay questions? Everyone is different, but you know what styles work for you. If you like multiple-choice questions on tests, then go for the instructor that tests that way. Don't spend too much time enrolling in classes that only fit your party, sleep, or work schedule without considering who the instructor is. Your success in the class is more important than the time it is being offered.

You can find out about the instructors by going to the department office and looking at the type of tests the teacher has given in the past. You can interview students or look up the professors' classroom assignments at the library. Or you can simply introduce yourself to the instructor. Don't be shy! After all, it's your money, time, and education on the line here.

Stay Organized

Once you have your school schedule finalized, share it with your boss at work. Let him or her know what you are doing behind the scenes –not for pity but to keep your manager informed. He or she could direct you to certain projects for you to lead or assist that may help you "kill two birds with one stone" because of the work involved and its school application. Keep your schedule in front of you and carry it with you as it will help you stay on track and not over-commit when you are asked to do things on or off campus. It's all fun and games until someone misses a deadline or an important event!

Keep a different folder for every class and keep all of your class work in one place. Have a Tuesday/Thursday class section and a Monday/Wednesday/Friday class section so you can find your work easily. Don't throw any paperwork away until the class is over!

Birds of a Feather Do Study Together

Studying is essential important to your success. Studying with others can increase you knowledge exponentially. However, study groups can either be a waste of time or exactly what you need to keep your academic "ball" in the air. There are a variety of ways to identify the right group for you to study with. You have to ask the right questions and be perceptive. Consider looking for students who have time and appear to have things in balance. Steer away from the individuals who have a rocky home life or are over-committed. Look for the students who come to class on time. Try finding out who is getting the best grade in class. Don't go by who is cute, nice, in the "right" fraternity, or sorority–this is business. Interview them wisely.

Raise Your Hand if You're Full!

Once you have established a study/support group, make sure you are getting what you need out of it. Act as a leader, student, and tutor. Study groups are a give and take. Make sure your group is productive and always choose neutral places to study (libraries, cafés, 24-hour restaurants). There are too many distractions when students try to study at their homes or places of business. If things are not working for you in the study group, do not be afraid to tell the group. It's not that you're blaming them or putting them down; let them know that too much time is being wasted or that you aren't learning at the same pace. Whatever the reason, you have to figure out what you have to do in order to make it work.

Decisions, Decisions…
"Hey girl! Kathy's having a party tonight. It's going to be awesome! And you know Kevin is going to be there. Are you coming?" Well, if you haven't heard that question yet, you will. It will come in different forms and be posed by different well-meaning people but it's all the same. Are you going to study or party? Or are you going to get to the real business of being in school?

Don't get me wrong, having fun is important. However, it all depends on when the party is happening. Do your best to plan for fun. I know at your age this might sound corny, but it is essential to your survival. You simply will not be able to make every party, family gathering, Sunday dinner or girl's night out! But you can plan for them. It's no different than requesting time off from work. You have to let your manager know in advance that you don't plan on being at work at a certain time on a certain day. So do have fun, but build it into your home, work (if necessary), academic, and financial schedule.

Your bachelor's degree is a ticket into the game;
it will keep you from being eliminated!
– Richard Harris

Work

Because of my experiences struggling for my undergraduate degree, I was somewhat prepared for the lifestyle of working for a living, taking care of home, and going to school. What I wasn't prepared for was being a professional. The "corporate games" blindsided me. However, through lots of coaching and mentoring, I was able to stay the course. I found supportive bosses, family members, and friends to motivate and encourage me on several levels. Asking for and being open to help are the first and most valuable lessons you must activate in order to be successful at work. The following tips will help you juggle your work life:

Just Gimme a Job, Man!

If you have or are seeking a job and not a career, then treat the job as if it is a career. The seeds you are planting at the job may turn into excellent letters of recommendation for you in the future. Your current employer might want to promote you at some point because of your track record. You never know. Also, try to work in the field you are studying. It's a lot easier to get your company to pay for your schooling (even if they don't have an official reimbursement program) if you are studying in the field that you're working in.

Look the Part

When managers are considering staff members for promotions, appearance and attitude are usually at the forefront. If you are wearing inappropriate clothing, letting everyone in the office know how you "feel," are known as a pessimist, the starving student, a "not-my-jobber," or anything other than a true professional, you will likely not be considered for the promotion. You've just stunted your income.

Regardless of whether or not you like or want the job, act like you do. Trust me, an academy award awaits you and it's all green, honey!

Get Ahead!

Getting organized and maintaining this organization at work as you have done at home and school is very important. Get ahead as much as you can with projects, reports, or presentations at work. You don't have the luxury of staying late at work every night. If you're not organized by nature and are sincerely hoping to bypass this area for reasons of your own, you are headed for failure. If you are not in management and are at a more task-related level, you must be organized to give your customers (boss, clients, colleagues) what they need as quickly as possible. You will come off like the true professional. Start slowly and take maybe an extra half hour at work to sort through emails, voicemails, and articles in your read pile.

Find a "Fan"

You'll need someone at work with whom you can talk and who is not threatened by your goals at work, someone who is at a higher level than you, someone who is willing to take time to develop you. These people are mentors and they can be very useful to you as you change jobs and move into your profession. They have contacts!

Putting It All Together

For some of you, work comes before school and home because work is funding school and home. For others, school may come first because it's the very reason why you relocated and work may be your supplemental income. On the other hand, home may come before school or work because you may have children or have full responsibility for elderly family members at home. Whatever your first priority, keep it first. The home, work, school lifestyle are full of what I consider competing priorities. They all are important to your livelihood. Therefore, it is extremely important to establish which of these competing priorities is first in your life and know when one needs more attention than the others. This is where the juggling comes in and a vicious cycle begins.

The cycle of little to no sleep, not being able to hang out with friends often, feeling guilty when you're on a date, living in a pigsty (at times), always feeling behind, living on limited amount of money, taking no breaks, when you're out of school you're at work, when you need to take a vacation you can't because you're at work, you still have school work, and there usually isn't a lot money for a good vacation! Good grief! Remember, this painful cycle is not permanent! It is filled with intermittent periods of joy, like the end of a school term for example. So get a runner's high.

A runner's high is only experienced when a runner has gone past the distance he or she has trained for. Runners must run a long way before they can experience it. Right before runners get this high, they are fighting off the cramps, feeling a burning sensation in their chest, and finding it hard to breathe. That's when the high begins. They find their cramps are going away, their chest isn't burning any more, and their breathing has stabilized. They now see themselves reaching the finish line! You can reach this level too, but guess what? Quitters never see it. They will never know what a runner's high is because they fail to finish their race. In this race of juggling priorities and staying on top of your game, remember, it's not the smart who finish, the race is won by the determined–the ones who have stayed the course.

ABOUT THE AUTHOR

SANDRA SPAULDING HUGHES

Sandra Spaulding Hughes was a member of the Wilmington, North Carolina City Council for four years. On the City Council, Ms. Hughes distinguished herself as "the people's representative." She developed a reputation for tackling tough issues and being an independent and thorough thinker.

On the City Council, Ms. Hughes served on the Council of Governments, the Film Commission, Downtown Area Revitalization Effort, and the Cape Fear Convention and Visitors Bureau. She was a trainer for the North Carolina Council of Governments, and completed the Leadership Training Institute in Washington, DC.

Ms. Hughes has received numerous awards including: Outstanding Service and Excellence Award, Robert Earl Jones Award for Excellence in Education, Educator of the Year, Governor James B. Hunt Award to Influential Women in North Carolina, Woman of the Year from Delta Sigma Theta Sorority, and Citizen of the Year from the Alpha Psi Alpha Fraternity. She is the co-founder of the Community Action Group, a citizens group that was awarded Community Organization of the Year by the Human Relations Commission.

Ms. Hughes is a graduate of North Carolina A & T State University. She did further graduate study at North Carolina State University, the University of North Carolina at Greensboro, and Webster University in South Carolina. Ms. Hughes is also a graduate of the National Dale Carnegie Course in Public Speaking and Human Relations and numerous Career Track Programs.

Before retirement, Ms. Hughes worked for New Hanover Cooperative Extension Services as a family and consumer science educator, and for Progress Energy as a consumer consultant.

Presently Sandra Hughes is an associate of the Professional Woman Network (PWN) and vice president of the LifeSkill Institute, Inc. She conducts LifeSkill Workshops for Parents and Youth, Leadership Development Seminars, and classes in Etiquette & Social Graces. She is also a consultant for wardrobe planning and business etiquette in the workplace.

Contact:
LifeSkill Institute, Inc.,
P.O. Box 302, Wilmington, NC 28402;
910-251-0665/800-570-4009
connections477@earthlink.net
www.lifeskillinstitute.org
www.protrain.com

EIGHTEEN

WARDROBE PLANNING AND ORGANIZATION

By Sandra Spaulding Hughes

The clothes you wear give warmth, protection, and make a fashion statement. They also present a picture of who you are, what you are about, and where you are going. Your clothes can make you blend in unnoticed, stand out like a sore thumb, or help you make a positive first impression. Clothes have a lot to do with your image!

Your clothes make a statement about you to other people. To a large extent, people respond to you based on how they feel about your appearance and your clothing choice. We always say: "Don't judge a book by its cover," but people do it constantly—consciously or unconsciously. Granted, your clothes are not you. How you dress or appear on the outside is not who you are in the inside. But, in the real world, how you look, what you wear and how you move (to a large extent) will impact your possibilities for success and accomplishment.

So, even if your appearance–the way you dress–may not be important to you, it is extremely important to most of the people you will meet in school, work, or life in general.

Investment Dressing

The key to "investment dressing" is PLANNING. The satisfaction and value you receive from your wardrobe is determined by careful planning and buying. Planning involves three steps, each one building on the preceding ones.

The steps are:

1. Clothing Inventory

2. Activity Chart

3. Shopping List

1. Clothing Inventory

Garments currently in your wardrobe comprise your *Clothing Inventory*—the starting point for "investment dressing."

This inventory helps in:

• Knowing what clothes you have available

• Assessing the wearing frequency of each garment

• Evaluating the wearability of each garment

• Identifying the predominant family colors within the wardrobe

Begin by removing all clothing from your closet. Next, separate your clothing into these four categories:

1. Frequently worn

2. Less frequently worn

3. Least frequently worn

4. Not worn at all within the last two years

Ask yourself:
• Are there common *"likes"* and *"dislikes"* in each category?
• Why do you wear the clothes in the *"frequently worn"* category as opposed to clothes in the other groups?

Be honest with yourself. The more quickly you identify past clothing mistakes, the better off you will be in making future purchases. (Impulse items can cost you a lot of money in the long run if you never wear the pieces of clothing). You will get a wonderful "return on investment" if you are able to wear a certain piece of clothing (skirt, blouse, jacket) many times by accessorizing and "mixing and matching."

Try on all garments you have placed in the *"frequently worn," "less frequently worn,"* and *"least frequently worn"* groups. Look at yourself in front of a full-length mirror. With each garment do you:

• Like your visual appearance?
• Feel good about yourself?

Analyze why the *"less frequent"* and *"least frequent"* garments are not worn more often. Is the garment a special occasion item such as a prom dress or evening wear? Or is the garment not worn because it doesn't fit, needs repair, or you just don't like it? If any of these reasons apply, you should evaluate whether the garment is worth keeping in your wardrobe.

When considering whether a garment should be kept in your wardrobe, ask yourself:

- Is there enough "life" remaining in the fabric and styling to make keeping it worthwhile?

- Is it one of your more expensive garments?

- Do you have the expertise to revitalize the garment--make necessary alterations/repairs--or can you pay someone to do them for you?

- Will you wear the garment after revitalization?

- Will the garment compliment your "most frequently worn" clothes?

If your answer is yes to most of these questions, then spend the time and money needed to revitalize the garments.

For garments placed in the "not worn" category, your best approach is to discard them. If you do not wear a garment, there is probably something wrong with it or you are just tired of the clothing item. Unworn garments do not make the wardrobe more versatile. They are a waste of closet space!

Categorizing your wardrobe by groups also makes it easier to identify prominent color families. If you find more than two basic color families, you may have coordination problems. When you have two basic color families (i.e., black and khaki), you can mix and match clothing items and choose awesome accessories such as bracelets, earrings, purses, and shoes to make your fashion statement with basic pieces.

EXERCISE:
Clothing Inventory:

Make a listing of all the clothing pieces you will keep in your wardrobe:

	Blouses	Pants	Jeans	Skirts	Dresses	Sweaters
1						
2						
3						
4						
5						
6						
7						
8						
9						
10						

2. Activity Chart

Like all individuals, you possess a unique personality and lifestyle. Your clothes should reflect this uniqueness. To better understand the way you live and your particular clothing needs, it is helpful to make an *Activity List.*

An *Activity List* is a listing of all major activities in which you participate. Combine this *Activity List* with your *Clothing Inventory* to develop your *Activity Chart.* Use your *Activity List* to determine if you have:

• Appropriate clothing for your life style

• Wardrobe gaps

EXERCISE
Questions to ask yourself:

1. What type of clothing do you wear to school?

_____

2. What type of clothing do you wear to after-school extra-curricular activities such as cheerleading, choir practice, volunteer work?

_____

3. What do you wear to church?

_____

4. If you hold a part-time job, what clothing do you wear? How often do you work?

_____

Activity Chart

Activity Example:	How Often?	Clothing on Hand	Needed
Church	Weekly	Skirt/Sweater/ Dress Shoes	2 skirts

To make an Activity Chart:

1. List weekly and monthly activities, such as school, social, civic, church and employment functions.

2. List the garments you have on hand which can be worn for these activites. Check to see if:

   • Activities that take the major portion of your time have the most garments.

   • There is at least one garment designated for each activity. Some garments serve a dual purpose. Mix and match your work clothes. Instead of buying six complete outfits, buy one matching outfit and complete the rest of your wardrobe with complementary separates. The more garments you have to mix and match, the better the *clothing investment*.

- The major portion of your money should be spent for school clothing.

3. Identify additional clothing needs.

- Are there any activities that need more clothing?

- Are there any garments that need replacing?

- Are there any additions that will round out your wardrobe?

3. Shopping List

"Investment dressing" is based on developing and using a shopping list. Your *Clothing Inventory* and *Activity Chart* become the bases for the Shopping List. Planned purchases–your shopping list–deter making spur-of-the-moment buying decisions. By using your Shopping List, you know the items to be purchased that will fit into your wardrobe.

EXERCISE
Look at your *Clothing Inventory* list and your *Activity Chart*. Now you have a good idea of what you have in your closet and what activities take place in your life. In other words, it is now time to make a shopping (or needs list) for your future purchases.

Items you need to purchase in the near future, prioritized as:
A = Top priority. You REALLY need this!
B = Need it soon, but it's not urgent!
C = Need it someday (maybe a great birthday or holiday gift!)

Shopping (Needs) List

Skirts	Pants	T-shirts/ Blouses/ Tops	Jeans	Sweaters/ Jackets	Shoes	Purses	Other
1							
2							
3							
4							
5							

Organizing Your Wardrobe

An attractive wardrobe closet is a real asset. With everything in its place, you will know what to do with it. Start with placing all similar clothing items together, all jeans lined up on one end and all skirts on the other. Then divide them according to use. All school clothes on the right and special occasions on the left. Be sure all clothing items are ironed, repaired, coordinated, and ready to wear. Have at least seven days of outfits ready to go! Consider even putting out your clothing for school (or work) the night before. (You will be less groggy than in the morning and less frustrated when selecting your clothing).

Many of your projects, clothes, accessories, personal and school items, odds and ends, crafts, and hobbies require storage spaces.

• Begin with storage boxes such as cardboard shoeboxes and inexpensive clear plastic box sets. These boxes may be used as storage units for such items as hair accessories, CDs, greeting cards, and personal diaries.

• There are many other storage containers that include baskets, stacking trays, shoe bags, closet organizers, bins, pegboards, hooks, belt racks, cans, and jars.

• Always label the box or container. You can retrieve the contents quickly and save TIME.

- Organize your clothing wardrobe at least two times per year. (summer and winter)

- Envelopes may be used to organize small flat items. After labels are attached, organize envelopes in a shoebox.

- Hang your belts from small hooks in your closet.

- Have a special hanger or an organizer box for your scarves.

- Keep your hair accessories organized in a small clear container.

As a reminder, the best way to keep your clothes looking good is to take care of them. Don't throw your clothing onto the floor when you return from school. Instead, hang up your clothing. (It is best to check the condition of the pants, sweater or skirt before you put them away. NEVER put dirty clothing away. Put it into the laundry hamper).

Realize that to look your very best, you really just need some basic pieces such as tops in black, ivory, and perhaps vibrant colors such as red or purple. What you can do to individualize a piece of clothing is to accessorize. Some of your best fashion investments will be necklaces, earrings, belts, rings, and large scarves (which can be worn around the waist or over the shoulders on a chilly evening). Keep everything in its own place in your bedroom. The key to looking good is having your clothing at your fingertips in good condition and organized.

Young women can look great on a small budget that won't break the bank! Follow the guidelines about taking inventory of what you DO own, consider what activities you are involved in on a daily basis, and start a shopping list which you can post in your closet. When you have the funds (or your family inquires about what you want for your birthday or special occasion), you will have your fashion-needs list ready to share with others. And very importantly, you will have a list to use when you go shopping. Rather than buying impulsively, you will know exactly what you need and buy just the right piece of clothing, shoes, or accessory.

Wardrobe Planning is an effective way to look your best at all times. Understanding your body type, buying quality clothing and appropriate accessories will help you feel good about yourself and project an image of personal success.

Wishing you wonderful success in planning and organizing your fashions!

Recommended Resources

Conservative Chic by Amelia Fatt (Times Books, $9.95)

Fearless Fashion by Allison Bell (Lobster Press $19.95)

Get Organized with Heloise by Heloise(Perigee Books $10.00)

It's You by Emily Cho and Neila Fisher with Hermine Lueders, (Ballantine Books $7.95)

Life Strategies for Teens Workbook by Jay McGraw (Fireside $13.00)

Style Trix for Cool Chix by Leanne Warrick (Watson-Guptill $9.95)

The Complete Idiot's Guide to Looking Great for Teens by Ericka Lutz, (Alpha Books $12.95)

The Perfect Closet and Other Storage Ideas by Debra K. Melchior (Signet Special $6.99)

Working Wardrobe by Janet Wallach (Warner Books $8.95)

Notes:

ABOUT THE AUTHOR

CASSANDRA LEE

Mission: Education and Empowerment. Passion: Teaching through Speaking. These are the fuels to the existence of Cassandra "D.I.V.A. of Dialog™" Lee.

A certified trainer, national speaker, consultant, facilitator, and author, the "D.I.V.A. of Dialog™" is a messenger of soul-stirring and life-altering teachings.

In her interactive, theatrical seminars, she uses "divine inspiration vocally applied™" to fortify, inspire, renew, and energize the minds, bodies, and spirits of her audiences nationwide on such topics as communication skills, financial empowerment, goal achievement, health and wellness, leadership, professional development, and self-esteem.

Through her company, SSANEE, Inc., Ms. Lee has presented for various organizations including the Woman2Woman Health & Beauty Expo, V103 Expo for Today's Black Woman, U.S. Department of Education, Social Security Administration, SkillPath Seminars, My Sister's Keeper Program, Jesse White Tumbling Team, Illinois Alliance of Boys and Girls Clubs, Hugh O'Brien Youth Leadership Program, Chicago Public Schools, Chicago Public Libraries, and many others.

She is a member of the National Association for Campus Activities, the Professional Woman Network, Toastmasters International, and the G.R.A.C.E. Ministry of the Apostolic Church of God. She resides in Chicago, IL.

The "D.I.V.A. of Dialog™" is available to speak at your next event.

Contact:
SSANEE, Inc.
P.O. Box 804546
Chicago, IL 60680
(773) 592-2930
SsaneeInc99@hotmail.com
www.protrain.net

NINETEEN

"OUCH! IT HURTS!" HOW TO OVERCOME STRESS

By Cassandra Lee

"Stressed is desserts spelled backwards."
– Unknown

The Pain Begins

Imagine awakening one morning and as you attempt to get out of bed, you realize you can't move your neck or head, left or right, up or down. Imagine this is the second time in a two-week period when you have experienced this situation. Only this time, the pain is more severe and your range of motion is even more limited. Imagine that as your doctor is examining you, she gets a worried look on her face and tells you that she is sending you over to physical therapy IMMEDIATELY. Imagine spending about six weeks in physical therapy where you learn through a series of isometric exercises (singular, separated movements of muscle groups) how to increase your range of motion and make the pain go away.

Can you see this picture? Can you feel the pain? Can you imagine this happening to you? Well, this story may be an imagined reality for you; however, it was my reality in February of 2000. I can remember my doctor asking me a series of questions during my follow-up visit that left me feeling perplexed. She asked me questions such as, "What are you eating?", "How's your menstrual cycle?" and "Are you getting eight hours of sleep?" These normal, routine questions didn't cause me concern. It wasn't until she asked me, "Are you getting along with the people in your life?", "How many negative thoughts do you think per day?", "What else is causing you to have this stress?" that I became worried.

"STRESS? Wait a second! Did she say STRESS? How can the pain in my neck be STRESS? Furthermore, what did my thoughts have to do with my not being able to move my neck up or down, left or right? STRESS? What did STRESS have to do with it?" After these questions ran rapidly through my mind, I asked her, "What does stress have to do with the reccurring pain in my neck? Didn't I just sleep in a bad position which caused the problem?" She replied that sleeping in an incorrect position may have been one cause of the problem, however, based upon my answers to her questions, it appeared that stress had more to do with it than I was aware. She went on further to explain that stress effects people in a variety of ways. She helped me to understand how my answers to her questions were signaling a high level of distress. This meant that the stress in my life was beginning to affect me in a negative way. She warned me that if I didn't get a handle on my stress level, I would have worse problems to deal with other than digestive issues, weight loss, and neck pain. I would be dead! "Whoa! Dead? Was she trying to scare me?"

I sat up straight and took a deep breath. As I exhaled, I decided I was too young with too much to offer to be reaching a point of death. I knew in my heart I had not even begun to scratch the surface of living out my purpose. Sitting there on the examination table, I silently pledged to do whatever I had to do to keep S-T-R-E-S-S from hurting me any further and taking me six feet under!

The Missing Lesson

That experience has had a major impact upon my life! It was truly an eye opener! Although it was a painful experience, I'm glad I went through it because it has provided me with the motivation and insight to write this chapter for you. The primary objective for me contributing to this guidebook is to provide you with knowledge and recommendations on how to better manage stress. I want you to avoid going through the pain and discomfort that I went through. From my ordeal, I discovered that young women are not taught how to handle stress. Heck, truth be told, we are not really taught what stress is! The longer I thought about it, the more I realized that stress lessons were not taught to us. As we grew from little girls into young women, we were taught a variety of lessons on almost everything under the sun, except stress. Our earlier teachings included such lessons as:

1. Look both ways before crossing the street.

2. Don't talk to strangers.

3. Bend at the knees to pick up items off the floor/ground when wearing a skirt/dress.

4. Wear clean underwear every day in case you're in an accident.

5. Date boys/men that treat you with respect.

6. Save money for a rainy day.

The list of our earlier life lessons could go on and on and on, yet we won't find lessons on what stress is or how to keep it from destroying our minds, bodies, and spirits. Therefore, this chapter serves as your missing lesson on stress. It's an interactive foundation for discovering who you are and how stress affects you. Your journey toward effective stress management starts now! This chapter allows you to commit or re-commit to taking the steps toward living a healthier and livelier "stress-balanced" life. In short, this chapter becomes your life lesson on how to overcome stress today, tomorrow, and in the future. In this chapter you will learn what stress is and the difference between "good" and "bad" stress. You will discover the areas of your life that stress you out, as well as determine your current level of stress. Finally, I will provide you with techniques and strategies for combating stress in an effective way for healthy living.

The "Low Down" on Stress

The reality of life is that we will have stress. If we were to avoid stress, we would be living dull and monotonous lives. "Good" stress and "bad" stress co-exist in our worlds for a reason. Researchers have found that stress in moderation can provide us with some mental and physical benefits. It's prolonged stress, however, that can cause damage to our minds and bodies. Prolonged stress is the stress we want to properly manage. "Good" stress tends to disappear with the situation, circumstance or event that caused it. "Bad" stress tends to latch on to you and linger. It's almost like a pit bull biting your leg – you can't beat it off with a baseball bat.

"Good" stress usually does not make a person seriously ill or cause them death. "Good" stress is considered to produce excitement and productivity. Events such as, graduating from high school/college, getting married, starting a new job, joining a club/sports team, giving birth, buying a house, or starting a business allows us to "be, do, or have" in a positive and prosperous way. Our physical reaction to these "good" stress situations is appropriately balanced without causing us any problems.

"Bad" stress, on the other hand, is stress that exhausts and depletes our energy. "Bad" stress is destructive to our bodies, time, work, energy, relationships, efforts, and spirit. Prolonged stress tends to make us exhausted: depleting our energy, weakening our bodies, stifling our creativity, and clogging our minds.

What Exactly Is Stress?
Stress is more than physical discomfort. It's negative psychological energy that manifests into negative physical pain. Stress is a "mentally or emotionally disruptive or upsetting condition occurring in response to adverse external influences and capable of affecting physical health, usually characterized by increased heart rate, a rise in blood pressure, muscular tension, irritability, and depression," according to the *American Heritage Dictionary of the English Language*.

This definition helps me to understand why my doctor asked me the types of questions she did during my examination. She wanted to get to the psychological root of the problem in order to fix the physical side of the pain. Since there is a mind-body connection, she wanted me to see that the thoughts I kept affected the pain I felt.

Furthermore, this definition reveals to me that we must be careful of the thoughts we allow our minds to think because those thoughts can adversely affect what we do and how we relate to others. Therefore, avoid thinking thoughts of anger, fear, anxiety, guilt, worry, or resentment and you will avoid experiencing hives, headaches, ulcers, irritability, depression, and high blood pressure.

The History of Stress

We humans were designed to have stress. Our ancestors used stress to their benefit to fight off wild beasts and warring tribes. You know this syndrome best as the "fight-or-flight" syndrome. Their bodies would become revved up with increased blood circulation, rapid heart rate, tightened muscles, and rapid breathing. These sensations would serve as protection against threats, giving them the power to survive.

We humans were also designed to naturally combat stress. We have within us beta-endorphins that neutralize the effects of stress on our bodies. Alcohol and drugs won't do. When we use these unnatural healing sources, we block our bodies' ability to create the natural medicine needed for combating stress.

Beta-endorphins are the best natural chemical our bodies manufacture that counteracts the effects of stress. Beta-endorphins "operate like natural pain killers and tranquilizers." When our levels of beta-endorphins are high, we can endure more pain and stress. (SOURCE: Steve Bell, *Stress Control*)

We can create beta-endorphins by exercising our bodies and sense of humor. Meaning, we must make regular exercise and laughter a part of our lives. Since stress wears out our mind, body, and spirit, exercise and laughter will help us relax and better handle the natural occurrences of life.

A Critical Review

As a teen, you are at an age where you have probably experienced some sort of change, whether subtle or severe. How did you handle it? Did you embrace the change? Did you think negatively about the change?

Did you become stressed by the change?

From my transformational life experiences, I have come to the conclusion that we women must understand: life is change and change is life. Our lives are forever changing on an hourly, daily, monthly, and yearly basis. Whether we are full-time students, stay-at-home moms, ladder–climbing professionals, or innovative entrepreneurs, we must learn the most effective ways to handle our stress. Effective stress management is vital to our growth and sanity.

Even though it is important to know the background on stress, it is just as important to know if and when we are stressed in order to effectively mange it.

I recall telling my doctor what was "tap dancing on my last nerves." I rattled off "my family, job, and finances" as the sources of my stress. Even though I knew the sources of my stress, I did not realize I was stressed! I had not paid enough attention to the weight loss, shoulder pain, headaches, upset stomachs, fatigue, irritability, forgetfulness, acne, and chronic lateness as physical signs of stress until it was too late.

How about you? Do you know what "tap dances on your last nerves"? Do you know your stress symptoms? Let's take a few moments to find out.

In the exercises below, find out if you are currently stressed and the areas of your life that are causing you stress. (Remember: be honest! For it's when you are honest with yourself that you can more effectively resolve issues.)

EXERCISE: **The Stress Test**

Are you stressed? Answer the questions below to find out. Record a "Y" for "Yes" and an "N" for "No" in the space provided:

Do you feel sick at the thought of going to school/work? _____

Do you stay awake at night thinking about the course load/workload for tomorrow? _____

Do thoughts of grades/bills run a marathon in your head? _____

Do your family/friends do things that frequently irritate you? _____

Do you feel your body is carrying too much weight for your bone structure? _____

Do you have problems with acne, blemishes, or other skin issues? _____

Do you often feel tired? _____

Do you have stomach or digestive issues? _____

Do you often feel bored, sad or depressed? _____

Do you have negative social and intimate relationships? _____

Do you find yourself consistently late or unprepared for appointments? _____

Do you have constant pain in your shoulder, neck, or back? _____

Do you easily catch a cold or the flu? _____

Do you hold back in communicating with your family/boss/classmates/co-workers/friends? ___

Do you experience frequent headaches or migraines? _____

Do you have unexplained weight loss? _____

Do you have irregular or unusual menstrual cycles? _____

Do you consume drugs or alcohol to "escape from things"? _____

Do you constantly feel angry, irritated, or impatient? _____

Do you have high blood pressure or high cholesterol? _____

Record your scores here:
Yes: _____   No: _____

Here are the guidelines for interpreting your "Yes" responses to the Stress Test:

0-4   MINOR STRESS – your stress level is probably rather low; no need to worry;

5-8   MANAGEABLE STRESS – your stress level can probably be resolved with proper rest, exercise and nutrition;

9-12   MAJOR STRESS – your stress level probably needs your attention; identify the source(s) of your stress and take the action to reduce your stress symptoms;

13-20 MAXED OUT OF CONTROL STRESS – you are probably experiencing uncomfortable levels of physical pain and reccurring stress symptoms. SEE A DOCTOR!

EXERCISE: **Stress Areas**
In this exercise, check the areas of your life that cause you great levels of stress (check all that apply):

( ) Family
( ) Communicating with Others
( ) Finances
( ) Friends
( ) Relationship/Marriage
( ) Children
( ) Health
( ) Job/Career
( ) Commuting to Work/School
( ) Neighborhood
( ) Community Involvement
( ) Car
( ) School
( ) Co-workers/Classmates
( ) Social/Fraternal Clubs
Other: _____
Other: _____
Other: _____
Other: _____
Other: _____

Setting the Stage

Your results give you insight into how well you manage your stress or how badly stress is affecting your life.

As a young woman, I want you to understand that you are living during a time that has been reported to be more complex than a few years ago. It has been found that life today is estimated to be 44 percent increasingly more difficult than thirty years ago. (SOURCE: Holmes-Rohe scale)

With this in mind, understand that our generation is suffering from stress-related illnesses at a much higher rate than the generations of our parents, grandparents, or even great-grandparents.

Therefore, you must consciously and consistently take care of yourself. Getting proper rest, eating balanced meals, exercising regularly, and visiting your physician at least once a year, will allow you to reduce the effects of stress on your life. Moreover, this will increase your chances of being around to see your children, your children's children, and your children's children's children grow up.

Now that you have determined if you are stressed and the areas of your life that cause you stress, it's time to identify the things you can do to de-stress.

EXERCISE: **Personal Stress Busters**
In the area below, create a list of ten Personal Stress Busters. Make sure you list activities you can do to reduce the grip of stress on your life:

List of Personal Stress Busters
Example: Go for a walk along the beach; drive to St. Louis to visit best friend; ask for what I want/need
1. _____
2. _____
3. _____
4. _____
5. _____

6. _____
7. _____
8. _____
9. _____
10. _____

Daily Stress Management

From my ordeal, I discovered that the key to effective stress management is to do an activity EVERY DAY to de-stress. In the early stages of my stress management plan, I became more physically active by walking twenty minutes twice daily between the train station and my office. I also became a fitness enthusiast who exercised, ate, and read to strengthen my body and renew my energy. I joined the African American Association of Fitness Professionals to gain educational instructions on fitness. Finally, a gym membership and at-home exercise tapes (i.e., Tae Bo™ and Windsor Pilates™) rounded out my exercise plan.

In addition to exercise, laughter also became a part of my stress management plan. When I was in physical therapy, my doctor had challenged me to commit to doing something every day that would make me laugh. So I committed to watching Will Smith in *The Fresh Prince of Bel-Air* at 6:30 p.m. each evening, for it was a show I could watch and get a gut-wrenching laugh no matter how many times I had seen the same episode.

Even when I was done with physical therapy, I still kept watching *The Fresh Prince of Bel-Air*. I found that no matter the season or the station, I could find an episode of *The Fresh Prince* each day of the week to "get my laugh on." To this day, the show remains the number one way I consistently add laughter into my day. My stress management plan for humor also includes *Everybody Loves Raymond, Living Single, Will &*

Grace, and *My Wife & Kids*. The benefits of my show-watching routine help me release the daily tension of life. Additionally, I find I laugh more as I socialize and communicate with family, friends, clients, and colleagues.

I need you to understand that stress affects your mind, just as much as it affects your body. Therefore, you must maintain a balanced plan for a healthy mind and a healthy body. The best stress management plan is one that is done daily and focuses on the entire you: mind, body, and spirit.

Below are my recommendations for living a "stress-balanced" life. I call them "Diva De-Stressors" for the mind, body, and spirit.

Diva De-Stressors for the MIND

Diva De-Stressor #1: READING

My philosophy is that reading is to the mind what exercise is to the body. Therefore, spend fifteen minutes daily reading for inspiration, information, education, motivation, and a vacation. Read a variety of material from various genres (i.e., fiction, autobiography, self-help). This technique will allow you to increase the amount of material you read in a year while instilling new knowledge into your mind. Join a book club to help with variety and frequency of reading. My involvement with the Literary Vibes book club in Chicago for the past six years has influenced my reading habits. I went from reading one book a year to about 6-12 books/magazines/newspapers/etc. per month. Allow reading to relieve your stress.

Diva De-Stressor #2: MUSIC

Listening to music motivates the soul, relaxes the mind, and removes unwanted stress. When other stress combaters such as meditation or movement accompany music, it becomes an even more powerful force in relieving your stress. As with reading, variety is key. Classical, jazz, light rock, praise and worship, or instrumental will allow the mind to relax and renew. So turn on some smooth sounds today.

Diva De-Stressor #3: ACTIVITIES

Keeping the mind active allows it to remain equipped to resolve issues and handle conflict, hence, less stress. Engage the mind in activities such as chess, crossword puzzles, Taboo™, Scrabble™, and solitaire. Try a new hobby, take a new class, or join a community service organization. These activities will stretch your mind to see things from a new perspective and train the mind to become a creative problem-solving mechanism.

Diva De-Stressors for the BODY

Look to your health; and if you have it, praise God and value it next to a good conscience; For health is the second blessing that we mortals are capable of; a blessing that money cannot buy.
– Izaak Walton

Diva De-Stressor #4: NUTRITION

Eating a balanced meal will help you to better handle stress. Grains, vegetables, fruits, meats, dairy, and fats all make up the current FDA Food Pyramid. The main thing for you to remember is to eat a meal that meets your specific dietary needs. Consult your physician on the best nutritional plan for you.

Diva De-Stressor #5: EXERCISE

Daily exercise is another great way to keep your body from retaining

266 THE YOUNG WOMAN'S GUIDE *for Personal Success*

stress. An exercise regime that includes aerobic (builds your heart and lungs through moderate, sustained activities such as walking, jogging, swimming, and biking) and anaerobic (promotes muscle growth and definition through short bursts of intensity found in low repetition weight lifting, push-ups, and crunches) activities will not only promote a healthy body, it will also promote a healthy mind. Find an exercise (i.e., Pilates) or activity (i.e., washing cars) that you enjoy and commit to doing it at least 30 minutes a day, 3 times a week. When you commit to doing an exercise routine you enjoy, your body will feel good, your mind will become better, and stress will disappear.

Diva De-Stressor #6: MASSAGE
Massage is the rubbing or kneading of the body to aid circulation or relax the muscles. I found the medical and therapeutic benefits of massage to be phenomenal during my time in physical therapy. I want you to invest in yourself and receive a massage. Make a commitment to treat your muscles and relieve tension at least once every 3 months. Your body will thank you for the attention.

Diva De-Stressors for the SPIRIT
Diva De-Stressor #7: PRAYER

> *He makes me lie down in green pastures; He leads me*
> *besides still waters; He restores my soul...*
> NIV Bible, Psalm 23:2-3

Prayer allows you to connect with your higher power. Whether you call your higher power God, Jehovah, Allah, or Infinite Wisdom, prayer allows you private moments to have an intimate conversation where you give praise, ask for healing, request forgiveness, express thanksgiving, or affirm your future. Take a few minutes every day to pray. If you're uncertain of what to say, try these words: "Thank you for giving me this day. I am your ambassador. Allow me to be a light and model to those who enter my space according to your will. May your strength sustain me in all that I do." Add prayer to your life and you will receive abundant benefits for "stress-balanced" living.

Diva De-Stressor #8: MEDITATION

Quietly thinking at length is the primary goal of meditation. Meditation allows you to block out the distractions of the world. Use meditation in conjunction with silence. Sit quietly and visualize yourself as worthy of all that you want. Create pictures in your mind that show you as you want to be with what you want to have doing all that you want to do. Consistently meditating about positive things will allow you to manifest positive things into your life. According to Dr. Wayne Dyer in his inspirational book *The Power of Intention,* "Whatever you put your attention on, you will intend it into the world." Strive for a more fulfilling and productive life: meditate.

Diva De-Stressor #9: JOURNALING

Journaling allows you to discover who you are through the recording of your thoughts, experiences, and feelings. You are able to free your mind of negative thoughts, which frees your body of negative energy. Take time to journal daily. Write with freedom – don't worry about spelling, grammar, or punctuation. Write the thoughts that are on your mind using words, pictures, symbols, or cartoons. Your journal can be as simple as a spiral bound notebook or as creative as a decorated diary. Use what works best for you and allow the stress to leave your body with each stroke of your pen.

Final Thoughts

These Diva De-Stressors will allow you the opportunity to connect more with you. The better you know yourself, the better you will take care of yourself. Laughing and exercising are not enough. You must take further action. Tap into who you are through meditation. Use prayer to relieve the stress symptoms from the areas of your life identified in your journal. Eat nutritiously balanced meals on a regular basis. Allow a massage therapist to pamper your muscles and a fitness trainer to strengthen your muscles. Take time out to engage your mind in books, music, and games. Take time to care for you.

As long as you take care of yourself, you won't have to spend time or money in the office of a physical therapist as I did. The recommendations I provided to you in this chapter are solutions that work. Establish your stress management plan by using your ten Personal Stress Busters and my nine Diva De-Stressors.

Stress is a killer! It kills passion, productivity, careers, relationships, dreams, happiness, and lives! Create your stress management plan so that you may live: live your life, live your dreams, and live your destiny.

May the plan you set lead you through a prosperous and productive "stress-balanced" life. Peace and blessings.

Recommended Reading / Resources

AUDIO

The 7 Habits of Highly Effective People by Stephen Covey. (Also in book form)

The Success Principles: Your 30-Day Journey from Where You Are to Where You Want to Be by Jack Canfield and Janet Switzer. (Also in book form)

BOOKS

Girl, Get Your Money Straight by Glenda Bridgeforth.

In the Meantime by Iyanla Vanzant.

Maximize the Moment: God's Action Plan for Your Life by T.D. Jakes.

The One-Minute Millionaire by Mark Victor Hanson and Robert G. Allen.

The Principles and Power of Vision by Dr. Myles Munroe.

The Purpose-Driven Life by Rick Warren.

Think and Grow Rich by Napoleon Hill.

MAGAZINES

Black Enterprise

Black Enterprise's Teenpreneur

Essence

Money

O, The Oprah Magazine

ABOUT THE AUTHOR

YOLANDA MCINTOSH

Yolanda McIntosh is President/CEO of McIntosh Mo2vations (McM), a personal development academy for women.

Ms. McIntosh has been involved in personal and professional training and development for ten years. For three years, Yolanda served as Community Educator focusing on women's cancer issues for the American Cancer Society. Currently, as a Community Educator, her focus is women's self-esteem; the signature title of her presentation is "Who Do YOU Say You Are?" Yolanda has served as a professional trainer for such seminars as "Dealing with Difficult People," and "Stress and Resiliency in the Workplace" train-the-trainer workshops.

As a motivational speaker, Yolanda inspires both adult and young women to be their best selves. Her signature phrase is: "Here's to the Queen in YOU!" with an emphasis on the "royalty" that comes not from external forces, but the "royalty" that comes from within, for we are all children of the "King"! Yolanda inspires women of all ages to use obstacles as stepping stones toward their GREATNESS. She has also served as the Women's Ministries Leader and Women's Prison Ministries Leader for her church.

As a member of Toastmasters International (TI), Yolanda has served as President of her local Toastmasters Club and is now the District 6 Area Governor. Yolanda is a graduate of the Bill Gove Speech Workshop. She is a member of the American Society for Training and Development (ASTD) and is a certified Professional Woman Network (PWN) trainer for Women's Issues, with an emphasis on Self-Esteem and Empowerment for Women and Leadership Skills for Women.

She is a co-author of *The Young Woman's Guide for Personal Success* in the PWN Library.

Contact:
McIntosh Mo2vations
1360 University Avenue West, Mailstop 350
Saint Paul, MN 55104
(651) 768-9151
1-877-MO2VATE
mo2vate@qwest.net
www.mo2vate.net
www.protrain.net

TWENTY

WHY ME? A VICTIM NO MORE!

By Yolanda McIntosh

They said I wouldn't ever amount to "nothin"! They teased me because my nose was too big. They called me "bald-headed" because my hair wouldn't grow. I would be beaten by day and molested by night. I guess you could say I was a cross between the Black Sheep and the Ugly Duckling, with no hope of becoming a beautiful swan. But that was then. What about you? Are you struggling with getting through the school day without feeling inferior to other young women who may appear to be smarter than you, more popular than you, or what you perceive as being prettier than you? What about your work life? Are you feeling stuck in a job that not only pays little but seems to be going nowhere? At home, are you feeling smothered by rules, rules, rules, and very limited freedom? Besides, you are old enough to make your own decisions, right?

Like me, you are being taken captive by the "victim" mentality. The "victim" mentality says: "It will always be this way. You might as well accept it. You don't deserve any better than what you have going for you right now because…(I'm sure you can fill in the blanks)." But guess what? You CAN break free from this "victim" mentality and begin to live the life of a "VICTOR"! But your victory must begin—WITH YOU!

You see, some people still believe that I will never amount to "nothin"! My nose is still too big and my hair still won't grow. And although I am no longer being physically beaten by day and molested by night, the emotional scars from these tragic events still remain. So what happened? What changed? My perception is what changed. My perception of who I had been yesterday, who I am today, and who I will become tomorrow! You see, yesterday, I was a victim, but today I am a victor! Tomorrow has already been conquered because it never comes! It is always today!

I wanted to be a "VICTOR" and no longer a "victim"! I longed to define who I **would** become. I desired to determine **my own** value. I yearned to be respected by others. I also knew that I had to take it a step further. If I wanted to see and experience these changes, wanted to be able to define myself, and wanted respect, admiration and appreciation, then it had to start–WITH ME!

I had to relinquish the control that others had had over my life for so many years. I literally had to learn how to love and accept myself regardless of the negativity that others had projected onto me. And I must be honest. The process has not been and still is not always easy and I don't always get it right. However, even my failings at staying on top of the mountain are better than my wallowing at the bottom of the sea.

In this chapter, I'm going to share some practical ideas for your consideration as you make the transformation from being a "victim" to becoming a "VICTOR"! From living the life of defeat to living the life of a "CONQUEROR"!

Before we move forward, let me first say this: For all of the pain, disappointment, betrayal, deception, agony, anguish, humiliation, and intimidation; for all the fears and all the tears that you shed at the hands of those who were supposed to love and protect you and on behalf of your family members, family friends, religious leaders; your teachers, coaches, other adults, and other children, for anyone and everyone who has ever hurt you, taken advantage of you, exposed you, or caused you to experience any other type of abuse; on behalf of those who mistreated you…(as I take a deep sigh), I want to say to you, "You didn't deserve it and I'm sorry."

Although I can't change what happened to you in your past, I can offer you hope for your future. You deserve it! And it's yours for the taking. Are you ready?

Some of the first steps of living the life of a "VICTOR" are:

1) Knowing the Truth

2) Accepting the Truth

3) Living Out the Truth

Knowing the Truth
Knowing the truth about who you really are has nothing to do with how others have defined you. It has nothing to do with how others have treated you. It even has nothing to do with how negatively you may have treated yourself. You see, your negative outward expression is a result of your inward turmoil. When I ask you who you "REALLY" are, I am asking you to reach back and pull forward the truth about yourself. I am asking you to let go of the façade of being who you are not, in order to protect yourself from being hurt.

For just a few minutes, I am asking you to break down the wall that not only keeps others out, but barricades you in. Deep inside, are you a sensitive person although you act like you don't care and nothing bothers you? On the outside, are you a bully, although you genuinely care about people and long to give and accept affection? Or maybe, because of some past negative experiences, you now dress and express yourself in a more masculine fashion. Yet deep down, you long to release the sensual, sensitive, feminine side of the "REAL" you? I ask you again.

EXERCISE
Not being defined by what others have said and done, or by your own negative actions and experiences, tell me, what is the **truth** about who you "**REALLY**" are?

_____

_____

Are you convinced of this truth?
_____ Yes   _____ Not yet, but considering it
_____ No

If your response is **No**, what would it take for you to become convinced of the **truth** as to who you "**REALLY**" are?

_____

_____

What steps can you take today to start convincing yourself of this truth?

_____

_____

If your response is **not yet, but considering it**; what would it take for you to become convinced of the **truth** as to who you "**REALLY**" are?

_____

_____

What steps can you take today to start convincing yourself of this **truth?**

_____

_____

If your response was **Yes**, what did it take for you to become convinced of the **truth** as to who you "**REALLY**" are? How do you maintain this truth?

_____

_____

Case in Point

As a child, I never felt accepted; I never felt that I was good enough because of the things that were said and done to me by my caregivers and others. Over time, I convinced myself that the abuse I experienced was somehow my fault; that I deserved it. As I blindly accepted these misconceptions as truth, these truths became **"My Reality."**

What misconceptions have you accepted as truth–making them your reality?

_____

_____

The following is a short list of suggestions for your consideration to assist you with discovering and knowing the truth about yourself:

- **Study Self-Development Materials**
  Whether it's books like the one you are holding in your hand, or whether it's inspirational materials, etc., study them and apply them to your life! Study materials that will help build your confidence and increase your self-esteem. If you don't have a lot of time to read, listen to books on tape or CD. Study what you want to become.

Case in Point

My ultimate goal is to become a motivational speaker. I therefore study materials on how to make this happen. I also study motivational speakers whom I admire, not only to see what has worked for them, but to figure out how to apply appropriately some of their successes to my own life.

- **Study the People Around You**
  The types of people we spend the most time with are a reflection of our "REALITY" as it relates to ourselves. This may be a conscious or unconscious reality on our part. But it is our reality just the same.

You have heard the cliché, "Birds of a feather flock together." Surround yourself with people who want to see you succeed! People who will not only encourage you and empower you toward your next level of GREATNESS, but will, in return, allow you to do the same for yourself!

Case In Point

I decided that 2005 was "my year"! It would be the year that I was going to invest in my success! One of my investments included surrounding myself with those who wanted to see me succeed and move toward my next level of GREATNESS! However, this investment also included sacrifice. It meant that I had to take a microscopic look at my relationships and rid myself of relationships or individuals who had proven themselves to be what I call "poison" from my life…for my sake! This doesn't mean that I no longer speak to them or that now I am rude to them. It means that I have drawn the line on allowing them to inject their "poison" into my spirit.

- **Empower Yourself!**
  If negative words spoken to us result in damage and destruction, and positive words spoken to us result in empowerment and exhortation, how much more powerful are the words we speak to ourselves? It is so important that we use our words to encourage and empower OURSELVES! So many times we are quick to cause damage and destruction to ourselves, yet we are slow to encourage and praise OURSELVES. Somehow, we have convinced ourselves that it's okay to put ourselves down; but it's not okay to speak words of appreciation or admiration. As a result, we cause more damage and destruction to ourselves than what anyone could ever speak to us. This ought not to be.

We have a purpose and we have to learn to encourage OURSELVES so that our purpose can be fulfilled. Also, there will be times when we will have to stand alone; times when others may not be around to encourage and empower us. We need to learn NOW how to encourage OURSELVES! We also need to learn how to encourage and empower ourselves because it's the words that we tell ourselves that ultimately dictate our DESTINY!

EXERCISE
As a "victim," what damaging and destructive words or phrases did you use to refer to yourself?

_____

_____

Now, erase these negative words or phrases from your vocabulary!
As a "VICTOR," what words or phrases will you now use to refer to yourself?

_____

_____

Be sure to add these words to your vocabulary **permanently!**

And last, but certainly not least:

• **Empower Others!**

When you take the time to empower others, you are ultimately empowering yourself! There is such a feeling of satisfaction in knowing you have made a difference in someone else's life! You never know who may be on the brink of suicide, murder, chasing that next high, and so on. However, your offering of a smile, a kind word, a listening ear, or a helping hand as a means of offering them hope in the place of their hurt and pain could ultimately save their life. Besides, when you empower others, you develop your character, compassion, and accountability. Need I say more?

Once you **know** the truth as to who you **"REALLY"** are, the next step is **accepting this truth**. Are you ready?

Accepting the Truth

There is a distinct difference between having an intellectual knowledge of something and the acceptance of the intellectual knowledge we possess. We may have an intellectual knowledge of the fact that we deserve to be loved. However, if we allow someone to continuously hurt us and/or we hurt ourselves by repetitive negative choices, we are ultimately communicating that we have not yet accepted the fact that we deserve to be loved. The messages we communicate reflect the fact that our negative outward expression is a reflection of our inward turmoil.

Case in Point

You may wear the finest of clothes, shoes to die for, with perfectly matching accessories. Your hair and nails are as smooth and as classy as only YOU can do. Your make-up is fresh and your lips look voluptuous! Yet, as you walk down the street or into a ballroom, your stance is one of sloping shoulders with your head bowed and eyes that say, "I don't really deserve to be here, I don't deserve to be complimented." As a result, your non-verbal communication is sending a message to others that says: "I may look good on the outside, but on the inside, I don't feel good about who I am or how I look." "I don't deserve to be treated like the "Queen" that I am representing." Well, honey, I'm here to tell you: That is a lie! You are a "Queen" and you deserve to be treated as such! But your royalty status must start—WITH YOU!

What do I mean when I say "You are a Queen and you deserve to be treated as such?" Simply this:

"You are lovable and you deserve to be loved!"
"You deserve to be cherished by YOURSELF and others!"
"You deserve to love YOURSELF!"

"You deserve to DREAM BIG!"

"You deserve the opportunity to pursue your dreams!"

"You are worthy of RESPECT."

"You don't deserve to be mistreated or abused!"

This is the truth! However, these truths can only become "Your Truth" when you accept them and make them Your Reality!

Case in Point

Have you ever noticed that Queen Elizabeth II has the respect of everyone who crosses her path? Mind you, I did not say that everyone likes Queen Elizabeth II. However, everyone, even those who may not like Queen Elizabeth II, respect her when they are in her presence. Why is that? It's not just because of her title; for there are many people with elaborate titles who are not respected. It's not just because of the stylish, elegant clothing she wears, for there are many people who dress just as stylishly and elegantly who are not respected.

So what is the difference between those who are respected and those who are not? Well, the difference for Queen Elizabeth II and others who are respected is how they carry themselves. They have a stance that communicates, "I respect myself and am worthy of respect." It's in their walk; it's in their conversations; it's in their mannerisms; it's displayed in their appearance. You see, it's not about the cost of an outfit, but how well the outfit is worn. The outfit should not have to complete you; you should complete the outfit! Titles are nothing more than outfits. It's whether or not our titles are completing us or whether we are completing our titles that will make the difference in being treated like royalty.

Those who have proven themselves to be respected are the ones who respect themselves and know their roles. They are the ones who have made respect a lifestyle; it oozes out of their very character; therefore empowering them to walk in the authority of royalty status! What about you? You may not be the Queen of England or of any other country; but does that disqualify you from being treated like one? Absolutely not!!! But you must learn how to respect yourself and accept your new royalty status! "You are a Queen and you *deserve to be treated as such!*"

EXERCISE: **Royalty Status**

What steps can you take to begin learning how to respect yourself and **accept** the **truth** about the royalty status you possess?

_____

_____

_____

_____

Now that you know and have accepted the truth as to who you "REALLY" are, it is time to live out your royalty status, to live like a "VICTOR"!

Living Out the Truth

It's time to prepare to live out these truths and activate "Your New Reality"! Let's review:

• Hope for your future starts – WITH YOU!

• You are a "Queen" and you deserve to be treated as such!

• You are no longer a "victim" but a "VICTOR"!

As you prepare to make the transition from "victim" to "VICTOR," let's define some of the differences between the two:

A Victim

- Holds onto the negative experiences of the past by acting out their past experiences in the present. Because of being abused as a child, the victim abuses other prominent people in their lives, their children, or significant other.

- Holds onto a "Poor Me" mentality. Because the victim did not have a positive relationship with her father, she convinces herself that she is not capable of having successful relationships with men.

- Allows the negative experiences of the past to paralyze their future. Because the victim was always told how stupid she was, she has convinced herself that she is not qualified to further her education or other positive learning experiences in order to obtain the better things in life.

EXERCISE
What other examples of a "victim" mentality can you think of?

_____

_____

Erase the "victim" mentality from your memory bank. You will no longer be needing it! Now, using the above scenarios, let's examine the perspective of the "VICTOR"!

VICTOR!

- YOU release the negative experiences by making a conscious decision to not project the abuse that you experienced onto others.

- YOU release the "Poor Me" mentality by learning to not hold all men accountable for the actions of one.

- Although you were always told how stupid you were, you have since had a revelation of the truth as to your capabilities and your gifts and are now determined to successfully further your education and your positive learning experiences in order to solidify your "New Truth," your "New Reality"!

EXERCISE

What other examples of a "VICTOR" mentality can you think of?

_____

_____

_____

Now replace the "victim" mentality with the "VICTOR" mentality and put your examples to work!

Remember, being a "VICTOR" is a lifestyle! It encompasses your whole character, your very being! It takes consistency and determination! So stick to it! "VICTORs" are not quitters! Negative words are not a part of the "VICTOR's" vocabulary! However, the reality is this: "VICTORs" are not produced overnight. Be patient with yourself. Know that it will take some time to uproot the years of damage from the past. You may have to take small steps, one day at a time, but whatever you do, take steps daily! Success is possible and I know you can do it! Be Blessed!

Notes:

ABOUT THE AUTHOR

DR. JOYCE ROLAND PH. D. MSN

Dr. E. Joyce Roland is a doctorally prepared registered nurse with expertise in women's health from a holistic perspective (mental, physical and spiritual). She is currently an adjunct associate professor of nursing at North Carolina Central University, Durham, North Carolina. She is also president and founder of The Roland Group, a service that focuses on Wellness Training, Leadership Development, Stress and Conflict Management, as well as the mental, physical and spiritual health of women. She is a teacher, writer, and researcher in mental and physical wellness for women, and especially African American women.

Dr. Roland received a BS in Nursing from Winston-Salem State University, a masters degree in Nursing from Seton Hall University, South Orange, NJ, and a doctorate in Community Psychology from North Carolina State University, Raleigh, NC. Since 1978 she has worked as a nurse educator and research psychologist. From 1997 to 1999 she completed post-doctoral studies in Alcohol and Substance Abuse Epidemiology (as it relates to women) at the Alcohol Research Group, University of California, Berkeley (1997-99), and most recently completed research on posttraumatic stress disorder among women veterans (2004-06). She enjoys working with women and young girls, teaching them self-care and self-improvement strategies and providing mid-career advice to women.

Her most recent community work has been with a Durham-based Rites of Passage program for African-American girls and volunteering with the Urban Ministries of Durham—a community agency for the homeless—teaching life skills development for women and preparation for re-entry into society. She likes to travel and has visited Mexico, Haiti and other Caribbean Islands, and most recently traveled to England, visiting Coventry Cathedral to learn more about strategies for promoting peace and reconciliation in the world.

Dr. Roland is a member of The Professional Woman's Network, a life member of Delta Sigma Theta Sorority, and a member of N.C. League for Nurses. She is an active member of St. Paul AME Church in Chapel Hill, NC serving on the Trustee Board and the Health committee. She also sings in the choir.

She is married to her husband, Lewis, and has three adult daughters: Leslie, Kaifa, and Lisa, and two beautiful granddaughters, Cameren and Asha.

Contact:
E. Joyce Roland, RN, PhD, MSN
125 Hidden Springs Drive
Durham, NC 27703
(919) 598-1917
jaylew@intrex.net
www.protrain.net

TWENTY-ONE

FOLLOW YOUR DREAMS: PATHWAY TO SUCCESS

By Dr. Joyce Roland

"If you can dream it, you can achieve it."
– Walt Disney

Dreams–ah, the magic of dreams! Do you believe in dreams? Do you believe dreams come true? What if you could wave a wand and the fantasy of a lifetime became yours? What would you wish for? What if dreaming about your future could actually make it come true?

Well, it's not quite that easy, but dreams often lead you to your future. What are your dreams for the future? This chapter provides an opportunity for you to look inward and outward and to consider your future. How often do you stop to think of what your future holds for you? Do you dream of becoming an astronaut, an attorney, a journalist, a star athlete, or a TV anchor? What is your dream?

EXERCISE
Let's take a few minutes and explore that question.
Make a list of what you dream for your future.

1._____

2._____

3._____

4. _____

5._____

So what did you come up with? Was this an easy task? Writing your dreams down helps you really focus on what you want your future to be like, doesn't it?

Let's talk about achieving your dream. First, whom do you know who is doing the one thing you think you would like to do when you do grow up? To answer this question, you must take a look at yourself. Where are you headed? What do you know about yourself? What are you good at? Who best portrays the example of what you'd like to be when you grow up: Brittany Spears or Fantasia? Halle Berry or Angelina Jolie? How about Oprah? Or perhaps Star Jones or Jennifer Lopez? Venus Williams or Paula Zahn? Condoleeza Rice or Laura Bush? Perhaps the person you admire is not a TV or movie personality. Maybe it's your mother, your aunt, your hairdresser, or your teacher. Stop a minute and answer these questions. Am I stimulating any thoughts for you? Are any ideas popping into your head? Who most inspires you?

EXERCISE
Let's put it on paper. Begin by writing down the names of people you most admire. Write beside each name what you like about the person you've identified. Do these individuals have a quality you'd like to emulate or further develop? Can you name that quality or what you specifically like about that person? Might the qualities be personality, communication style, attractiveness, or talent, style of dress, occupation, the money they make? Stop right now and write down your answers!

Admired person:

1. _____
2. _____
3. _____
4. _____

Qualities I like about this person:

1. _____
2. _____
3. _____
4. _____

What did you learn about yourself from listing attributes of those you admire? What were the qualities of the person you admired most? Were these qualities superficial or were they qualities that are lasting and worthy of imitation?

EXERCISE
All right, let's make another list. This time, write down some of your own qualities that make you special and uniquely you, qualities that make you different from anyone in your family or any of your friends.

Personal qualities of others:

1. _____
2. _____
3. _____
4. _____

My own personal qualities:

1. _____
2. _____
3. _____
4._____

What did you learn? What did you put down? This little exercise should have stirred up some ideas in your mind. Let's continue our talk about how to achieve success in life by following your dreams. Now that you have had a chance to think about people you admire, what will it take for you to achieve your dreams?

First, you begin by acknowledging who you are. In order to move toward your dreams you must know yourself. You must understand yourself. You must recognize your strengths and weaknesses.

Take another few minutes and write a list of five or more positive characteristics (strengths) that you have that you like about yourself. Make another list of qualities that you don't like about yourself. What are your strong points? What qualities would you like to change? What would you keep? What do others like about you? What do they dislike?

EXERCISE
Stop now and make your list.

Things I like about myself:

1. _____
2. _____
3. _____
4. _____

Qualities I don't like about myself:

1. _____
2. _____
3. _____
4. _____

Some of my strengths include:

_____
_____
_____

What would I like to change?

_____
_____
_____

What do others like about me?

_____
_____
_____

What don't others like about me?

_____
_____
_____

What did you come up with this time? Do you know more about yourself now than you did before that exercise? As was stated earlier, the first step in achieving your dreams is knowing yourself. Know what you like! Understand what you don't like! Visualize yourself doing that thing that makes you happiest. What is it? How can you make it uniquely yours? Can it bring you happiness and success?

Defining Success

Just what is success? *The Merriam-Webster Dictionary* defines success as "a favored or desired outcome as a result of effort" or the "attainment of a proposed goal." You set a goal. You develop a plan toward reaching that goal. You create a road map toward making that plan work. You put all your effort into achieving the desired goal. Sound like hard work? Well, it can be. There is an old saying that goes "nothing ventured, nothing gained." If you don't attempt something that seems hard, you will have no way of knowing what you can do. So you set a goal and figure out how you are going to achieve the goal.

The Path to Success

Let's talk about the path to success. What is the path like? Is it a winding, curvy path? Is it a straight and narrow path, or is it a path filled with hills and valleys and potholes? There is no perfect path to success, but achieving success is possible only if you want it badly enough. The path to success is very akin to putting your goals for the future into an organized step-by-step plan and taking appropriate "action steps" to ensure the plan comes alive for you.

To attain your goals, however, your life does not have to be a tedious, boring, and predictable grind. On a daily basis, live life to the fullest, following the path you've chosen, and by so doing, you will learn things about yourself while you make progress toward the goals you set. Once you have achieved these goals, you can say, "I was successful at fulfilling that dream." I can do it again! That is what making those lists was about—discovering what you want in life and determining how to accomplish it.

Someone once said "If you don't know where you are going (in life), any road will take you there." What do you say to that? I'm sure you want a bit more control over the path your life takes than just taking any road or the first road you come upon. I'm sure you also have given some thought to what you'd like to be when you grow up. Maybe you are already doing some of those things, like singing in the choir at school, or playing on the basketball, soccer, or cheerleading team. Oh, I can just imagine lots of possibilities for an energetic, forward-thinking young lady like you.

Let's Take a Trip

Sit back for a moment and let your mind take you on another fantasy trip. What are you doing? Maybe you have a desire to write songs, or poems or books, or to be a fashion designer. The world, you know, is your oyster! Do you know what that means? That means you can be whatever you want to be if you want it badly enough and have the passion to work hard to achieve your goals against all odds.

Fantasy trips are like daydreams. They help you put your wishes and hopes into pictures in your mind. Remember, "If you can conceive it, you can achieve it."

Believe in Yourself

The next thing that will lead you to success is believing in yourself. You learn to believe in yourself by focusing on the good things that have already happened in your life.

EXERCISE
What are you most proud of that has happened to you up to now?

_____
_____
_____
_____

What personal attributes did it take for you to accomplish that task?

_____
_____
_____
_____

Sometimes we find out what we are good at by simply attempting a task that no one else will try, regardless of our age. So think about it. Begin to volunteer to do some things that no one else agrees to do, something that really challenges you. Volunteer at the local hospital or even the library. Chaperone a group of younger students on a field trip; lead a group of Brownie Girl Scouts, or teach a Sunday school class.

Your journey through school and life will give you an opportunity to learn what you are good at. Your friends will also let you know what they think you're good at. At some point have a conversation with your friends and ask them what they like about you and why. These conversations will help you learn more about yourself. Are the other person's impressions of you the same as your impression of yourself? If so, you are on the right path.

If I were visiting your school, your home, or your church, what would I likely find you doing? What would your parent, teacher, or principal tell me about you? Again, take a few moments and write a paragraph, about fifty words, about what your teachers, principal and friends would say about you.

EXERCISE
My friends, teachers or principal might say:

_____

_____

_____

_____

_____

_____

Taking Risks

Now it is very likely that you will not experience success if you don't seek to do something that is somewhat challenging for you. You must think outside the box. Do you consider yourself a risk-taker? A risk-taker is someone who acknowledges that something appears difficult to do, and maybe highly improbable, but decides to tackle it anyway, despite the odds of being successful.

One way, however, to assure success at attaining your goal is to break the scary task involved into manageable parts. Look at the big picture, then began to break the tasks down into individual, "easy-to-accomplish" units. Write your plan for accomplishing the goal down on paper. First, I will do this, and then I will talk to other people who are already doing this thing. I will find out what it took for them to be successful. Are you willing to challenge yourself in that way? Perhaps you need to take lessons to gain more skills. Are you willing to put aside the money you spend on make-up and clothes to pay for singing or piano, or even tennis lessons? Can you sacrifice one or two pleasures for a long-term goal you greatly desire?

Preparing for Success

Ideas for successful goal-setting often come from very unlikely sources. You may be just wandering along, taking care of your neighbor's dog or cat, when an idea hits you. I like to care for animals. Maybe I can be a veterinarian. YOU are the one who must identify your talents, your likes and dislikes, and start early to dream of what YOU want to do and what it will take for you to do it.

What are the keys to success? The keys to success are many. First, the dream comes, then comes the required preparation. Is a certain level of education required? Will you go to college? You must prepare yourself with the best education possible. That means if you are in school you must stay in school. Oh, sure, there are a number of successful people who dropped out of school and still achieved their dreams. But having the right credentials, such as a high school diploma, is becoming more and more the ticket to getting what you want out of life, regardless of race, creed, color, or class. Often so many people are competing for a certain job that having the right credentials is the only way to separate those who are prepared from those who are not.

Tooting Your Own Horn

What unique quality do you have that would catapult you to success? Are you an outgoing person or do you prefer to be by yourself. What do you do when you are alone? I'm asking lots of questions, aren't I? Well, this is to get you to thinking about yourself and the path you must follow to achieve your unique dream.

Many times, we, as young women are reluctant to brag about ourselves. In fact, we are taught most of our lives not to brag about ourselves. It's okay to brag about someone else, but certainly not ourselves. Well, my dear, sometimes it is perfectly all right for you to toot your own horn. Doing so gives you a sense of self, a feeling of pride, and a good feeling about something you can do that perhaps not many of your friends can do. Discover what it is that you are good at and get better at it. Go back to your list of what you are good at.

Dream Boards

Another helpful way to get in touch with your inner desires is to be aware of what excites you when you look through magazines. What pictures remind you of yourself or something you'd like to do when you grow up? When you come across such pictures, cut them out and paste or glue them on a poster board or large piece of white cardboard. You can get poster board from an office supply or art supply store. Cut and paste the pictures that capture your eye. Do you like nature? Horses, flowers, sports? Rocks, science, bugs, art, cooking? Cut these pictures out, put a picture of yourself in the middle of all this, and imagine yourself having a special place in this array of life, and a special assignment. You begin to take steps to achieve the dream you have shown in the pictures you chose. This creation is called a "dream board." This "dream board" helps you imagine and create your dreams and sets you on your way to your future and to your reality! Creating a dream board is a very visual and graphic way to get your dreams in front of you. Try it. It's fun. I did one myself once. It was the most creative thing I ever did to move me toward new personal goals.

Every so often you'll want to create a new dream board as new dreams replace the old. Dreams change AND so do you. You can expect to change as you grow older. Always try to move forward. Always strive for a bigger and better dream. Try also not to make the same mistake twice.

Creative Energy from Your Creator

The one affirming thought I'd like to leave you with is that you can do anything you put your heart into when you depend on a source in your life greater than yourself. I want you to remember also that you are a creature created by God, and like the birds and other creatures God created, you are unique, and you do have a place in this world–a unique place and a special reason for being here. In fact, God did not make another person like you in the world. You are very special. You, more than anyone else, will have to identify what that uniqueness and specialness is. Sometimes we find our dreams (and ourselves) by talking to God about what we want.

To sort out this overload of information and decision-making, you must find time to be alone with yourself. Be quiet. Take walks. Write your thoughts and dreams down in a journal. Often without your realizing it, God sends you messages about what your life's work should be. So stay in tune with God through prayer and thoughtful meditation. Connect with your innermost thoughts, and stay in touch with even the dreams you dream.

Your subconscious self also sends you lots of messages and picture images. It is God's way of providing ideas to you. If you wake up and remember your dreams and what you were doing, write them down. Writing dreams down helps you find meaning in them. Ask yourself, what did this dream mean? If I could imagine a message coming from this dream, what would it be? Again, you are using your imagination, and by doing so, you continue your dreams even when you are awake, and you bring meaning to the dreams you experience in your subconscious mind at night. Who will help you achieve your dream?

Getting Help
Do you need help fulfilling your life's aspirations? If you are to accomplish your dreams, whom do you need to know? What do I mean

by that? I mean, who will help you reach your goals? Take a few minutes to think of whom that might be.

EXERCISE
Who will help me reach my goals?

_____

_____

_____

Will it be your teacher, your neighbor, your pastor, your principal, friends, your parents, or even some of your parents' friends? Can these people guide you toward your goals? What kind of help can they provide? Sometimes they can be helpful just by listening to you share your life's goals. People also like to be asked for their advice. So choose well the people you ask for advice. Such persons are often called mentors. Mentors may help you clarify your ideas, then they may help you to talk through a plan for reaching your aspirations, and may also introduce you to people who can help you find the right path. Who comes to mind right now to ask to be your mentor? Most people are quite willing to listen to a young girl's plans for achieving success in her life. So don't be shy.

Getting from Where You Are to Where You Want to Be
Write down your plan now for reaching the goals you've identified in a journal, and answer the following questions. What do you think you have to do to reach your goal? Where do you want to live? By age 21, what should you have accomplished? How about age 18? Surely at that age you should have finished high school. Does everyone have to finish high school? No! If for some reason you dropped out of school, you can go back and complete your basic education. There are the GED or General Education Diplomas that allow you to test out of or show your

mastery of certain knowledge and content. This diploma is accepted at many colleges just like a high school diploma. Again, you must get involved in doing your search. Ask questions. Ask your teacher. If you play a sport, ask your coach. Your coach is a good resource.

If going to college is part of your pathway to achieving your dreams, how will you accomplish this? Will your parents be able to send you to college? And what if they can't? Does that mean you can't go? NO! You just have to find another way to get there. If you have the desire to go to college and see higher education as part of the path to your goal, then there are many avenues to this goal. Don't let obstacles of any kind keep you from finding your way on the path you have chosen for yourself.

Visualizing the Path

I have already suggested that you create a dream board to help you identify and visualize your dreams. Now, on a separate piece of paper, draw an actual path. Where does the path begin? Where does it end? What are the obstacles along the way? Put yourself at the beginning of the path. Put your long-term goal at the far end of the path. How do you get from where you are to where you want to be? Create one-year goals, then five-year and ten-year goals. Again write out the steps that get you to your goals. Writing things down helps them gel in your brain.

EXERCISE
Steps to Achieving My Goals
1. _____
2. _____
3. _____
4. _____

Today's Date: _____

My 1-year Goals:
_____

Make your goals achievable ones and identify the possible obstacles on your path, if you can. The journey toward achieving your goals is very much like the journey of life. There are many hurdles in life, but mastering one hurdle prepares you for the next. Then one by one, the hurdles are overcome. You get to the end, you look back, and you'll see how far you've come and how well you've done. There is a saying that you should remember, "The race is won, not necessarily by the swiftest, but by (s)he who endures to the end." Do you have it in you to endure to the end? Of course you do! Remember: "Nothing ventured, nothing gained."

Now find some quiet time to reflect on what has been presented here and before you know it, your path to success will begin to take form and become real in your imagination.

Author's Note

After you have finished reading this chapter, create a list of all the ideas we talked about. Then go back to your list and prioritize it. As you prioritize, some of your desires and goals will become more concrete. You may discard or strike some of them. That's fine. Now you are becoming more discriminating and more realistic about your path. You know what? I think you have what it takes to achieve your dreams no matter how daunting they are. I issue this challenge to you. Follow the guidelines in this chapter. Follow your heart! Find your path! Get out there, get busy, and success will be yours. START TODAY! Remember: The thing you seek is seeking you!

Notes:

ABOUT THE AUTHOR

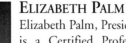

ELIZABETH PALM

Elizabeth Palm, President of Palm Consulting Group, is a Certified Professional Consultant located in southeast Michigan. Her expertise includes corporate training, human resources, and business management. Ms. Palm has a degree in Business Management and is certified in Human Resources. She is an active member of The Professional Woman Network and serves as a senior member of the PWN International Advisory Board.

Ms. Palm is highly knowledgeable about issues regarding customer service, human resources, diversity, self-improvement, women's issues, and professionalism.Ms. Palm has conducted training in both formal and informal settings nationwide for thousands of corporate employees including executive management teams. Ms. Palm has a passion for sharing knowledge and guiding others on their journey toward success. Her presentations are interesting, insightful and thought-provoking. She is also a co-author *Customer Service & Professionalism for Women* in the PWN library.

Ms. Palm is available as a keynote speaker and seminar leader on a local and national basis.

This chapter is dedicated to her children Angela, Tina, and George for whom she has the utmost respect. They are her inspiration, her encourgement, and a tremendous source of happiness. They learn continually from each other and share many valuable life lessons.

Contact:
Palm Consulting Group
PMB 343
19186 Fort St.
Riverview, MI 48193
(734) 282-8442
www.protrain.net

TWENTY-TWO

PREPARING FOR INDEPENDENT LIVING

By Elizabeth Palm

Becoming independent can only be accomplished by recognizing that you live in an interdependent world. There will be highs and lows. If you are prepared, then neither will catch you off guard. If you prepare, you will delight in a lifetime of success and wonderful adventures. What you will find is that independent living requires you to be resourceful, set realistic goals, and manage your time.

Be Resourceful

Living in an interdependent world provides us with valuable resources. Your desire to be independent, for instance, is not a new concept; therefore you have at your fingertips a world of resources to help you attain independence to any degree you would like. There are many examples around you of others who are striving for the same objective. In addition, there are a multitude of examples (resources) you can choose from, such as: your parents, peers, teachers, relatives, mentors, and friends, to name a few. Being independent, as well as interdependent, mean that you can lean on others as you step out on your own and gain the confidence necessary for independent living.

EXERCISE
To whom can you turn to as a resource for independent living? Who could be your mentor and provide ideas and support?

Person #1: _____

Person #2: _____

Person #3: _____

Others: _____

As you prepare to venture out on your own, it is wise to know who you can count on. To whom will you go in an emergency? How will you handle setbacks? What will it take to get back on track when your motivation slows down? We forget sometimes that we are not alone on this planet; there are many people and activities to help us. Identify your key resources, people you can count on, who will provide you with the information and support you need. The important thing to remember is that the more self-sufficient you are, the less dependent on others you become.

Being resourceful does not mean depending on others to give you everything you need; it means knowing how to communicate your needs to others, and getting the results you want. For example, if you want to live on your own, you will have to pay rent along with a few other necessary things like electric, phone, and gas bills. You will need a job—it's a resource for money brought to you by all those customers you have to wait on everyday. You will not want to work at a job you hate, so it's helpful if you prepare yourself by learning a specific skill that you can live with until you find your perfect job.

It's not surprising to know that five to eight percent of young adults don't graduate from high school in many metropolitan communities.

They jump into the workforce unprepared for what it takes to survive and become a second statistic in unemployment and welfare. This is a time of transition. It helps to be prepared.

There are five subjects that are usually not formally taught in school, yet are necessary for independent living (followed by some insight on each) they are:

• Decision Making

• Planning

• Communication Skills

• Self-esteem

• Social Skills

Decision Making:
Usually, in everyday life, we have to make decisions quickly. There are things to consider that we don't always have time to think through so we trust our intuition. A few key things to consider when making a decision: whom it will impact, what are your options (there are always at least two), what are you basing your decision on (something you heard, personal experience, etc), and can you live with your decision regardless of the consequences?

Planning:
Once you decide where you're going, plan your way there. Keep your eye on your outcome. Be flexible. Always have a plan B; it's an alternative that you can live with. Know what it will take to get from where you are to where you ultimately want to be.

Communication Skills:

You will want to know how to get your message across to someone else. Remember, we live in an interdependent world. If you can't say it, learn how to write it, and then learn how to say it. Above all, if you want to be heard, learn how to listen.

Self-Esteem:

Accept your strengths and weaknesses; you will learn from both and no one is perfect. Listen to yourself: if it's good for you, you'll feel good about it; if it's not, move away from it. Be who you are. There is no one better to be. You are special and unique.

Social Skills:

It is important to know how to interact with others. Know your environment, speak positively and clearly, and do your best to observe and listen at the same time. Try modeling the social skills of someone you respect.

EXERCISE

List a role model. Whom do you know who has excellent social skills, is a good planner, and an awesome communicator?

Person #1: _____

Person #2: _____

Could you ask them questions and gain insight into these skills?

Goal Setting

Life is an adventure, and every adventure has a goal. Getting through the jungle is the goal; the adventure is how you decide to get through it. Goal setting is intended to help you create your own path. You are the best judge of what your strengths and weaknesses are; setting goals will help you overcome your weaknesses and put momentum behind your strengths. The best part is that you are in control. The benefits and insight you gain are all part of the adventure. Goals help you focus your energy and get you on your way.

There are three easy steps to get you started on setting your goals:

• First, decide what it is you want to do;

• Next, identify what it will take to get there, and

• Then put the ball in motion.

It is helpful to understand the differences between short-term and long-term goals. Long-term goals are those big ticket items we want in our future, whereas short-term goals are the stepping stones that lead us in that direction. For example, your long-term goal is to live independently; you know there are things you have to do first, these are your short-term goals. They might include getting a job, saving money, or learning how to budget. Let's say you have a job, but you are not very good at saving for an apartment. Learning how to live on a budget would be a good short-term goal. What will it take to accomplish this goal? It may mean doing without that new pair of shoes or working extra hours. The object here is to keep the short-term goals simple, but focused on moving you toward your long-term goal.

There are always things that come up to interrupt or distract you from reaching your goal; we'll call them obstacles. As a matter of fact, the minute you decide what you are going to do, two or three of them will show up unannounced. My recommendation is to acknowledge them, list all the obstacles you think will occur, write them down, and determine how you will handle them. Once you acknowledge an obstacle, you will know if you have to go around it, over it, under it, or through it. Your objective is to get past it and reach your goal. Decide how much time you want to spend on the obstacle and then move on.

The most important factor in goal setting is to keep the target realistic. Short-term or long-term, it must be achievable. The intent is to choose something meaningful and self-fulfilling, and then set the bar just above your reach so you will experience a greater level of satisfaction when you succeed. Keep the short-term goals consistent with your long-term goals, and above all, believe you can do it. Set your own goals–don't let someone else set them for you. No one knows your ambitions and dreams as well as you. If you own your dreams, then the chance for success is much higher. Run your own marathon; condition yourself for success. Go farther than you thought you would by setting achievable short-term goals and you will celebrate each time you reach the finish line. Remember, you are in control.

EXERCISE: Goal-Setting Exercise
Identify your goals and write them down (long-term and short-term):

Long-term goal 1:_____
Short-term goal 1a:_____
Short-term goal 1b:_____
Short-term goal 1c:_____

What other goals do you have? Keep on writing them down in a journal or notebook.

Determine what it will take to get you there: energy, time, and effort.

What I will need to accomplish these goals?
1._____
2._____
3._____

Outline your plan of action. Make a list of those who can help you.

People who can help me:

1._____

2._____

3._____

List any obstacles and decide how you will overcome them.

Potential obstacles and how I will overcome them:

1._____

2._____

3._____

By following these few steps, you will set a clear and defined path to success. In addition, your new approach to overcoming obstacles will give you a new perspective on dealing with difficult situations. An added benefit will be the confidence you feel when you succeed.

Time Management

Time management is an essential part of preparing for independent living, as well as an extension of setting goals. It's a subject we all have to deal with throughout our lives. Balancing family, friends, careers, goals, and our health can be a challenge for even the most organized person. Managing your time successfully will raise your awareness and help you prioritize your activities.

By investing the time to plan your day or set your goals, you are increasing your level of success. One way to begin is by using a planner to schedule activities, track your progress and setbacks, and to serve as a reminder of where you are heading. It's even beneficial when you schedule personal time to meditate, relax, or exercise.

The best-kept secret of time management is that you really don't manage time at all. There are only 24 hours in a day and we have to work within certain parameters. For instance, there are only a certain number of hours of daylight to accomplish all those things on our list. So what we really end up managing is ourselves. Your objective here is to capture the big picture (that is your life) and see where you're going or where you've been.

A good time management plan will get you organized, keep you in control of your life, give you balance, and increase your performance in school or work. So go to the office supply store and get a planner. There are many varieties to choose from; I suggest something that has space to write in the columns and calendar areas so you can fill in any appointments. Whatever style works best for you is the one you should choose. You may need to adjust between basic models or fancy ones. Personally, I like the basic models with motivational or positive quotes to keep me thinking positively when I schedule my day. Once you make your selection, go through and fill in all the things that start pouring out, like birthdays, doctor appointments, interviews, parties, vacation time, or other special occasions. After all these areas are filled in, you will be able to plan current activities in more detail.

There should also be a space where you can jot down little things that you have to do later. A planner is a great way to reduce your stress level and improve your memory because it will all be right there in front of you.

And let's not forget the benefits that come from good time management skills: in addition to the reduced stress of trying to remember everything, you'll find more time to be creative and productive. Think of all the things you want to do but simply don't have time to do because things are disorganized or you have to spend too much time looking for something because it's not where it should be. A little less frustration is always welcomed. Everyone will wonder how you manage to stay on top of everything.

Another benefit of time management is the satisfaction you will feel when you realize the number of tasks you're able to accomplish. At the end of the day, as you review your accomplishments and write your to-do list for tomorrow, you can look at your writings and see your progress. You will see where you stretched outside your comfort zone and highlight any new skills you learned along the way. And finally, by writing your to-do list before you go to bed at night, you will rest better and feel more refreshed the next morning. Great rewards for fifteen minutes of effort!

EXERCISE
Let's begin! Make a to-do list for tomorrow and check off what you have accomplished tomorrow evening before you go to bed!

My to-do list for (date)_____:

_____
_____
_____
_____
_____
_____

Concluding Thoughts

Certainly, as you read these chapters, you will find that the sum of all its parts will help you on your journey to independence. We all count on others to help and support us with advice, information, and understanding. Know what independence means to you and realize two things: it will not happen the way you want it to overnight and you will be the one to make it happen. Remember that when you experience a setback, it is all part of the process! You will learn from it! Better yet, record it in your planner along with a note or two on how you got through it. Enjoy the other chapters in this book and count them as part of your collective resources for independence.

EXERCISE

This exercise will help you incorporate the three key features of this chapter: time management, goal setting, and resources.

• Get a planner. An inexpensive style can be found at any office supply store.
• Set a goal to use a planner for 30 days.
• Spend a few minutes getting familiar with the planner. Note how it is set up.
• Go through the calendar and write in birthdays and special occasions for the year.
• Go to the addresses section write names and phone numbers (valued resources).
• Go back to the current week and write down all the things you must do.
• Next step: write in those activities that are flexible.
• In the margin (or somewhere on the daily page), write your to-do list.
• Write in one long-term goal and three to five short-term goals to help you get there.

The initial time you spend getting organized might take about an hour. The purpose of the exercise is to get you started on your way to a few good habits. Make the commitment to bridge the gap between your potential and your performance. You'll be amazed at how easy it is to get organized.

Recommended Reading

The Back Door Guide to Short-Term Job Adventures: Internships, Extraordinary Experiences, Seasonal Jobs, Volunteering, and Working Abroad by Michael Landes.

The 7 Habits of Highly Effective Teens by Sean Covey.

Notes:

_____

_____

_____

_____

_____

_____

_____

_____

_____

_____

_____

_____

_____

_____

_____

_____

_____

_____

_____

_____

_____

_____

_____

_____

ABOUT THE AUTHOR

LAURA SWANSON LEEZER

Laura Swanson Leezer consults professionally in the areas of clothing and figure analysis, style definition and development, non-verbal communication skills, and professional development. She has held management positions in the retail field including sales, buying, and training and is currently Vice President and Director of Marketing in the financial industry.

Ms. Leezer holds a master's degree in education and teaches classes in fashion, marketing, and business in higher education. She is certified in Diversity and Women's Issues by the Professional Woman Network and serves on The International Advisory Board.

Her true passion is mentoring and helping people develop their skills and talents. Her future plans include travel, writing and furthering her education, which is a never-ending process. She is a co-author of *Becoming the Professional Woman* in the PWN library

Contact:
Laura Swanson Leezer
10680 E. 1000th
Macomb, IL 61455
(309) 837-2325
lldl@macomb.com
www.protrain.net

TWENTY-THREE

THE ART OF TRAVEL: PLANNING, PACKING, AND TRAVEL ORGANIZATION

By Laura Swanson Leezer

There is an art to traveling. The art is based on proper planning. The timeliness of your adventure can be planned to the hour and your itinerary can give you room for unexpected surprises and delays. The art of travel is also about traveling light and with confidence. As a young woman, you may be traveling to visit relatives, leaving for college interviews, traveling for a job interview, or leaving on a fun vacation with friends. But to have great success on your trip, consider the three elements of travel that are going to be covered in this chapter: Planning, Packing, and Travel Organization.

After reading this chapter, you will be able to:

• Understand how to prepare for a trip

• Understand how to pack for travel

• Understand key travel tips and learn valuable resources for traveling

• Understand common pitfalls when traveling and how to overcome them

Proper Planning

Planning is the essential first step of traveling success. Start by determining when and where you are going and what you are going to be doing while you are there. If you are going for a job interview and hope to include some site-seeing time, arrange this prior to your arrival. As a young woman, you may be working for a company that sends you out of town for business conferences. A business trip can include rewarding excursions, as well as attending seminars or meeting with clients. Is your trip a long-overdue vacation or are you attending an important function for work? Defining your purpose is important for covering all details.

Some of the key questions you need to ask yourself about your trip are as follows:

1. Are you traveling for business or pleasure?

2. What is your budget?

3. When are you departing and returning home?

4. What is your mode of transportation?

5. Are you traveling alone or with another person?

6. Do you need a passport?

7. What are the weather conditions at your destination?

8. Are you traveling during peak season, off-season, or during
    a holiday?

9. If traveling with a friend or companion, are there special needs
    and expectations?

10. Make sure your travel companion is aware if you smoke, have
    unusual habits such as late-night television watching or rising early.
    Do you really want to share a room?

Now that you have answered some basic questions, start by researching
your destination. The more information you have about the location,
the more prepared you will be when you get there. Learn about the
historic areas, business district, shopping, attractions, and other details
that make that city unique. Spend time reviewing the hotel options in
that area as well as places to eat. Ask individuals who have traveled there
about their experiences. Learn about unusual festivals or tourist
attractions the city may have. You might even consider enlisting the help
of a professional travel agent.

Travel Agents

A travel agent can help with all aspects of your trip. A professional travel
agent can provide information regarding air flights, vacation packages,
and often is able to offer experience regarding locations, hotels, and
transportation. Travel agents can help make last-minute changes if
necessary. They can do the searching for you. A professional travel agent
can stay within your budget and help with special needs. Utilizing a
professional can eliminate the worry.

Travel Purchase over the Internet
Another option is online booking. This is where you go to a specific website and make your reservations for your hotel, airline, train, or excursion tickets over the Internet. For example, www.travelocity.com has awesome rates and schedules! You can receive special deals and discounts and plan your trip online. The number of sites that offer hotel and travel packages is endless. Shop around and review several sites before making your final purchase. You can order airline, train, and bus travel online, as well as rent a car. Be aware of all options. If you enter a destination into a search engine, chances are you will pull up some travel site that will allow you to check hotel prices and availability, as well as connect you to links of special sites giving pertinent information regarding your destination. It is important to be very clear and exact when booking online. You need to be aware of what restrictions apply and cancellation policies if you have an emergency and need to cancel your trip at the last minute. Make sure you read all the information and get a confirmation number. If you have never made a reservation online before, have an experienced friend help you through it the first time.

Check the Weather
Learn about the weather and check weather sites online and on television to see what the climate will be.(Check out www.weather.com for local weather in your destination city). The Internet weather sites are up to date and you can print off extended forecasts to take with you.

There is a variety of other resources to use for research, which include:

• Local area Chamber of Commerce websites

• The city's official website

• State and local tourism offices

• Embassy sites and U.S. State Department for foreign destinations

• Travel magazines and books

• *Consumer Reports* Travel Letter

• Fodor, Knopf, AAA, Blue Guides, and Frommer's travel guides

• Visitor centers and travel bureaus

Having done your research on your destination, now decide how to get there and where to stay. Again, your pre-planning research will be useful. Your budget will dictate the next two travel issues.

Transportation

Trains, planes, buses, and automobiles are means of transportation to consider. How much time do you have for your travel? If you have limited time but flying is not in your budget, check the train and bus schedules in your area. Maybe driving is your best option. If you drive to your destination, remember to allow for parking costs and space availability. Many larger cities have parking garages that allow hourly, daily, and weekly parking for a price. If you choose to drive, consider parking your car and taking public transportation such as a taxi, buses, subway, or hotel shuttles. This will allow you to avoid extra parking costs and the chance of getting lost.

Make sure you have asked the hotel about certain modes of transportation in that area. Some subway systems might be confusing or unsafe for tourists. If you are arriving by air, train, or bus, determine what your hotel's shuttle schedule is in advance and where the pick-up locations are. Allow for transportation at your destination such as taxi fares and tipping. Just because you have flown to your location, you still need to get around once you are there.

Hotel Accommodations

Now that you have your location, time frame, mode of transportation, and the purpose of your trip (whether it's business or pleasure, or both), you have the fun of choosing where you stay. The best way to choose a hotel is to ask yourself what your specific needs are. Is it just a place to sleep or do you want to spend most of your time there? You need to ask yourself what you are going to be doing and is the location important. What hotel services are important? If you want to have breakfast in bed every morning, room service is a necessity. Maybe you need a great pool or workout facility. Answer these important questions and then choose the best place for you within your budget.

If you are going to a city for a conference, try to stay at the hotel where the conference is being held. This will be convenient and allow for quick trips back to the room at breaks and let you to sleep longer in the morning! If you are traveling and want to see the local sites, pick a location that is close to popular landmarks or attractions. Choosing a hotel is based on many factors. What are your priorities? If you want to walk the streets of the city, does your hotel location allow for that? Is the neighborhood safe for a woman traveling alone? Maybe shopping is the key to your happiness and you want to be located near a shopping complex. Do your research and check out the local maps for that area.

Long-Term Travel or Traveling Abroad

The overall pre-planning schedule or itinerary depends on the complexity of your trip and the distance you will be traveling. The further you travel from home, the more time you will spend planning. Many of the details you need to cover for traveling abroad is the same for traveling within the United States. If you are traveling abroad or long-term, your travel timetable and checklist could look like this:

Six months or less:

☐ Research the destination, and secure air travel, and a hotel.

☐ Apply for a passport if you don't have one by going to the local passport agency, or for more information call the U.S. State Department at 202-647-0518 or go online.

☐ Check with the U.S. State Department for security or safety warnings for your destination.

☐ Understand any medical issues that need addressed such as vaccinations or medications you will need, and get a check up for medical and dental issues.

☐ Learn the exchange rates for U.S. money and learn what some costs may be by visiting the U.S. State Department's website on Foreign Per Diem Rates by going to: www.state.gov/www/perdiems/.

☐ Understand local language and learn basic skills and secure a guide or book.

☐ Understand your personal insurance coverage and what it covers when traveling locally and abroad.

☐ Make arrangements for someone to watch your home and pets.

When traveling abroad or long-term, the closer to your departure, the more exciting and detailed it becomes! The following should be completed two weeks prior to departure.

☐ Confirm all reservations and have copies of confirmation numbers.

☐ Get travelers checks and small bills for traveling and tipping.

☐ If traveling by car: check oil, tires, spare tire, etc. (Don't miss a flight because you can't get to the airport!)

- ☐ Enlist a friend to watch your home and water plants.

- ☐ Make clothing and accessory purchases and break in walking shoes.

- ☐ Check your luggage for damage.

- ☐ Start gathering necessasary travel essentials.

The day before your departure, make sure you take care of the following:

- ☐ Confirm travel schedule with your place of employment.
- ☐ Pay outstanding bills.
- ☐ Re-confirm flights, hotel reservations, and transportation.
- ☐ Pack your suitcase and check packing list and make copies of documents.
- ☐ Water plants, empty refrigerator, take out garbage.
- ☐ Check with your housesitter one last time and provide emergency numbers/key.
- ☐ Turn down heat/turn off air.
- ☐ Set any alarms or automatic safety lights.
- ☐ Check house windows and doors.
- ☐ Unplug electrical items such as computers and televisions to protect against storms.
- ☐ Confirm that you have all of your travel documentation, airline tickets, and money.

Packing Tips

The way you pack for a trip depends on how long you are going to be gone and what you are going to be doing. The key to any trip is pack light! Taking too many items makes your luggage heavy, prevents you from dressing quickly because of so many choices, and does not allow room for purchases you make on your trip. Choosing your luggage according to your mode of transportation is one way to go. If you are flying, a structured suitcase on wheels is a great choice. Moving through an airport is fast and painless. A structured bag allows weight to be placed on the bag without the bag losing its form and crushing your clothes. If you are going for a weekend, casual clothes can fit nicely into a duffel or small carry-on-sized suitcase. If you are attending a business function and are taking suits or dress clothing, then a garment bag works well.

Regardless of the style, remember to purchase or borrow luggage with sturdy and re-enforced wheels. Choose a suitcase that will not tip over easily. What is the point in taking a suitcase that tips over every time you pull it or stop to look through your purse? You are going to end up hurting your back from picking it up repeatedly anyway! With all the luggage options available, the most important thing to consider is what the suitcase will be like to handle once it's packed.

Select a bag that is durable but not so expensive that if it's damaged, you've lost a fortune. Choosing a designer bag or flashy suitcase draws attention and can look worn and dirty after just one use. The zippers should be metal and heavy on larger suitcases. Make sure you test the zipper and wheels in the store before purchasing. Many suitcases come with locks, but remember airport security wants to be able to look inside your luggage if necessary. Do not lock your bags until they have gone through security and have been scanned. A good theft deterent is using wide straps to help keep suitcases closed or protect suitcases from popping open from broken hinges or bad zippers. The straps are made of nylon and have a very simple clasp for easy opening and closing. The straps are easily removed by security if necessary but others may not want to bother with removing them.

Many suitcases look the same so clearly mark you bag inside and out. Having a luggage tag on all handles makes it easy for you to verify your bag and help others quickly recognize they have picked up the wrong bag. Always inventory your items so that if you are flying and your bag is lost, you can replace those items. Airlines are responsible up to a certain amount and you can purchase travel insurance if you need additional coverage. Include a copy of your packing list and your trip travel itinerary inside your suitcase. If your bag is lost, you know what needs to be replaced. If security personnel find your bag, they will know where to take your luggage because you included your travel itinerary.

Airlines have strict carry-on policies and weight limits for checked bags. Call the airline before you leave home to make sure you know the rules. Remember that less is always better. When traveling by air, turn your computer and cell phone off before you board the plane.

Clothing Packing Tips
The following tips are helpful in packing and make travel more enjoyable.

• Make a list of all activities and assign an outfit for each event. Write it down and stick to your list. Include accessories and shoes on the list.

• Coordinate your wardrobe by color and utilize your shoes for several outfits.

• Pick two basic colors and build your travel wardrobe around them. Black is a good basic for traveling; it doesn't show dirt, can be worn for dress or casual, doesn't show wrinkles, can be worn more than once, and goes with everything.

• Layer your clothing for comfort and warmth and to utilize your best garments.

- Wear your most comfortable shoes for traveling. Pack other shoes in plastic bags to keep dirt off clothes.

- Place undergarments and socks inside shoes to utilize space and keep the shoes shape.

- Choose clothes made of wrinkle-free microfibers or wool crepe for suits and knits under your jackets to eliminate ironing.

- Pack garments on their hangers with the dry cleaning bags over them to prevent wrinkling and allow for quick and easy unpacking.

- Hang wrinkled items in the bathroom while you shower to release the wrinkles.

- Include in your carry-on clean underwear and one top in case luggage is lost. You can always buy other items if necessary.

- Rolling, stacking, and staggering are three ways to pack clothing. Rolling consists of rolling from the bottom of the garment upward. Stacking is folding your clothes neatly and placing them in stacks in your suitcase, and staggering is when you crisscross items and interweave side to side.

- Carry a light sweater or jacket for comfort any time of year.

- Dress comfortably, look pulled together and nice. You never know who you are going to meet.

- Laptops should be easy to access and in a protective case you carry on board planes and can be purchased in attractive styles that match your purse or luggage.

- Computer cases count as a carry-on so utilize one with extra pockets and a shoulder strap.

- Consider using a small purse that fits inside your carry-on or around your shoulders such as a backpack style to free up your hands.

• Carry a special zipped case, purse, or document sleeve that will allow you to store travel documents in an easy-to-access place that is always carried close to your body.

Travel Safety and Health Tips

• Always allow plenty of time, arrive early to avoid confusion and delays.

• Carry valuables such as jewelry, eyeglasses, camera, and important documents with you.

• Make copies of your driver's license, passport, insurance cards, all travel documents, and carry them separately from the originals. This will help you if anything is stolen or lost, prove your identification, and help with replacement.

• Consider using traveller's checks as well as cash and credit cards.

• Have the 800 number of your credit card company in case your credit card is stolen.

• Don't carry all of your money in one location. Separate it and hide in various locations on you, such as a money belt, neck pack, zippered pockets, or hidden compartments in your jacket or pants.

• Do not leave any items unattended in airports and utilize hotel safes.

• Always be aware of your surroundings and keep your personal space protected. Walk with confidence. Do not wear flashy jewelry and stay low profile. Use your cell phone as a deterrent from unsolicited attention; just pretend to be talking to keep others away.

• Keep your hotel and car doors locked at all times and be aware when you enter elevators and hallways.

• Carry a small flashlight for travel emergencies and unfamiliar hotel rooms at night.

- Know the exits in your hotel and where the stairwells are located.

- Take bottled water and snacks in case of delays. Assorted nuts, dried fruits, etc., are good choices as traveling by air is dehydrating

- Remember to carry medications with you and include such items as sunscreen, antacids, stomach soothers, bug repellent, and eye drops for tired and dry eyes.

- Try to carry medication in the prescription bottles for security purposes.

- Place liquids and other toiletries in zip-locked bags and pack extra bags for the trip home.

- While traveling on business, carry extra business cards with you and in your suitcase for identification if your luggage is lost.

Make a copy of the checklist on the following page for any trips you might be planning.

Basic Checklist of Necessary Items

- ☐ Brush and comb
- ☐ Toothbrush, paste, floss
- ☐ Shampoo and conditioner if you don't want to use the hotel's brand
- ☐ Blow dryer if not in hotel room (call ahead and ask)
- ☐ Deodorant and cologne and moisturizer with sunscreen
- ☐ Shaving items
- ☐ Contact lens supplies or eye glasses if necessary
- ☐ Personal hygiene items
- ☐ Medication and pain reliever
- ☐ First aid travel kit
- ☐ Lip balm and eye drops
- ☐ Towelettes
- ☐ Make-up
- ☐ Camera and film with extra batteries
- ☐ Travel alarm
- ☐ Cell phone and charger
- ☐ Hat or visor
- ☐ Travel packs of stain remover
- ☐ Small umbrella
- ☐ Extra luggage tags
- ☐ Tote bags for shopping and souvenirs
- ☐ Computer accessories and discs
- ☐ Brief case with shoulder strap
- ☐ Sewing kit
- ☐ Paper and pen

Traveling for business or pleasure can be exciting and educational, but you should allow for the unexpected and plan for delays. There will always be some waiting time so plan accordingly. Start a travel journal and bring a good book, as well as your favorite magazine, which can always be left behind for someone else to enjoy after you are finished! Striking up a casual conversation with the person sitting next to you can be enlightening and fun if he or she invites the interaction. Above all, remember to plan in advance, pack light, arrive early, and have fun!

ABOUT THE AUTHOR

LaSonya McPherson Berry

LaSonya McPherson Berry is an entrepreneur, trainer, consultant and personal/professional mentor. She is a dynamic speaker and motivator who inspires individuals to reach their potential. LaSonya has a B.S. in Industrial Engineering, Masters in Human Resource Development, and will complete her doctorate in 2008. She has obtained certification in Leadership, Personal Development, Diversity and is a certified Youth Trainer.

Prior to starting McPherson, Berry & Associates, Inc., LaSonya began her career as a counselor. She became a charter member of Jasper County Teen Peer Counselors. She was trained to counsel in areas of teen pregnancy, drug abuse, peer pressure and all adolescent situations. LaSonya worked with the Department of Social Services with their teen pregnancy program, and facilitated workshops with teenagers who were a product of generational mothers of teen pregnancy.

LaSonya understands the need for community involvement. She is an alumna of the United Ways' Volunteer Involvement Program that provides board training. Her community involvement and training resulted in a director position for Operation Dignity's Bankhead Courts Human Resource Center. The center offered training classes that were parallel to the Welfare to Work Program and that is what inspired LaSonya to start GET POISED, a training and development business designed to help people reach their destiny. She obtained additional training, certification and became affiliated with The Professional Woman Network, an international training organization, as an International Advisory Board member and trainer. The business was later expanded and became McPherson, Berry & Associates, Inc. She currently serves as president. She is a co-author of *Becoming the Professional Woman* in the PWN library.

Contact:
McPherson, Berry & Associates, Inc.
PO Box 360669
Decatur, Georgia 30036
(404) 243-7926
Fax: (404) 241-5795
www.mcphersonberryassoc.com
lasonya@mcphersonberryassoc.com
www.protrain.net

TWENTY-FOUR

MONEY MANAGEMENT: WATCH HOW YOU SPEND IT!

By LaSonya McPherson Berry

It is no secret that money is a key factor in today's society. If you are part of Generation Y, then it is on your mind, too. Are you looking at the "bling bling," trying to figure how to get you some? You are on the verge of starting your adult life. To create a strong foundation, every penny counts. I am not saying you should not get the things that are a part of the hip society. However, if you spend wisely now, you can have more for later. Perhaps part of your future plans includes attending college or entering the workforce to start life on your own. Either way, you will need money. Let's take a look at those two avenues and see how you can prepare.

Independent Living

You are preparing to enter an area full of new freedom and tough choices. Now is a great time to start using that allowance wisely. Sure, at the moment, you might think that there is no greater resource than your parent, parents, or guardian. Let me forewarn you! That well does dry up! Be smart; don't spend it all on the latest shoes, that dazzling bag, or another cool piece of clothing. Consider these ideas on making a compromise for your "tomorrow fund."

Start off by setting your financial goals. Yes, financial goals! You will not know where you are going if you have not decided on where you are trying to get. Consider these for instance:

Goals:

• Save for a down-payment or purchase of a vehicle

• Save for your college life

There are many opportunities to travel or attend college activities. Your parents or guardian may not be so quick to send the funds to support your fun. Think ahead to the opportunities that may be before you.

• Save for furniture

• Save for your career wardrobe

Suits and business casual attire can be expensive when you attempt to buy them all at once. If you are going to college, it may not be feasible to have such a wardrobe at this time, but you will need it later. Be proactive and prepare for it. It will not be long before you will be going on a job interview.

What are some of your goals? Write them down here:

_____

_____

_____

_____

After you have established your goals, there are other things to consider. It would be beneficial to set up due dates for each goal you have set. Include a dollar amount for each goal to be able to track your progress. Your goal may seem to be a large challenge right now, but take small steps to achieve your goal. Do this the same way you would eat a steak. One piece at a time!

Secondly, you can begin saving ten to fifteen percent of every dollar you receive. Just think of it as doubling the sales tax you spent on that last DVD. Doesn't sound like much but a little can add up. It a great time to even determine rather you really needed that item in the first place. Before you buy in the future, consider these two things: Can you borrow that item from a friend to handle your immediate desire? Or just get to the core of the reason why you are considering purchasing. Is it a need or a desire?

Here comes that pep talk on making the right decisions. You don't have the time or the chances for mistakes these days. The earlier you prepare, the better your financial future will be. You have to begin acting with maturity with your finances, and that begins by practicing self-control. Remember everything that looks good may not be good for you. More importantly, can you get it cheaper by waiting for it to go on sale? Or just compromise and get a cheaper brand. Marketing ads are designed to appeal your senses. Look beyond your desires and remember your goals.

Here are a few more tips. On birthdays and gift-giving holidays, provide family members with a list of items you will need for college. You can start a hope chest. They can begin to buy you items you will need for college such as a comforter set, microwave, refrigerator, or linens for instance. This will save you and your parents from having to finance those items needed once you get there. More importantly, it will show them how responsible you are. That can win you a lot of brownie points!

Workforce Bound

Many of the suggestions and tips above can be applied to your household as well. That's right! You should be spending time right now understanding how your parent's household runs. Spend time with the individual responsible for paying the bills in your household. It may not be the most exciting thing to do but you are getting an idea of how to run your own mini-corporation. Learn from others so that you do not make the same mistakes or decide on choices that may yield less than expected returns. It always helps to read about areas in which you might be weak. However, there is nothing like experiencing things in "living color!" Talk to your parents and ask how they have set up their budgets. You will learn a lot from their suggestions and mistakes!

Part of the job "shadowing" with your "household finance officer" should include how to balance a checkbook! Learning to write the checks is the easy part. Maintaining the records and tracking the expenditures are something else. Your math and computer skills will pay off while doing this task. Here are a few tips to begin:

• Only consider banking institutions that offer free checking.

• Find out which of those institutions are along the route you travel to school or work, and are convenient.

• As you narrow down your choices, review the different charges and fees associated with their services.

• Know what you are getting into up front. Eliminate all potential surprises.

Creating Your Household Report

Establishing a budget is essential to your financial success. I have developed a Household Report for you. Remember, you are operating like a mini-corporation! This is your "operations" report.

Start by preparing a place for the supporting documents. This will be your "home office." Prepare a folder for every bill that you pay or might have to pay. A final folder can contain tax preparation material, such as receipts or documents that could assist you during tax season or in the event of an audit, like pay stubs if you are working. Even though you are in your teen years, thinking down the road and getting your systems in place now will make a big difference. This system is a big deal and will be beneficial for years to come. It is REALLY important to create such a system if you are going to college! You are learning to become more responsible for your financial affairs.

The key to maintaining your finances is operating on a budget. A budget is a system to track what is coming in and what is going out. Take a look at the Sample Household Report on the next page.

You can adjust the spreadsheet to include all of your expenses. Be sure to include the actual amount of each payment for fixed expenses. For those that are not fixed, include an estimated amount. The "Actual" column would be used to input the actual amount paid. It will be helpful to include the due date of each item. The "Status" column would be used to indicate where you are that month with payment. A check mark would indicate that it has been paid. Leave it blank if it has not been paid. The last column is for notes. Here I like to include account numbers, payment information (online or by phone), and account contact numbers. Your level of responsibility is very important. Entering your account information requires you to treat it as confidential.

Household Budget Report

September 2006

Summary	Budgeted	Actual			Notes
Total income	3,000.00				
Total expenses	2,911.10				
Income less expenses	**88.90**				

Income		Actual			Notes
Base Salary	2,000.00				
Part Time Salary	1,000.00				
Other	$0.00				
Total income	**3,000.00**				

Investments	Budgeted	Actual	Due Date	Status	Notes
IRA	100.00		1st		
Household Money Market Acct	100.00		15th		
Total withholdings	**200.00**				
Percent of expenses	**6.87%**				

Finance Payments	Budgeted	Actual	Due Date	Status	Notes
Capital One - Credit Card	75.00		1st		
Auto loan - Ford	543.00		1st		123-456-7890 Acct# 1234567
Mortgage/Rental	993.10		1st		
Student Loan	200.00		1st		
Total finance payments	**1,811.10**				
Percent of expenses	**62.21%**				

Household Expenses	Budgeted	Actual	Due Date	Status	Notes
Charitable donations	100.00		1st & 15th		
Auto insurance	135.00		1st		
Water and Sewer	30.00		10th		
Cellphone	4.00		15th		
Life Insurance	35.00		1st		
Cable TV	40.00		15th		
Telephone / DSL	50.00		1st		
Electric	120.00		1st		
Total household expenses	**245.00**				
Percent of expenses	**8.42%**				

Variable Expenses	Budgeted	Actual	Due Date	Status	Notes
Household					
Groceries	200.00				50 wkly
Auto upkeep and gas	180.00				
Other travel expenses					
Furniture					
Clothing					
Grooming	75.00				
Medical/prescriptions					
Allowance	200.00				50 weekly - every Tuesday
Other					
Total variable expenses	**655.00**				
Percent of expenses	**22.50%**				

If you do not yet have your own checking or savings account, try it in your current household with the help of a parent or guardian. Again, it is key for you to do as much preparation and learning from others as possible before starting out on your own. You could even ask your parents if you could take over the household accounting and bill paying for one month so that you might gain experience!

Other Money Management Ideas

Spending or Saving

Above, I discussed ideas about saving money. At first, you might not be able to think of ways to cut back. Perhaps you don't consider the money you are receiving enough to do or buy what you would like. Well, consider these ideas for reducing your spending.

• Create an abbreviated version of your financial goals. Keep it in your purse. It will serve as a reminder.

• Carry small amounts of cash. The less you have on hand, the less you will spend.

• Try not to shop just for fun. That would be just looking for money trouble.

• Buy what you need, not what is on sale. "Good deals" may destroy your financial goals.

• Always shop for the best deal on items you must have. Don't always buy what you need at the first place you see an item. Shop around for the best price!

Now what are you going to do with the money you have gained by curbing your spending habits? Consider this option: Pay Yourself! What do I mean by that? Put it into your Tomorrow Fund. If you save $5 dollars a week for a year, you would have paid yourself $260. That may not seem like much right now, but to increase the amount, think of other ways you can save! Instead of buying that soda for $1 at school every day, bring water or something healthy. Put the money you save in your Tomorrow Fund. Now you have increased your original $260 by $180, for a total of $440. If you put that into a savings account, you may be able to increase your savings by one percent.

Credit Cards

Credit cards have been called the "little plastic wonder." It is a plastic card you present in lieu of money to purchase items. They are convenient to use, especially if you are not the one paying the bill. Because you are taking the time to read this book, you have determined that preparation is important. Now let's pretend you have a credit card. Do you understand the rules and responsibilities of credit cards? You use now and pay later. If it is not handled properly, you can pay considerably later. Here are a few things for you to consider about using and selecting a card.

Understand the interest rate represented with the use of the card. The term for this is the Annual Percentage Rate (APR). The rate can be fixed or variable. The best choice is a fixed "low" rate.

Review all the associated fees with a card. There could be annual membership fees or membership fees that are applied on a monthly basis. Neither of these would be the preferred one to select. There are late fees associated with every card. The point here is to avoid them and pay your bill on time.

Determine the grace period with the credit card you are considering. The grace period is the time before the interest will be applied to your current and previous purchase. It is beneficial to have one with a grace period of 20 days or greater.

Your card options are also secured or unsecured. With a secured card, you must provide a deposit or collateral for your potential purchases. An unsecured card is based on your good credit and the best choice to make if given an option.

The points above will help you determine the best selection for applying for a credit card. There is another point I would like to make, however. It is not a must that you obtain a credit card. But if you have determined you want one, what now? If you have found the best card for your situation; consider these tips when using the card:

• Don't charge what you can't afford to pay off when the bill comes.

• Use your credit card for emergencies only.

• Don't give others permission to use your card.

• Place your credit card in a secure place so that others cannot view the numbers.

• Review your statements in detail for unauthorized charges.

• If you lose your card, report it lost immediately. It is better to be safe than sorry.

Using credit cards can create massive debt. Being responsible in your spending is something that should not be taken lightly. Credit cards are beneficial if you do not leave a balance each month or if you need to establish credit. The continued theme here is to manage your money in its entirety.

Managing your money is an important responsibility as you prepare to become an adult. While you are determining where you will go to college and what career field you will pursue, it is important for any diva or princess to learn how to handle the riches she has or will obtain. Much is expected from those who have been given much. Managing your money is a sign of responsibility. It may be cool to have the latest fads, but what price will you be paying for these things besides what is on the tag? Building lasting assets are better than satisfying temporary wants. Start getting your financial structure in order today. We all have dreams; it takes a determined and responsible individual to accomplish them.

ABOUT THE AUTHOR

KAREN R. FREEMAN

Karen R. Freeman, President and Founder of The E.T.N Group, believes wholeheartedly in the power of self-discovery and action planning. Her strong background in human services, human resources and training provides her with an excellent foundation to assist her clients with their stated goals.

The E.T.N. Group is a personal and professional development company designed to "unlock" the client's potential for further growth and fulfillment.

The E.T.N. Group workshops are designed to provide a higher level of awareness-whether for a business professional seeking better customer relation skills, a mother-daughter who want to enhance their communication, or a child who has questions about those different from him/her.

Karen Freeman and her daughter, Victoria, live in Charlotte, North Carolina.

Contact:
The E.T.N. Group
P.O. Box 480635
Charlotte, NC 28269
(704) 921-3052
ETNgroup@bellsouth.net
www.protrain.net

TWENTY-FIVE

LIVING A FULL LIFE: MIND, BODY & SPIRIT

By Karen R. Freeman

To me, living a full life means finding peace and acceptance with the things I cannot change, yet, do everything within my power of influence and control to change the things that are not fulfilling to me. My ultimate life goal is HAPPINESS!"

That is my definition of living a full life. Now take a moment to reflect on and write down your own personal definition.

_____

_____

_____

_____

_____

EXERCISE
Ponder this: Where are you on the journey to living your definition of a full life?

_____

_____

_____

_____

When you think about your life, you may get exhausted with all the pieces that make up your existence. There's your home life, school life, spiritual life, and maybe work life. There's developing a healthy self-esteem and body image. Wow! So many things, right? It may be hard to figure out who you really are as you go through the motions of your very busy day. Yet, to live life to its fullest, it is important that you begin working through some of these areas as soon as possible.

Let's look at three essential elements that make up the foundation for your happiness: mind, body and spirit. In other words, you! For you to reach a successful level of contentment in each of these areas, you first need to define what success looks like to you. What would it take for you to be truly happy and fulfilled? Throughout this chapter, I will ask you to stop for a moment and write down "what does success look like" in each of the three elements. Writing down and believing in your own "definition of success" will begin a process of achieving your goal of living a life full of purpose.

Your Mind

Let's look at the first element of "you"…your mind. By that, I am referring to your view of yourself: your self-esteem and self-worth. What do you like about who you are? What do you think others would say about you and how you interact with them? Do you believe that you are smart, funny, courageous, sensitive to others' needs, etc.? Do you believe that what you value is important?

You have total control of you. Yes, I know, you probably still live at home. Your parents or guardians may make many of the decisions that affect you. But, only you have control of your thoughts, feelings, actions, and ultimately, your success and happiness.

EXERCISE
Ponder this: When I think about the person I am today, and the person I want to be, my idea of success is:

_____

_____

_____

_____

Nathaniel Branden, in his book *The Power of Self-Esteem*, wrote, "Self-esteem is confidence in our ability to think and to cope with the basic challenges of life. [It is the] confidence in our right to be happy, the feelings of being worthy, deserving, entitled to assert our needs and wants, and to enjoy the fruits of our efforts."

To say it a little differently, developing a healthy self-esteem and self-worth begins with being honest about the kind of person you are and how you treat yourself and others. It's making the best decisions that you can for your personal happiness. Sometimes these will be tough decisions, and sometimes they may not work out. But, it's being true to your choices with the understanding that no one is perfect. You have the right to make a different choice the next time.

Moving toward healthy self-esteem is a continuous circle of action and decision points. The first stage is self-discovery through personal feedback and feedback from others. Embrace the good stuff about yourself and develop a plan to improve the areas that challenge you. Secondly, begin to put those new skills into practice and you will grow from your learning. Finally, you will probably receive more feedback about how you're doing with the new skills. Are they working or not? Hopefully, you will be successful! Then, guess what? You start all over again with another component of your life. During each of the stages in the circle, you must decide for yourself "Is this important to me?" Remember, to achieve your definition of success, it must be important to you.

No one succeeds alone. During your journey of self-discovery and understanding, remember that you do not have to travel by yourself. There are always resources or people who can answer questions or give you direction. But, you have to begin by asking for help.

How many people do you think succeed all by themselves? I think very few. Often successful people identify others who have expertise in specific areas. They question and listen to the ideas and wisdom of others who have taken the journey before them. Success is not always immediate and there will be times when they fail. However, failure does not define or stop them. Failure may simply slow them down for a moment, until they figure out a new way.

Building a mentor relationship can provide you with a wonderful chance to talk with, listen to, and learn from someone who has "been there and done that." An effective mentoring relationship should be based on reciprocal trust and respect. It should give the mentee (you) an opportunity to ask questions and seek advice regarding circumstances that affect you.

Mentors can come in many packages, which means that you may build a mentoring relationship with a family member, a teacher, clergyperson, or older friend. It's important that the two of you have an understanding regarding the goal of the relationship. In mentoring relationships, the most important objective is for your personal growth and betterment.

EXERCISE

Ponder this: The greatest gift I can give the world is:

_____

_____

To help build up my self-esteem, this is what I can do:

_____

_____

These are my best qualities:

_____

_____

These are areas I need to improve:

_____

_____

I view failure as:

_____

_____

From now on, if I fail at something, I will:

_____

_____

This is what I believe my parents think of me:

_____

_____

This is what I believe my friends think of me:

_____

_____

I am a good person, so this is what I can do to better my relationship with my parents:

_____

_____

I am a good person, so this is what I can do to better my relationship
with my friends:

_____

_____

I would like to build a mentor relationship with _____.
By this date _____, I will approach him/her about being my mentor.

My mentor can help me in my personal growth in this way:

_____

_____

In sixty days, return to this chapter and check your feelings about what
you wrote. Have you made any progress on the action items? If so,
congratulations! If not, try and figure out what's holding you back from
getting it done. Then, try again.

The Five "Be's" of Developing Healthy Self-Esteem and a Peaceful Mind

- Be honest with yourself about what's great about being you and
  what's not so great.

- Be open to change if it's in your best interest.

- Be true to yourself when making personal decisions. Don't let others
  push you into doing something that doesn't feel right.

- Become the daughter and friend that you would want to have.

- Believe in yourself and your ability to make your dreams come true.
  It may not be an easy road, but if it's something you want, go for it!

I believe that healthy self-esteem and self-confidence has a direct effect on
your perception of your body image. Let's talk about that a little more.

Your Body

Unique! Matchless! Distinctive! Exceptional! Wonderful you!

Those are great words! Do you believe them about yourself? You should try, because we are all exceptional people, and we each come in unique and amazing shapes and sizes. However, have you noticed that often times we are not happy with our uniqueness? Currently, there's a trend in plastic surgery to not only have a celebrity's nose, but now the paying public can come close to duplicating a celebrity's hair, body, and face! Wow!

Nobody is perfect. That bears repeating. Nobody is perfect. Personally, I have neither met nor seen a perfect person. Have you? With the reality television shows that are so prevalent now, Hollywood would have you believe that physical perfection is what life is all about. It can be easy to get caught up in the excitement of liposuctioned thighs or veneer-covered teeth. However, at the end of the show, often times the "new and improved" recipients look like the previous guest or the guest before that. They may believe they look better, but have they truly changed their inner perception of themselves?

Let's be truthful: it can be very hard not to wish for a perfect body or perfect teeth, etc. During a recent photo shoot, I looked in the mirror and wished a few pounds away and wanted whiter teeth! You know, the "if only" statements, like "If only I had pearly whites like my friend." The "if only" thoughts are human nature and can creep into your mind before you realize it. I believe that most people can name a body part or two that they wish were different. I'm sure that even Miss America goes backstage, looks in the mirror, and has an "if only" moment. The key to overcoming the "if only's" is to do your best to ignore them and not let negative thoughts take control of you and your behavior.

Sometimes the negative talk may come from a classmate or even someone you love. Just how do you ignore those "in your face" put-downs? How do you stand out as an individual in a world of teenage conformity? It's hard to do, but not impossible. It goes back to the first elements of being you...your self-esteem and self-worth. Discover who you are, build up your confidence, be true to yourself, and be original. Step out on the belief that a "perfect" body is not the pre-requisite of a quality individual. You are so much more than that.

EXERCISE
Ponder this: When I think about my body, my definition of a successful self-image is

_____

_____

_____

As you grow into womanhood, your body will change often. If you are too shy to ask your parents or friends about the changes, a good first step is a visit to your family physician. Before you go, write down all the questions that are floating around in your head, even if they sound silly to you. It's important to know if you are in good health for your age and body type. Just because a person is skinny or thin doesn't mean she is healthy; by the same token, a person who is pleasantly plump isn't necessarily unhealthy.

With the continual growth in teenage eating disorders such as anorexia and bulimia, teenagers now, more than ever, need an excellent support system to discuss their concerns about self-image. Because there are many types of mentoring relationships, as you build a trusting connection with a female mentor, you may find her to be an excellent outlet to voice your concerns and questions. However, as with most personal questions, your parents may have the answers you seek.

EXERCISE
Ponder this: These are five great things about my body:
1._____
2._____
3._____
4._____
5._____

Overall, do you feel comfortable with and in the body you have? What are your honest thoughts about your body?

_____

_____

Have you ever struggled with an eating disorder?

_____

_____

If so, have you told anyone about your struggle with food?

_____

_____

If you have shared your concerns about possible eating disorders or poor body image with someone, that's a wonderful first step in helping yourself! If you haven't, please tell an adult as soon as possible so that you can become a stronger and healthier you with the help of physicians and counseling. Remember, many eating disorders begin as a simple diet. Become aware of your eating patterns and how food makes you feel.

The Five "Be's" of a Positive Body Image

• Be pro-active in researching information and understanding your changing body.

• Begin a fitness program to better your health. Be consistent. Don't give up even when you find it to be challenging.

• Be open to help that may be offered.

- Be mindful when you are less than kind to others. Remember, words hurt.

- Believe that your uniqueness is WONDERFUL!

As you begin the process of self-discovery and growth, the foundation of a healthy self-esteem and positive body image is what makes you the person you are…it's your inner-self, your soul, your spirit… .

Your Spirit

Look to this day
Look to this day, for it is life,
The very life of life,
In its brief course lies all the realities
And verities of existence:
The bliss of growth, the splendor of action,
The glory of power.
For yesterday is but a dream
And tomorrow is only a vision.
But today, well lived, makes every yesterday
A dream of happiness!
And every tomorrow a vision of hope.
Look well, therefore, to this day!
–Sanskrit Proverb

EXERCISE
Ponder this: When I meditate on my existence, my dreams of happiness, and visions of hope, my definition of a successful spiritual life is:

_____
_____
_____

Your spirit cannot be touched with your hands, but it can truly be felt with your heart. It's that inner voice that directs your choices, gives you peace, and confirms your self-worth. It lights you up from the inside out. Have you every heard someone say, "She has such a kind spirit (or happy spirit or peaceful spirit)? People have also been known to say, "She is so mean-spirited."

Your spirit is the essence of who you are and the energy that guides your decisions. It doesn't necessarily involve your religious life, but for many it means just that. For them, their spirit or spiritual self is directly connected to their belief in a higher being. You may feel this connection as well. Your spiritual self is where you can go to renew your strength and personal power.

Sometimes in your busy life, situations may arise that spoil your day. Maybe you had an argument with your best friend or your pet became ill. You may not feel that anyone else can possibly understand what you are going through. How could they? It is your pet who's sick or your friend who yelled at you, right?

When faced with challenging times, consider talking to someone you trust. If that doesn't bring you peace or understanding, find a quiet place and write down all that you are feeling about the situation. Be honest with yourself about everything that is happening. What you may discover is that when you calmly and honestly reflect on the circumstances and your feelings about it, you are able to see things more clearly. Yes, there may still be pain associated with the issue, but writing it down (journaling) will give you an opportunity to work toward the next step, and maybe a solution.

Journaling to renew your spirit is an excellent way to find peace through self-reflection. I recently picked up a copy of *Journalkeeping: Exploring a Great Spiritual Practice*, by Carl J. Koch. In his book, Koch states, "We know that we are growing spiritually when each choice we make nurtures and aligns with our beliefs, and our love becomes more and more inclusive."

A healthy and happy spirit brings you to a place of satisfaction and contentment within yourself, but it does not mean that you become complacent (settling for things the way they are). It's knowing that your heart is "in the right place" when you make decisions and being open to new experiences that challenge you to grow.

EXERCISE
Ponder This: If I could see a mirror reflection of my inner self, would I like what I'd see? Why or why not?

_____

_____

When I think about someone who has a kind and happy spirit, I think of:

_____

_____

She or he displays these qualities, which I admire:

_____

_____

These are the things that bring me joy:

_____

_____

I nourish my spirit/inner self by doing:

_____

_____

Because I take responsibility for my spiritual health and energy in the world, each day (week or month) I will do one thing that truly encourages my growth. I will begin with this:

_____

_____

The Five "Be's" of Honoring Your Spirit

• Be in meditation and learn to listen to your inner voice.

• Be committed to finding time for yourself, even during busy days.

• Be honest about the negative energy you may be putting out. Take steps to find out what's behind the negativity and work toward a change.

• Be sure that the decisions you make are what you want (feels good in your spirit) and not what friends want you to do.

• Be happy!

Your Mind, Body, and Spirit

My Journey, My Prayer

Dear God,
Today, I begin my journey to living a full life: mind, body, and spirit.
I am stepping out on faith with the belief that you will open my heart to a new way of thinking about my happiness and my purpose.

I know that personal growth and change can be challenging. Please guide me when I lose my way, encourage me when I become stubborn, and shelter me when I fall.

Let me look to you always with honor; knowing that your strength and love will heal all.

God, today I begin my journey to living a full life of happiness: mind, body and spirit. Thank you in advance for your guidance and love.
Amen

The prayer I've written above is based on a Christian faith in God. However, regardless of your religious beliefs, the thought behind the prayer is for you to be true to yourself by living your life with purpose and not by chance.

My continued hope is that you embrace all of the possibilities and opportunities that life has to offer. Make choices that are not always easy, but that may provide you with excitement and adventure and purpose. Step out on faith with the belief that you will fulfill your definition of success!

Recommended Reading

Fat Talk: What Girls and Their Parents Say about Dieting by Mimi Nichter.

Journalkeeping…Exploring a Great Spiritual Practice by Carl Koch.

The Power of Focus for Women: How to Live the Life You Really Want by Fran and Les Hewitt.

The Power of Self-Esteem by Nathaniel Branden, Ph.D.

Reviving Ophelia: Saving the Selves of Adolescent Girls by Mary Pipher.

Strong, Smart & Bold: Empowering Girls for Life by Carla Fine.

THE PROFESSIONAL WOMAN NETWORK
Training and Certification on Women's Issues

Linda Ellis Eastman, President & CEO of The Professional Woman Network, has trained and certified over one thousand individuals to start their own consulting/seminar business. Women from such countries as Brazil, Argentina, the Bahamas, Costa Rica, Bermuda, Nigeria, South Africa, Malaysia, and Mexico have attended trainings.

Topics for certification include:
- Diversity & Multiculturalism
- Women's Issues
- Women: A Journey to Wellness
- Save Our Youth
- Teen Image & Social Etiquette
- Leadership & Empowerment Skills for Youth
- Customer Service & Professionalism
- Marketing a Consulting Practice
- Professional Coaching
- Professional Presentation Skills

If you are interested in learning more about becoming certified or about starting your own consulting/seminar business contact:

The Professional Woman Network
P.O. Box 333
Prospect, KY 40059
(502) 566-9900
lindaeastman@prodigy.net
www.prowoman.net

The Professional Woman Network
Book Series

The Young Woman's Guide for Personal Success
Becoming the Professional Woman
Customer Service & Professionalism for Women
Self-Esteem & Empowerment for Women

Forthcoming Books:
The Christian Woman's Guide for Personal Success
Survival Skills for the African-American Woman
Overcoming the SuperWoman Syndrome
You're on Stage! Image, Etiquette, Branding & Style
Women's Journey to Wellness: Mind, Body & Spirit
A Woman's Survival Guide for Obstacles, Transition & Change
Women as Leaders: Strategies for Empowerment & Communication
Beyond the Body: Developing Inner Beauty

These books will be available from the individual contributors, the publisher (www.goblinfernpress.com), Amazon.com, and your local bookstore.